SUSTAINABLE DEVELOPMENT GOALS IN LAOS

Insights from Southeast Asia
Multidisciplinary Approaches towards the Region

Volume 7

Supitcha Punya

SUSTAINABLE DEVELOPMENT GOALS IN LAOS

Insights from Southeast Asia
Multidisciplinary Approaches towards the Region

Volume 7

GALDA VERLAG 2022

Insights from Southeast Asia
Multidisciplinary Approaches towards the Region

ISBN 978-3-96203-215-9 (Print)
ISBN 978-3-96203-216-6 (E-Book)

Bibliografische Information der Deutschen Nationalbibliothek
Die Deutsche Nationalbibliothek verzeichnet diese Publikation in der Deutschen Nationalbibliografie; detaillierte bibliografische Daten sind im Internet über http://dnb.ddb.de abrufbar.

Direct all inquiries to Galda Verlag, Franz-Schubert-Str. 61, 16548 Glienicke, Germany

Originally presented in earlier versions as the author's bachelor thesis (mainly section 2) and master thesis (mainly section 3), Humboldt University of Berlin, 2012 and 2018

ABOUT THE SERIES

Developments in the field of area studies—goaded by the analytical deconstruction of world regions from their geopolitical sense—have deeply affected the knowledge production from societies and cultures located in the politicized compartmentalization of the globe. With this series, the editors and authors wish to contribute to a reformulation of sensibilities in area studies which emphasizes the epistemic value of contextualized knowledge production. Starting with the notion of Southeast Asia, books published in this series will contribute to a more nuanced understanding of regionality based on a multidisciplinary approach. The series represents an outlet for young scholars intending to publish their degree theses; and for established scholars who are looking for a place to republish out-of-print books. We also encourage scholarly collectives from the regions to publish collaborative works or edited volumes on topics that usually will not attract the attention of big presses due to their transdisciplinary orientation.

FOREWORD

Writing about the politics of development in the Lao People's Democratic Republic has always been one of my academic passions since I started graduate school. It is incontestable that Lao development has always been a product of the interplay between the international community and the Lao government, in turn shaping the country's development policies. Having observed this relationship, and given the socialist identity of the country, gave me an interesting starting point in my doctoral study to further explore Lao development under the Sustainable Development Goals. This book is the sum of my ten-year research journey in Laos and my contribution in providing additional material on the subject of Lao development for those who are interested in Laos and socialist countries in general.

This book would have been infeasible without the support of my former supervisor—Prof. Dr. Boike Rehbein—who inspired in me a sense of critical thinking which I find very useful upon writing this book. I thank Galda-Verlag for allowing me to be a part of the *Insights from Southeast Asia* book series—giving me a chance to be read and heard. I thank my friends and colleagues in Berlin, Chiang Mai, and Bangkok for the wise conversations, suggestions, and support. More importantly, I would like to express my gratitude to my family. I would have not come this far without their unconditional encouragement and patience. Lastly, my sincere thanks go to Adam who always motivates me to fulfill my passions—including the writing of this book.

Chiang Mai, 2022

DEDICATION

To *Prof. Dr. Boike Rehbein*

CONTENTS

PHOTOS

TABLES

GRAPHS

DIAGRAMS

1 INTRODUCTION

The first time I was in the Lao People's Democratic Republic (Lao PDR or Laos) was in 2009. I took a slow-moving boat ride from Chiang Khong in Thailand to Luang Prabang to enjoy the so-called "slow life" in Laos. Having watched the romantic movie titled "*Sabaidee Luang Prabang*" (Good Morning, Luang Prabang—in English), which revolves around the story of a Thai-Lao photographer from Bangkok who traveled to Laos for work and eventually falling in love with a Lao girl who happens to be his tour guide, I had developed this perception that Laos is a passionate country. The movie conveys the notion that life is simpler and slow-paced in Laos. After that boat-ride experience I had as a tourist, and without any knowledge on the context of Lao development, I came to the conclusion that indeed life in Laos is slower paced and less chaotic. Since then, I longed to visit again to experience that nostalgic feeling. However, when I revisited the country in 2012, I realized that my generalization was too shallow.

The rapid Lao development I personally observed after my trip in 2012 has been quite impressive. Development can be seen in the abundance of rubber, cash crop plantations, and trucks from China. There were newly constructed casino buildings, entertainment complexes, hotels and guesthouses for tourists in northern Laos and the capital city resulting in an increase in the country's capacity to invite foreign investors and tourists. The slow-paced life in the country that I experienced during my first trip was far from the present pace of living in many cities, giving the impression that Lao development had been dynamic in recent years. Being identified as a socialist country in the midst of what can only be described as western development, one can only be curious and attempt to investigate how these developments is being carried out in a socialist country and much more the importance of these developments for the Lao government more precisely, the Lao People's Revolutionary Party[1] (the LPRP or simply the Party). Upon my investigation, I came across an economic development based on the market-oriented economy that was adopted in 1986—a critical juncture for Lao development in which the country reached a point of no return.

Before 1986, the country was mostly reliant on the USSR for its development. Due to this reliance, the country was seen as hermetic (Phraxayavong, 2009). After the Cold War, Laos remained a socialist country. Being a land-locked country in Southeast Asia, the country was characterized as a least developed one. Given this context, many scholars and international organizations had faced difficulty in accessing information about the country. The study of Laos was rare and often dubbed as "one of the lesser-studied countries in Southeast Asia" (Boute & Pholsena, 2017, p. 1). Since then, however, after the Lao government's unprecedented opening of its economy to the international community— and to global capitalism—information about the country has become more accessible.[2]

For a socialist country adopting a market-oriented economy, the diminished influence of Marxist-Leninist principles will be an accentuated consequence in the areas of economic realms, economic growth, and human development. More so, the concept and influence of a democratic process—which is a foundation of all market-oriented economies—will creep into the country as development assistance flows in. Development partners will make known that this assistance should play along with the democratic process in turn influencing any development policies the Lao government will formulate. Development in Laos after 1986 has always reflected an interplay between the external forces (e.g., the development partners and Lao neighbor countries) and the Lao government. The Lao government is receptive to meeting the international development standards by complying with the development norms stipulated in the Official Development Assistance (ODA) and actively becoming a member of the economic integration at regional and sub-regional levels (Pholsena and Banomyong, 2005). The country then transitioned from a "land-locked" to a "land-linked" country by using its

1 There exists an institutional overlap between the Party and the Lao government (see Croissant & Lorenz, 2018). To avoid confusion between the Party and the Lao government in this chapter, the Party — for the purpose of discussion—will be defined as the acting body that possesses the state power while the Lao government as the state authority that implements the Party's policy in both national and local level development.

2 The international community in Lao development includes the international organizations, aid-donor countries and Non-Governmental Organizations and private sectors. Currently, these actors are called "the development partners" in Laos.

geographical potential and natural resources to accelerate economic growth resulting from this economic connectivity.

Although an outcome of the open economy in Laos has been notable economic growth, the contradiction between socialism and capitalism is problematic and the Lao government has encountered many difficulties as a result. The first difficulty is that Laos is classified as the Least Developed Country, according to the United Nations Development Programme (UNDP). In terms of the Human Development Index (HDI), the country was ranked 137 out of 189 countries in 2020 (UNDP, 2020). The second difficulty is that capitalism itself widens the development gap between the rich and the poor[3] where the rich get richer, but the poor remain poor. The last difficulty stems from an increasing number of development projects that have received backlashes due to a range of worrying issues such as environmental degradation, human rights violations, corruption, drug trafficking, inflation, and the COVID-19 pandemic affecting the Lao economy and people's livelihood (Stuart-Fox, 1995; Pholsena and Banomyong, 2005; Lintner, 2008; Creak, 2011; Creak, 2014; Howe and Park, 2015). These difficulties, as I pointed out, may deteriorate the credibility of the Party as the leading nucleus in socio-economic and political development since its establishment in 1975. Due to this possible deterioration of credibility, the Party has been incessantly searching for legitimacy to maintain the status quo as the ruling party.

Many scholars have recently observed that the Lao government undoubtedly commits to improving socio-economic development, narrowing the inequality gap, reducing the poverty rate, and bringing the country out of the rank as a least developed country to legitimate the socialist ideology in the country (Evans, 1995; Soukamneuth, 2006; Rehbein, 2007; Mocci, 2016). With the difficulties mentioned above, support from the international community matters to carry out the Party's commitment to Lao development through the Round Table Meeting held every five years. This process is to shape Lao development policies, strategies, and plans to achieve the development goals and meet the international development standards. Without a doubt, the Lao government has to comply with the terms of "rule of law," "people participation," "civil society," and "decentralization" in the good governance program.

This has led to inquiries of the book: how the Party deals with capitalism, international development norms (e.g., democratization, good governance, and

3 From the Asian Development Bank (ADB) report shows the number of Gini coefficient in urban area is higher than the rural area from 1992–2013. In 2012–2013, the number of Gini coefficient in urban area is 0.38, whereas the rural area is lower at 0.33 (Asian Development Bank [ADB], 2015).

people participation), and maintains socialist ideology, at the same time. This book aims to provide insight into the regime's survival as a socialist country with one-dominant party by advancing an argument that development, in general, can be a source of the regime's legitimacy in the country. To prove the argument, the Sustainable Development Goals (SDGs) are chosen as a current international development norm supported by the United Nations since 2015. With the 17 goals of the SDGs (see chapter 2), this book will provide insight into Lao development under the SDGs by analyzing the political rhetoric of the Party members on Lao development, Lao development policies, and strategies to achieve the development goals. Seeing the Lao government or the Party as a primary actor in Lao development, this book will take the post-socialist approach to analyze the regime legitimacy of the one-party state and how the SDGs can support the regime's survival in Laos.

Post-socialist approach

Following the collapse of the Soviet Union in the late Cold War, many former socialist countries were in a transition from socialism to capitalism and democracy. The study of socialist countries seemed to meet a dead end as only five countries, including Laos, remained entrenched in Marxist-Leninist political ideology and structure. The socialist regime transition and survival become a driving force for the post-socialist,[4] or post-communist scholars. Their attention has been placed on two focal points which are "transitology" and "consolidology" (Kollmogen, 2013). In terms of transitology, many scholars have focused on capitalism, modernization, and democratization as a transition path and outcome. Generally, post-socialist scholars examine how socialist countries deal with capitalism while maintaining socialist regimes, and why some socialist regimes lost power after the collapse of the Soviet Union, while others did not. (O'Donnell and Schmitter, 1986; Di Palma, 1991; Walder, 1995; Linz and Stephan, 1996; Shleifer, 1997; Brown, 2009; Bolesta, 2012; Saxonberg, 2013).

[4] Due to the fact that Laos remains a socialist state, I will apply the term "post-socialist" rather than "post-communist." I am convinced that "socialist" is a word with a broader scope, including economic-institutional and political reforms from central-planned economy to capitalism, while "communist" per se is merely seen as political ideology and political mechanism that allow the communist party as a ruling party without a political contestation (Bolesta, 2012, pp. 56–57). Development in Laos under the SDGs, I argue that it could reflect the post-socialist transformation to reach the development goals by shaping development policies and arranging domestic institutions rather than consider the development goals as the fruits of the transition process.

For those socialist countries, after the transition, a step was needed to consolidate their respective regime for survival whether or not they remain a socialist state. Stephan and Linz (1996) highlighted democracy consolidation in post-communist countries in Eastern Europe after their transition. They noted that, "in Eastern Europe and the Soviet Union, in addition to making a political transition to democracy, the countries have simultaneously had to make a transition to a market economy." They elucidate how civil society, political society, rule of law, usable state,[5] and economic society function in post-communist Europe. After all, the institutionalization of democracy and capitalism in those countries is important to consolidate and stabilize the new regime. Nevertheless, the regime consolidation in post-socialist countries in Asia is different from Eastern Europe and the Soviet Union. The following topic dedicated to post-socialist studies in Asia, in general.

Post-socialist in Asia

Unlike the experience in Eastern Europe and the Soviet Union, a socialist regime's survival in Asia deserves a specific analysis. The transitions of socialist countries have appeared different in terms of both outcome and process. The first difference is the societal context, as Evans (1995) explains that many countries in Asia remain largely peasant societies. From this context, he analyzes that "the dispersed nature of peasant society and peasant relative isolation from the affairs of the cities, made them both less easily mobilizable than urban workers and less interested in remote political affairs" (pp. xii–xiii). The second difference is national pride, which could be seen from Saxonberg's study (2013). Stephan and Linz's framework mentioned above, further investigated the communist transition in China, Cuba, North Korea, and Vietnam. He presents key elements for sustaining regime survival including ideology legitimacy, pragmatic acceptance, and revolutionary potential. China and Vietnam, have both experienced economic growth and openly displayed national pride (e.g., nationalist ideology in the Vietnamese regime).

Similar to the above studies, moreover, Bolesta (2012) combined post-socialist transformation theory with the developmental state model to scrutinize the development trajectory in China, which is different from that of the Soviet Union. In his perspective, China's development relies on "state ideological background, and institutional solutions in terms of politics and economics

5 The usable state, as defined by Stefan and Linz (19960), is a usable state bureaucracy. They argue "Per se, bureaucrats are not democratic, but they have a function in making democracies efficacious" (p. 250).

draw extensively from DS [Development State] experience" (p. 12). His conclusion at least helped in clarifying how the Chinese government achieved to "maintain a type of authoritarian political system" and "to create some sort of embedded [state] economy" (p. 235). From the aforementioned studies, it can be concluded that the post-socialist transformation in Asia is different from the former socialist countries in Eastern Europe and the Soviet Union in which the communist parties remain capable of controlling the whole of society within its given border and play a leading role in socio-economic and political development. Legitimacy and legitimation of the communist party to obtain the state power and popular support are worth studying to understand the capability of the ruling party to do so. It could contribute a new theoretical debate in the remaining socialist countries in Asia, particularly Laos—the main focus of the book.

Post-socialist dilemmas and the regime legitimation in Laos

Before conceptualizing elements of legitimation in Lao politics, this book attempts to put a spotlight on the concept of legitimacy. This concept is always associated with the concept of legitimacy from Max Weber (1864–1920), and according to many post-socialist scholars (see Rigby, 1982; Le Hong Hiep, 2012; Szeleny, 2016). Weber (1978, p. 212–213) divides power (Macht) from domination (Herrschaft) to comprehend a power relationship between rulers who dominate the power and those who are voluntarily under the power. This power relationship is asymmetric. He contends that "the belief in the system" and "belief in legitimacy" could contribute to voluntary obedience for those who are under the power to some degree. Each regime therefore has various means to establish such belief, including the socialist regime which is unlike the democratic one.

During the transition process in socialist countries, a legitimation associated with regime survival nonetheless, go far beyond Marxist-Leninist ideology itself. Actually, many scholars have shifted their attention to critiquing economic development and suppression of civil society, and their antagonistic effects on the socialist regime. O'Donnell and Schmitter (1986, 15), for example, contend that "the socialist government has shifted the popular attention to accomplishment of economic development and social peace in order to mobilize regime legitimacy." I strongly agree to this and further argue that concrete outcomes from economic development, such as economic growth, modernization, and urbanization, can prove the capability of the rulers in the regime thereby obtaining support. This approach also worked in Laos after the Party had established political power in 1975 and has maintained this capability to control the societal groups up to the present.

However, the Party somehow is in dilemma in legitimizing itself under the rapid changes in national and global contexts. The first dilemma appeared after the revolution in 1975. The political conflict during the Lao civil war[6] left it difficult for the Party to stabilize the new regime. To achieve stability, the Party institutionalized itself from *Pathet Lao*—the nationalist movement—to Lao People's Revolutionary Party with adherence to the Marxist-Leninist ideology in both political and economic realms. Moreover, the Party constructed the new national symbols by removing the royal family and the nobility and placing more emphasis on the Lao proletariat and the nationalist movement in the public sphere. The outcomes from the national construction and centrally-planned economy under the socialist regime were not as successful as the Party's expectation (Evans, 1995; Rehbein, 2007). This has led to the open economy in 1986 the same as the Soviet Union and Vietnam which contradicted the socialist ideology in the country. Such contradiction thus became the second dilemma for the Party.

The integration to global capitalism and the influence of globalization gave rise to the second dilemma for the Lao socialist regime and one-party system that could deteriorate their legitimacy. This gave rise to a new task for the Party, as Evan (1995) suggests, and this was to "promote the capitalist stage and guide it towards socialism in the long run" (p. xv). This new task required reforms in the country to meet the standard as Rehbein (2007) affirms the main threats for the Party from capitalism and globalization are the standardization of the state and reforms encapsulated in the international and regional cooperation, distinctive identities among the ethnic groups, the new middle classes, material expectations and demands from Lao people. Particularly, the emergence from the middle class in Vientiane and urban cities may increase public awareness and therefore a demand for "participation or a higher degree of political pluralism than is the case today," according to Litners (2008, p.172).

The third dilemma is related to the second one. As mentioned earlier, economic integration at regional and sub-regional levels is a process occurring

6 Briefly, the Lao Civil War or the Secret War (1959–1975) was a consequence from the proxy war during the Cold War. At that time, the *Pathet Lao*, the communist nationalist movement supported by the North Vietnam and the Soviet Union, separated from the Royal Lao Government, the ring-wing and neutral movement, to fight against the US. The outcome of the Lao Civil War is that the *Pathet Lao* gained the victory and institutionalized itself into the political party in 1975.

rapidly in Lao development. The Party needs to pursue the development standard to not fall far behind its neighbor countries (Stuart-Fox, 2009). Moreover, the influence of the international development norms in Laos also has changed the national slogan of the Lao government from "solidarity, progress, discipline, patience, consensus and so on" to the rhetoric of the international development norms such as "alluring argots of projects, growth sustainability, and good governance," according to Creak (2014, p. 152). The new approaches to Lao development have unavoidably created challenges for the Party to deal with the dilemmas and maintain its power in Lao political and socio-economic domains. This book attempts to demonstrate the current regime legitimization of the Party under the SDGs by arguing that the Party could turn the challenges from pursuing the SDGs into an opportunity to retain its status quo in Lao politics.

My attention here is not only directed at the Lao socialist transition and how the Party deals with the dilemmas from capitalism and international development standards, but also how the dilemmas, in turn, contribute to legitimizing the Party's power and the socialist regime survival of the country. This book takes the post-socialist approach from Saxonberg (2013), and Croissant and Lorenz (2018). Both similarly contend that the regime legitimacy in socialist countries rely on ideological and nationalist legitimacy, pragmatic acceptance or performance-based legitimation, and revolutionary potential.

For the ideological legitimacy, it could be seen the Marxist-Leninist ideology in Laos is unique as the ideology is legacy from the nationalist movement—*Pathet Lao*. Without a doubt, the socialist ideology in Laos is blended between the Marxist-Leninist and nationalist ideology that remain crucial to legitimate the Party's political power in the country. The term "ideological legitimacy" defined here is how the Party employs the socialist ideology of the country to obtain popular support while under capitalism. This book aims to investigate the formation of the socialist ideology to understand why the socialist ideology in Laos is different from other socialist countries. Another investigation for the ideology's legitimacy is how the Party constructs and reconstructs the ideology to legitimize itself to deal with capitalism and the international development standards like the SDGs. These investigations thus lead to the last inquiry—can Laos reach a socialist utopia in the future?

With regard to pragmatic acceptance or performance-based legitimation, Saxonberg (2013) defines, "given certain external and internal constraints, the regime is performing reasonably well (p. 18). I further identify that the constraints and dilemmas mentioned earlier are equivalent. Therefore, "development legitimation" should be considered in the analysis of pragmatic acceptance because it plays a significant role in the perceived capability of the ruling elites. The source of such legitimation could be derived from concrete outcomes of development. Currently, I argue that these outcomes are abilities to improve economic growth to bring prosperity and wealth to the Lao people, and to meet the 17 goals of the SDGs. This book attempts to examine how the SDGs could serve the Party's legitimacy.

The last component relevant to the regime's survival as investigated here is the revolutionary potential that emerges from the legitimation crisis. What could cause the legitimation crisis in post-socialism? Saxonberg (2013, pp. 23–25) proposes emotive scenarios for the revolution that may arise when the regime loses some of its legitimacy. The first scenario could happen from an economic downturn giving rise to civil unrest. Another scenario is that the "expectations for wide-ranging reform or more radical change are rising." The last scenario is "the regime does something to anger the population." When these scenarios happen, people could lose their belief and faith in the regime, particularly the intellectuals. They better know how to mobilize, and promote the democratic process and human rights to people by "either building a civil society or confronting the regime more directly." From his argument, both civil society and intellectuals in Laos are worth taking into consideration. According to the fact that the civil society becomes the third sector under the SDGs to cooperate with the government and the private sectors to achieve the goals. This has led to questions of how the civil society and intellectuals work in Laos and their potential to revolve for the new regime. Could they bring democratization to Laos eventually?

Process tracing and elite interview as a method

Process tracing and elite interviews are chosen as methods to collect the first and second-hand data to analyze a connection between SDGs and regime legitimacy in post-socialist Laos. Process tracing was defined according to the definition of Bennett and Checkel (2016, pp. 6–8) which is "the examination of intermediate steps in a process to make inference [sic] about hypotheses on how that process took place and whether and how it generates the outcome of interest." Using within-case analysis and allowing for equifinality, it examines causal mechanisms for theory testing and development by connecting observations to an explanation of the case study. Taking a historical approach, the process tracing relies on thick description and historical narratives to identify causal chains and mechanisms between independent and dependent variables (George & Bennett, 2005, p. 206).

Unlike other analytical tools, Beach and Pedersen (2013, pp. 3–5) argue that process tracing contributes "theory-testing, theory-building and explaining outcome" due to the way in which it "investigates the workings of mechanism(s) that contribute to producing an outcome. Process-tracing methods go beyond correlations by attempting to trace the theoretical causal mechanism(s) linking X and Y." By taking Lao development policies as the outcome or dependent variable, process tracing can be used as an analytical tool to simplify the set of possible causal factors embedded within the actions and historical processes influencing Lao development. In this sense, there are two actors, which play influential roles in Lao development. First is the net effect of the development partners or the international community, which was taken here as the independent variable. They play a role in propagating their development agendas at the Round Table Meeting in Laos and providing development assistance based on what they support. Second is the Lao government as the policy-makers. In 2015, both the development partners and the Lao government promoted the Sustainable Development Goals in Lao development. However, this development norm has been politically interpreted by the Party as functioning as an intervening variable. Through the Party Congress further described in Chapter 2, the Party's members have shaped the Lao development trajectory by blending international development norms and Lao-style development norms. Thus, it can be argued, that the Lao development reflects an interplay between these external and internal forces which is likely to work to sustain the legitimacy of the Party.

In order to scrutinize the mechanisms that give rise to the dependent variables, I divide the research into two levels of analysis. The first level of analysis sheds light on how the Party has a legitimate right due to endogenous factors, to obtain the state power to play a leading role in Lao development. I hypothesize that the Party legitimized itself by using the legacy of the nationalist movement and development achievements to maintain its political power. Viewed from this angle, I take a post-socialist approach to investigate the socialist state formation and regime survival in Laos. Understanding historical context with regard to the socialist and nationalist movements and socialist ideology in Laos, both before and after the open economy, is a necessary first step to investigating the regime legitimacy of the one-party state in Laos based on the framework above.

The second level of analysis focuses on the influence of the development partners in Lao development. The development partners have become increasingly influential in Lao development since the economy opened up in 1986. They provide development assistance to the Lao government in accordance with their development norms, which are currently the SDGs. I argue that the Lao state power is being transformed and constrained by these exogenous forces in various ways. Both levels in this analysis are hypothetically shaping Lao development, and process tracing allows for the conversion of this complex historical information into an analytical causal explanation.

The history of the political struggle of the nationalist movement contained in Lao literature forms a massive puzzle. It will therefore be necessary, for convenience and clarity, to split this trajectory into distinct time periods. I will distinguish between three periods in the internal and external examination of the regime legitimacy of the Party. The first selected period includes the Party's rise to power. This section will utilize historical information about the formation of the Party during the colonial era and the country's independence (1955–1975). The second will detail how the Party maintained its Marxist-Leninist ideology from the establishment of national independence to just before the open economy (1975–1985). Data collection for these periods relies primarily on secondary data including, for example, historical information in Lao texts and literature published in Lao, Thai, and English.

As the establishment of the open economy and the failure of the Soviet Union were turning points for Lao state power, the third period focuses on the New Economic Mechanism, a policy that attempted to strike a balance between the planned economy of earlier socialist Laos and the international capitalist economy, starting in 1986 and continuing to the present. Since the Lao government has begun to welcome capitalist influence and international development assistance, it is obvious that Lao state power has been transformed. This third period will therefore be utilized to illustrate how the Lao government and the Party cope with the exogenous forces, and how these forces influence Lao-style development norms. In this period, both primary and secondary sources are utilized.

To obtain first-hand, or primary data, I established working relationships with several key informants who are closely tied to projects directly impacting Lao development. This is the methodological approach known as elite interviewing. The function of the elite interview, according to Richards (1996, pp. 199–200), is to "provide the political scientist with an insight into the mind-set of the actor/s who have played a role in shaping the society… and an interviewee's subjective analysis of a particular episode or situation." Who should be chosen for an elite interview? It could be "a group of individuals, who hold, or have held a privileged position in society... [and who] have had more influence on political outcomes than general members." Referring to the Vientiane Declaration issued in 2015, the appropriate interviewees for this project are therefore policy-makers, country directors, representatives or specialists from the Lao government, and members of organizations that are considered development partners. It should be noted that due to the quality of information that can be obtained from elite interviews, the number of informants is less important than the informants' respective positions in and contributions to Lao development. According to Mason (as cited in Edwards and Holland, 2013, p.3), the common features of qualitative and semi-structured interviewing include "[1] the interactional exchange of dialogue (between two or more participants, in face-to-face or other contexts), [2] and a thematic, topic-centered, biographical or narrative approach where the researcher has topics, themes or issues they wish to cover, but with a fluid and flexible structure, [3] a perspective regarding knowledge as situated and contextual." Semi-structured interviews allow for flexibility when faced with time constraints. Combining this approach with focused group discussion [7] one can easily interview more than two people with the same questions.

To crosscheck for reliability and validity in first-hand accounts, triangulation was used with the help of primary and secondary sources. To support my argument about the ideology, for example, I analyze the secondary sources like the political leaders' speech in Lao news with the interview data from the Party member and the National Assembly member. This data can be used to generalize the influence of socialist ideology among Party members after the open economy. In summary, process-tracing and elite interviewing are employed to help classify the primary and secondary data and to select the key informants, while triangulation helps ensure the reliability of the sources.

Limitation of the study

Criticizing the Lao government and the politics in Laos creates a vulnerable situation for development partners and even the Lao government officers and the Party itself. I will therefore not disclose personal or organizational names

[7] Blaikie (2009, p. 235) further clarifies that focused group discussion "allows for group interaction and provide [sic] greater insight into why certain opinions are held."

of development partners, members of the Lao government and the Party, Lao experts, or civil society members who fully cooperate and participate as key informants in this book.

Book outline

I believe that the regime's legitimacy in Laos has no final answer, it is rather resilient and adjustable based on the new circumstances and dilemmas. With the six chapters in the book, hopefully, it could contribute insight into the politics of development in Laos and theoretical debate for post-socialist scholars and Lao scholars for their own further studies. The content in each chapter could be further described as follows.

Chapter 2 traces the process of development in post-socialist Laos and its debate. This chapter sheds light on how Lao modernity has been constructed and reconstructed to understand why development from the development partners matters for the Party and why they have played a crucial role in Lao development. After that, the chapter dedicates to the interplay among the Party and the development partners, Lao-style development, and the Party's long-term development aspiration with its debates from Lao scholars.

Chapter 3 investigates the regime's legitimacy in post-socialist Laos to comprehend Lao political and economic transitions in the late Cold War. Taking the post-socialist approach, moreover, this chapter deals with the regime legitimization of the Party before and after the open economy and under the SDGs by dividing it into three analyses—ideological legitimacy, performance-based legitimation, or development legitimation, and revolutionary potential. Lastly, the Lao political structure is worth analyzing to understand the socialist regime consolidation to maintain the status quo of the one-party state.

The analysis of the SDGs in Laos and how the goals have shaped Lao development plans, policies, and domestic institutions are investigated in chapter 4. The chapter begins with sustainable development as an underlying concept of the SDGs and the SDGs in a nutshell and their critics. The main idea of this chapter is to prove how the Party employs the SDGs as the source of its legitimacy by taking the elite interviews with policymakers in Lao development. Last but not least, the state capacity of the country to achieve the goals could serve a regime legitimization as well.

Chapter 5 deals with the Lao state capacity to achieve the ultimate goal—graduation from the LDC status. However, the global pandemic in 2020 has delayed Lao development and potentially plunged the regime legitimacy into crisis. This chapter further analyzes how the Party tackles the unexpected outcome from the pandemic and what will happen next if Laos is out of the Least Developed Country status. The final chapter provides a summary of the SDGs in Laos and how the goals legitimize the Party to stay in power.

2

DEVELOPMENT IN LAOS AND ITS DEBATE

Why development from western countries is good for Laos?

This question seems simple, but profound. To answer this question, it should be noted that Lao development has always reflected an interplay between the international community and the Party to shape Lao development policies, plans and strategies to reach the country's development goals. This chapter aims to explore the exogenous forces in Lao development from the colonial era to the present, how the forces advocated their development norms in Lao development and the debate on Lao development from a Lao scholar's perspective. Process tracing was selected as the method to explore the trajectory of Lao development.

The construction of Lao modernity

Western development standards may seem inapplicable for analyzing development in a socialist regime due to the different socio-economic and political contexts. Laos however has been receptive to development assistance from the development partners and has worked to reach development thresholds in economic growth and human development. The present locus of Lao modernity in terms of economic development, and the country's projected graduation from being a least developed country, shows compatibility to western modernization approach[8] and thus come to the fore for the Party. For this reason, it is worth considering how Lao modernity has been constructed and perceived by the Party. It can then be argued that the sense of

[8] The "West" in his book includes rich countries in North America, Western Europe, some countries in non-Western Europe, and professionals who get involved with foreign aid (see Easterly, 2006).

modernity in Laos has been constructed by external factors that follow the format of western modernity. To support this argument, three external factors will be highlight based on the history of Lao development. These factors include the French interventions during the colonial era, the United States during the cold war, and the international community.

While the makings of modern Laos started during the French colonial era, prior to the French establishing their colony in the country, Laos was known as the Lan Xang kingdom, a tributary state of Siam, and Vietnam from the late sixteenth to the end of the eighteenth century (Stuart-Fox, 1995). Unlike the western concept of a modern state, Southeast Asian kingdoms according to Tambiah (1977) were established as *galactic polities*, a concept derived from the *mandala system*.[9] Referring to PHOTO 2.1, it can be observed that the Lan Xang kingdom also covered some of the northern and north eastern parts of Thailand. The ambiguous nature of the relationship and organization of traditional and tributary states often confused the colonial powers (Winichakul, 1994). They used such ambiguity as an excuse to apply the principles of "civilization mission" (*Mission Civilisatrice* – in French), claiming that these tributary states were backward and needed to be civilized. Southern Vietnam, what was then Cochin-China, was the first of the many places that fell under the principles of "mission civilization" that the French colonial power implemented. The French then successfully expanded its rule to the whole of Vietnam, Cambodia and Laos.

Before the French occupation, Laos was under Siam influence. This influence made it hard for the French to take Laos as a protectorate state without resistance from Siam. Both Siam and France competed against each other to establish authority over Laos and one way of accomplishing their goal was by making maps to assert their territorial control (Winichakul, 1994; Ivarsson and Goscha, 2007). Such power struggle for control led to the Franco-Siamese dispute in 1893 that ended with a French warship's river blockade of the Chao Phraya River.

The blockade forced the Thai king to sign the Franco-Siamese treaty legitimizing the ceding of Laos to France. After the treaty took effect, Laos existed as a modern state, much like Cambodia and Vietnam; administrated as a French colony under the French Indochina.[10]

---

[9] Paik and Vechbanyongratana (2018) conclude characteristics of the mandala system from Tambiah (1977) that this system "consists of a core (*manda*), the center of authority, and a periphery (la) that encircles the core." The power relation between the core and periphery was not equal as the core had more power to control the periphery.

[10] Ivasson and Goscha (2007) contends that the Luang Prabang, Xiengkhuang and Champasak were "recognized officially and given an administrative identity. While Luang Phrabang

source: author, 2018

PHOTO 2.1 Lan Xang Kingdom map at the Lao national museum in Vientiane

The objectives of the French 'civilization mission' in Laos were intended to modernize the political administration, education, transportation, and commercialization of natural resources (Stuart-Fox, 1995; Rehbein, 2007). These objectives were successfully achieved while at the same time gaining influence towards the royal family and the Lao elite. For example, Prince Phetsarath, the second son of the Viceroy Boun Khong and the first Lao prime minister, gained his education from French-controlled Vietnam, France, and England. His educational background and travel experience enabled him to help build Laos as a nation-state based on Lao culture and religion. After he returned home in 1912, he became a member of the French colonial administration and travelled throughout the country to explore the transportation routes used by the French colony. He then united the Lao people and local civil servants outside Luang Prabang who, at that time, never had a mutual sense of Lao national identity. This contribution influenced the Lao elite to express their desires regarding Lao development through the Indigenous Consultative Assembly for Laos. He then attempted to create a Lao culture separate from

Kingdom was administrated as a protectorate, the rest of Laos was rules directly by the French either as a colony or as military territories (p. 58)."

Siam, through the construction of Lao Buddhism and the writing system. Through these efforts, he is considered as "one of Laos's most important modernisers" (Ivasson, 2008, p. 107). During the colonial era, modernity in Laos was constructed under the influence of the French and was warmly embraced by the Lao elite. This sense of following emanated from their change in dressing style to architectural design of buildings; all embodying the concept of French modernization (see PHOTO 2.2). Western modernity seemed more enticing, perceived as a more civilized option compared to the native's concept.

source: author, 2012

PHOTO 2.2 French colonial architecture in Luang Prabang, Laos

After the French colonial period, the United States and the international community, as new aid donors, began to spread their influence in Laos during the Cold War. The Geneva Convention in 1954 resulted in Laos becoming decolonized by the French, who withdrew their troops and reduced financial and development assistance to Indochina. As a newly independent state, the Lao government sought to open its country to new aid-donor countries to continue with the socio-economic development that began with the French. At the same time, the U.S. provided development assistance to defeat the influence of the Soviet Union in Vietnam and Laos by supporting the Royal Lao Army (RLA—in short), Royal Lao Government (RLG—in short), and the anti-communist movement in Laos. Referring to Phraxayavong (2009, pp. 71–72), since 1951, the U.S. began giving economic assistance to Laos for military, infrastructure and human development. The US government built schools, trained Lao teachers, and improve the standard of living in the rural areas. As a result, he notes, "an association of Lao 'Young Turks' was formed… Calling itself the Committee of the Defense of National Interests (CDNI) and adopting a strongly anti-communist and pro-Western orientation" (p. 72). This group became another agency to localize the wave of western modernity to Laos, but its mission was not as successful as expected. After the withdrawal of the US troops in Laos, the *Pathet Lao* movement gained astonishing victory and replaced the western establishment with socialist-style modernity (see chapter 3). The Party introduced "the socialist bypassing capitalism" as a development aspiration to reach the communist stage.

A conceptualization of Lao modernity under the communist construction was shaped by the socialist-style development. The Party took control over Lao development by adopting the centrally-planned economy and modernizing the agricultural and forestry sectors under the cooperative system. Moreover, the Party moved to monopolize the private sectors from the French colonial era to be state-owned enterprises; particularly the infrastructure and public service sectors. Under the socialist regime, Lao modernity focused more on improving food security for Lao people, and in distributing modes of production and public service equally before reaching the communist stage. The result of such modernity nevertheless did not meet the Party's expectation. According to a report of the Lao National Institute of Social Science and Humanities (2011), there were unexpected outcomes from the centrally-planned economy. For instance, the average income was 70–80 USD per year and the agricultural products were lower than expected. Also, poverty and food shortage reflected the economic vulnerability of the country which posed a possible factor in plunging legitimacy for the Party, which could have resulted in a crisis.

For this reason, I argue that the mind-set of modernity in Laos still follows the trajectory of western modernity that was shaped by western countries and localized by the Lao elite in the past. Once the mind-set of this modernity is perceived in Lao people, it is infeasible for the country to be back to the pre-colonial era. Viewed in this light, the open economy in 1986 thus was the answer to pursue the country's modernity and enhance the Party's legitimacy in doing so.

After 1986, the Lao modernity was again reconstructed by the Party based on external factors. The first and second factors are capitalism and globalization after the Cold War. The country has faced an influx of foreign direct investments and external cultures from western countries and other Asian countries These factors have shaped Lao people's lifestyle to be materialistic and capitalistic. For example, the malls in Vientiane could reflect the new lifestyle of people in the capital city in which people could spend their leisure time shopping or watching movies. The last external factor is the influence of the international community, or the development partners, in Lao development. With this factor, the Lao modernity was reconstructed to be indictable with the international development standard (for example, economic growth, and rate of literacy, life expectancy and so on). Their influence on Lao development could be seen from the so-called "Round Table Process" (RTP) which will further clarify their influence in Lao development in the following topic.

The interplay between the development partners and the Lao government under the Round Table Meeting

The Party alone does not determine development in Laos. Convincing evidence (See Phraxayavong, 2009; Khennavong, 2014) reveals that the Lao government and the development partners have shaped the Lao development plan mutually. The Party became more receptive to taking on development partners following the collapse of the Soviet Union and Laos' subsequent economic downturn. As mentioned previously, in 1986, the Party began to rethink economic reform and opened up the country to the international community. Aid-donor countries, international organizations, and financial institutions immediately provided assistance through the Official Development Assistance (ODA) organization, which offered a grant and low-interest loan to the Lao government, as Laos is listed as one of the least developed countries. Since Laos alone lacks the capacity to do so, the ODA is indispensable to the Lao government for meeting development standards. Since 1983,[11] these agreements have been negotiated at the Round Table Process (RTP), where the Lao government and the development partners go over de-

[11] After Lao gained independence in 1975, the Party needed development assistance to build its new regime and to mitigate economic difficulties. At that time, the Lao government appealed for help from the Council for Mutual Economic Assistance (CMEA) supported by the Soviet Union, the International Monetary Fund (IMF), and the United Nations Development Programme (UNDP) that allowed Western countries to take part in Lao development. In 1983, Laos participated in the Round Table Process in Geneva, Switzerland. Since 1983 the Lao PDR has been participating in the Round Table Process (RTP), with the support of the United Nations Development Programme (UNDP) (see Pharaxayavong, 2009).

velopmental issues and discuss assistance needed from the ODA, as well as how to implement ODA in the country's developmental plan effectively.

In 2000, the RTP was officially launched in Laos as a "unique platform for policy dialogue on the country's development agenda" allowing for the strengthening of "development effectiveness and aid coordination in the country" (Lao PDR, 2015). The RTP in Laos is special as the country is landlocked and least developed. All the countries of concern and all the donors or other stakeholders join together in the RTP. Primarily, it works to set up development priorities and determine what specific resources will be needed. The whole process of the RTP starts with the High-Level Round Table Meetings, which are held every five years. These meetings shape development policy in the national development plan and set up strategies to implement the plan in the country under the development partners' supervision. After policy implementation, the Round Table Implementation Meeting (RTIM) is held every year to re-examine progress made and to set up development priorities for the following year. This process is typical for aid-donor and recipient countries.

However, the relationship between the Lao government and the development partners has been re-shaped twice. First, by both the Paris Declaration and the Accra Agenda for Action that were endorsed in 2005. Second, by the Busan Partnership for Effective Development Cooperation that was endorsed in 2011. These development frameworks were shaped by the international community and implemented in many aid-recipient countries. The purpose of each was to improve the quality of aid, the impact of programs on development, the overall monitoring system, and the transparency and shared responsibilities between the state and the partners (Organization for Economic Co-operation and Development, 2011). There are five core principles of the Paris Declaration: Ownership, Alignment, Harmonization, Results, and Mutual Accountability.

Specifically, the principles of the Paris Declaration addressed the partnership between the Lao government and the development partners through the Vientiane Declaration on Aid Effectiveness (or VDI—in short) in 2006. The primary objective of the VDI is to "take appropriate monitoring actions to make aid more effective and assist the country in achieving the Millennium Development Goals by 2015, and the long-term development goal of exiting the status of least developed country by 2020" (United Nations Development Program [UNDP], 2006, p. 1). Based on the Paris Declaration, the five key principles of the declaration were set to fit in to the country's political context. They include:

1. Increased country ownership over development policies, planning, implementation and aid coordination;
2. Better alignment of development partners' support to national policies and plans, and increased support to and use of national systems;
3. Harmonization and simplification of development partners' procedures and activities;
4. Managing for results in order to ensure effective use of resources;
5. Both government and development partners have mutual accountability for progress (UNDP, 2006).

To achieve the development goals and provide development assistance efficiently, moreover, Sector Working Groups (SWGs) were introduced as "the main mechanism for coordination and dialogue between the Government and the partners in development at the sectoral and thematic area levels" (UNDP, 2006, p. 27). Focusing on four thematic area levels,[12] the Country Action Plan was formed from these dialogues to address, and ultimately achieve, the development goals. For example, the development partners and the Lao government set up the Ministry of Education, Australia Aid, and UNICEF to cover the Education and Gender Sector Working Group. SWGs continually shaped the role of the Lao government and the development partners with regard to the Sustainable Development Goals, which I will further clarify later.

Since the RTP aims to promote the global development agenda and guide the Lao government to implement the agenda, the development standards set by the development partners which have become the target figures indicating the development achievements of the Lao government. The interplay between the development partners and the Lao government, recently, could be reflected from the three open policies initiated by Thonglun Sisoulith, the current President of the State and the former Lao Prime Minister. These policies focus on the concepts of open door, open minds, and open barriers (The Strait Times, 2018). Even though the policy reveals a stronger turn toward the international community, the RTP is not the final process for policy formulation. The following topic will describe another crucial process in Lao development which is so-called the Congress of Lao People's Revolutionary Party —or the Party Congress.

[12] The four thematic areas of the SWGs in the MDGs are: 1) Health, Gender, and HIV/AIDs, 2) Education and Gender, 3) Infrastructure and 4) Agriculture, Rural Development, and Natural Resource Management.

The Party-led development in Laos under the Party Congress

Since the LPRP came to power in 1975, the Party has dominated the developmental supreme policy-making organs in Lao development, and are referred to collectively as the Congress of the Lao People's Revolutionary Party (the Party Congress—in short).[13] The Party Congress is normally held every five years. Every decision made by the Party Congress concretely becomes a part of the Five-Year National Socio-Economic Development Plan (NSEDP), the ten-year development strategy, and the fifteen-year development vision. The plan reflects the development norms that have mostly shaped national development and defines: 1) the ultimate development goals of the Party; 2) the economic sectors that have been prioritized for their contributions to the GDP; 3) the strategies for achieving the development goals under the Party's supervision, and 4) how external forces influence Lao development.

The Party Congress determines the political and socio-economic development direction in Laos for the upcoming five years, it is therefore always the center of attention for the Lao people and outside observers (e.g., Bourdet, 2002; Lintner 2008; Mocci, 2016). The Party Congress, first of all, reveals transitions in political leaders (Stuart-Fox 2007, p. 161). Transitions in the Party Congress further reflect intra-Party competition between political clans, reformist-liberals, conservative-moderates, and Pro-Vietnam and Pro-Chinese groups (see chapter 3; Stuart-Fox, 2007; Lintner, 2008; Sayalath and Creak, 2016; Mocci 2016). Second, the Party Congress represents the Party's hegemony and legitimacy over the country. At the Tenth Party Congress, Mocci (2016) concluded that the three pillars strengthen the Party's hegemony and legitimacy, these includes: "the idea of the heroism of the founding members of the revolutionary party," "economic growth," and "Laos's proactive and authoritative role in foreign affairs" (pp. 223–224). Third, the Party Congress reflects the interplay of internal–external forces that have shaped its role and that of the Lao government in national development.

The very first Party-led development plan emerged at the Interim Three Years Plan (1976–1980). During that time, Laos was considered a newly independent country, needing to stabilize its new regime and maintain a self-reliant economy. The main tasks of the plan, as Langer and Zasloff (1976, p.109) summarize, was to increase production in agriculture, forestry, and livestock breeding, and to improve the sectors of transportation, communi-

13 The Party Congress of the LPRP started in 1955. The first Party Congress focused on the fight against imperialism and the fight for national independence. The second Party Congress was held in 1972 to propose the third reconciliation government.

cations, and infrastructure. To achieve the development tasks, Phraxayawong (2009, p. 139) contends "the centralized command model of planning along Soviet lines" was employed by the Party to transition the country to socialism step-by-step, with the warm support of fraternal socialist countries. Though the interim plan was not as successful as the Party expected, development assistance from the USSR and other socialist countries, the IMF, and the World Bank supported the Lao economy to help avoid an economic downturn. Subsequently, the five-year National Socio-Economic Development Plan (NSDEP) endorsed at the Party Congress has reflected the influence of external forces in Lao development. In 1982, the interim plan became the blueprint for the first five-year NSEDP at the Third Party Congress.[14]

Since then, the Party Congress has always had similar speeches and commitments from the Party members based on the new circumstance. According to the Tenth Party Congress in 2016, for example, 685 delegates out of over 268,000 comrades throughout the country participated in this Congress. Similar to the previous Party Congress meetings, the speeches and reports delivered by the Party members at both central and local levels can be divided into four parts; 1) speeches about past political struggles and the heroic role of the nationalist movement; 2) reports on development achievements with target figures; 3) development constraints and challenges; and 4) development aspiration and target projections for the next 5 years, 10 years, and 15 years, respectively. Throughout all of this, the Party continued to commit itself as the leading nucleus and delegate of the Lao people in accomplishing the development aspirations of the country.

Long-term development aspiration and development debates in Laos

Since Lao modernity has been shaped by external forces, development goals in Laos are on the same path to reach western modernity. For this reason, the Party has been receptive to the international development standards from the development partners to shape the long-term development aspiration—to graduate from the least developed country status by 2026. This topic will shed light on the journey of Lao development from 2006 to 2015 to graduate from the LDC status and its debates from Lao scholars.

[14] Nouhak Phoumsavan, reported a set of nine major tasks enshrined in the First five year NSEDP to be achieved before 1985. The focal tasks, as Thayer (1983, pp. 88–89) concluded, were mainly in agriculture, forestry, handicrafts and small industries, transportation and public services, and economic development, through the enhancement of economic cooperation with Vietnam and Cambodia, and in utilizing economic assistance from the USSR and other socialist countries.

source: CDP Calculations; NERI (in MPI and UNDP, 2017, p. 31)

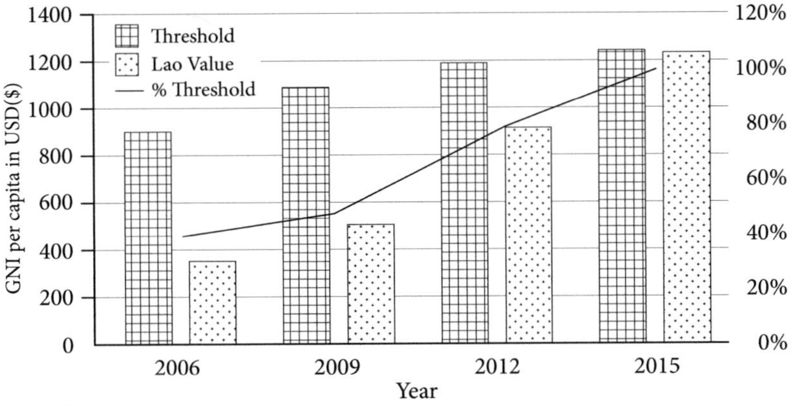

GRAPH 2.1 Progress of Lao PDR's GNI per capita in recent reviews (2006–2015).

The UNDP's criterion for classifying the least developed country (see United Nations, 2015) includes ratings on the following factors: Gross National Income (GNI) per capita, Human Assets Index (HAI), and Economic Vulnerability Index (EVI). For Laos, the UNDP and the Ministry of Planning and Investment (MPI) reported progress in each area in 2017 (Ministry of Planning and Investment & The United Nations Development Programme [MPI and UNDP], 2017).[15] The GNI had made progress by 2015, and it has been gradually improving from about $350 in 2002 to $1,232 in 2015 (see GRAPH 2.1). This number almost reached the criterion for graduation from the least developed country status at $1,242. The UNDP further forecasts, "the Lao economy is continuing to progressively develop and is expected to grow at an average rate of 7.5% per year" (p. 31).

Regarding the Human Assets Index (HAI), the report notes that Laos has made improvements, but not as significant as the GNI. HAI number fluctuated a bit between 2003 and 2015 (see GRAPH 2.2), indexing the country's slower progress relative to other countries. The report also addresses the possible reasons for this: "(i) the different indicators that constitute the HAI are generally slow to move compared with more volatile variables… and (ii) there has

[15] The three criteria for graduating from LDC status consist of an EVI of 32 or below, an HAI with a threshold of 66 or more, and a GNI per capita greater than $1,280. Each threshold for Landlocked Developing Countries and Small Island Developing States (UN-OHRLLS) has specific indicators according to the UN Office of the High Representative for the Least Developed Countries. For instance, the indicators of Economic Vulnerability Index (EVI) consist of: 1) population size; 2) remoteness; 3) merchandise export concentration; 4) share of agriculture, forestry and fisheries; 5) share of population in low elevated coastal zones; 6) instability of exports of goods and services; 6) victims of natural disasters; and 7) instability of agricultural production (see more UN-OHRLLS, 2018).

TABLE 2.1 Human Development Index and its components

Country	Human Development Index	Life expectancy at birth	Expected years of schooling	Mean years of schooling	Gross National Income (GNI) per capita	GNI per capita minus HDI rank	HDI rank (Global rank)
	Value	(years)	(years)	(years)	(2011 PPP $)		
	2017	2017	2017	2017	2017	2017	2016
Singapore	0.932	83.2	16.2	11.5	82,503	-6	8
Brunei Darussalam	0.853	77.4	14.5	9.1	76.425	-35	40
Malaysia	0.802	75.7	13.7	10.2	26,107	-11	57
Thailand	0.755	75.5	14.7	7.6	15,516	-7	86
Philippines	0.699	69.2	12.6	9.3	9,154	-7	111
Indonesia	0.694	69.4	12.8	8.0	10,846	-19	115
Laos	0.601	67.0	11.2	5.2	6,070	-13	137
Cambodia	0.582	69.3	11.7	4.8	3,413	3	146
Myanmar	0.578	66.7	10.0	4.9	2,471	12	148

source UNDP, 2018c

been a change in the database since 2012 in which the definition, coverage, etc. have changed" (MPI & UNDP, 2017, p. 32) As long as undernourishment declines and the literacy rate and secondary school enrollment rate increases every triennium, Laos will meet the demands of this criterion in 2018.

source: NERI calculations made from CDP database (in MPI & UNDP, 2017, p. 33).

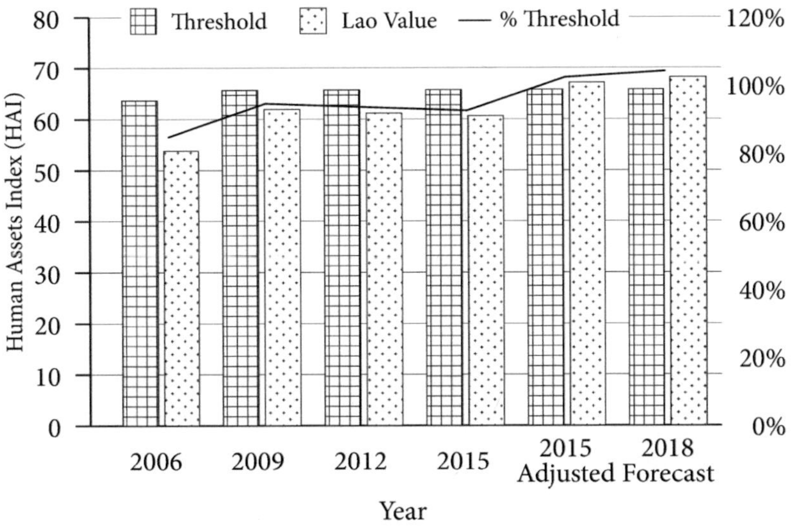

GRAPH 2.2 Human Assets Index (HAI) threshold and progress of Lao PDR

The Economic Vulnerability Index (EVI), the report (2017, p. 34) concludes that Laos reached 36.2 in 2015 (the graduation threshold of the EVI is 32 or below). This registers at 88% of the graduation threshold (see GRAPH 2.3).

Compared to the neighboring countries, Laos is not surprisingly behind relative to human capital and GDP per capita. TABLE 2.1 illustrates the Human Development Index (HDI) of the ASEAN countries and shows that Laos was ranked 8th out of 10 countries at 0.601. This data demonstrates that the Lao government is striving to accelerate economic growth and improve human development, surpassing the other ASEAN countries.

Without a doubt, the Lao government's ambition to graduate from being a least developed country status is reflected in its policy at the political, economic and social levels. In 2000, the Party announced its poverty reduction strategies at the 7th Round Table Meeting. This strategy was based on human resources development, rural development, and people's participation (Lao PDR, 2004). Moreover, the Lao government also initiated the so-called "2010 framework" to accelerate the implementation of plans for the MDGs.

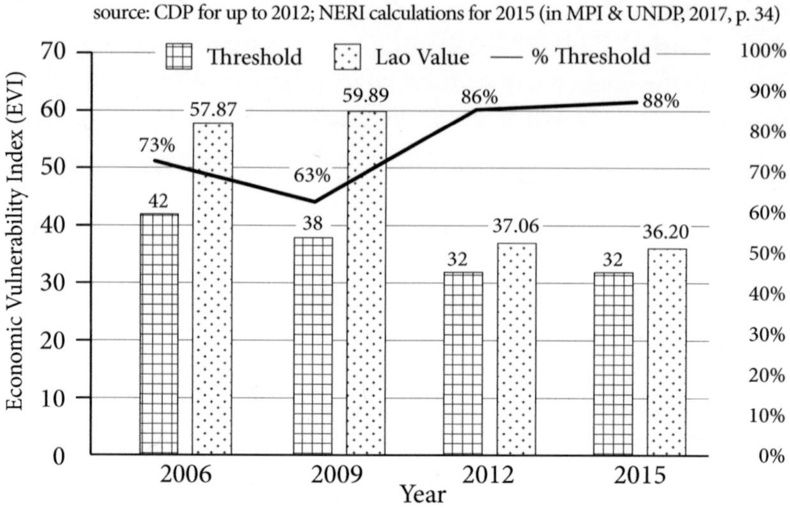

GRAPH 2.3 Laos' EVI evolution in comparison with the threshold

To achieve the MDGs, there are 1,400 current development projects amounting to more than 76 trillion Kips that had been assessed by the government before being included in the government's last five-year national socio-economic plan (Sengdara, 2015). An incremental number of business sectors expanded considerably, including those of hydroelectric power, mining, construction materials, agriculture and ecotourism (Stuart-Fox 1995; Creak, 2011; Howe & Park, 2015). These sectors are a result of economic integration at sub regional and regional levels, which has helped to change Laos from a "land-locked" to a "land-linked country" and become the "Battery of Asia" (see Gunn, 2008).

After the term for the MDGs expired in 2015, an assessment of the outcomes showed promise for the Lao government. The MDGs summary report in Laos (The UN, 2015a), notes that Laos has achieved universal access to primary education, gender equity in primary education, maternal mortality, reduced child mortality, safe water, and sanitation. Despite these achievements, Laos is continually facing challenges at achieving full and productive employment for its citizens, reducing malnutrition rates, increasing primary, secondary, and tertiary education rates, enhancing gender equity in secondary and tertiary education, improving the role of women in employment and political participation, decreasing mortality and disease rates, improving environmental sustainability, reversing forest loss, and clearing mines carpeted in the country after the secret war. These challenges also include Lao development under the SDGs since 2015.

Since the SDGs were introduced to Lao development, the Lao government has implemented the SGDs in the 8th five-year National Socio-Economic Development Plan (2016–2020), the Development Strategy of 2025, and Vision 2030. These plans include strategies to work toward green growth and sustainable development, to maintain steady economic growth, to achieve a constant reduction of poverty and to graduate from Least Developed Country status (Vientiane Time, 2016c). At the local level, the Lao government has been supporting local administrations to be more proactive and to drive the development process, strengthen service delivery functions, improve multi-sector coordination, and enhance participation, transparency, and accountability (Lao PDR, 2015). This shift yielded to the inclusion of International Non-Governmental Organizations and Lao Non-Profit Organizations as Lao civil society and the private sector in the RTP. As a consequence, the Lao government and the development partners endorsed the Vientiane Declaration on Partnership for Effective Development Cooperation (or the VDII) for the inclusiveness framework between the Lao government, the development partners and other stakeholders. This framework reveals the global and regional context to Lao development, the role of the development stakeholders, and the resources needed to implement the SDGs in Laos. With 18 goals of the SDGs in Laos, the RTM has broadened the SWGs from four to ten groups in order to achieve the SDGs efficiency and to better include stakeholders.

However, since Laos has been a highly aid-dependent country for over half a century, the role of the development partners in Lao development should be taken into consideration. As Pholsena and Banomyong (2006, p. 73) contend, “Laos is often designated as a ‘sponge’ which absorbs large flows of international aid.” There are many reasons why international aid matters to Lao government. Phraxayavong (2009) notes,

> The reasons for this are several: (a) the country is poor, (b) the government has perennially been in fiscal and sometimes political shambles, (c) most residents are still living in a “subsistence” economy, (d) the country’s administrative and economic expertise kept having to be rebuilt due to the constant wars and political changes, (e) the World Bank/IMF’s “structural adjustment” created new humanitarian needs that have had to be met in other ways, (f) Laos and its financial supporters want the country to graduate from the LDC status as soon as possible, and (g) the very attempt to connect the country to full participation in global capitalist markets—ostensibly as a way of improving the economy and standard of living (p. 258).

According to the normative diction of the SDGs, the terms "good governance" and "decentralization" have been used to advocate democratization indirectly. This has led to a debate about how the Lao government deals with these terms, which are incompatible with the hardline socialists and the socialist regime running the country. Since the development partners play an important role in improving good governance through development assistance under the Governance and Public Administration Reform Programme (GPAR) in 1993, its result is, as Khennavong (2014) argues, an improvement of some dimensions of governance in Laos. He contends there are two reasons for this improvement, "the first is that there is a good donor-government relationship… Second… aid has helped promote governance reform because the Lao government at least parts of it have wanted it to" (p. 170). His argument is more optimistic than Stuart-Fox's argument. As Stuart-Fox (2005, pp. 52–55) argues, the Lao elite has emphasized little with regard to democratization and, as long as "the levels of wealth in Mekong towns continue to rise…there is unlikely to be strong pressure for more democratic institutions." Indeed, "the Party cannot be expected to bring about its own demise by stepping aside to make way for a multiparty system." Likewise, Howe (2018) argues that the development partners per se do not strive towards democratization as an expectation because the development partners have "privileged the pursuit of economic growth over human rights, political freedom, environmental sustainability and a host of other social justice issues" (p. 131). In this book, it should be noted that the National Assembly and civil society are worth studying to understand how the principle of good governance functions in Laos (see chapter 3). The interpretation of good governance by the Lao government in its restructuring domestic institutions, formulating development policy, and legitimizing itself in the public eye will also be explored here.

Decentralization in Laos, many scholars argue, is like old whiskey in a new bottle. Though the Lao government attempted to decentralize power to local authorities, as I argue, this is inefficient since the decisive power, in turn, is mainly at the central level. As Creak (2014) argues, centralization is still masquerading as decentralization. Besides, there has been too little, if any at all, action to decentralize. Taking a regime-centered organizational approach to examine the political structure in Laos, Soukamneuth (2006) emphasized that decentralization in Laos is nothing but a development myth. Likewise, StuartFox (2005) has pointed out that the Party could maintain its power by appointing local governors and that corruption issues have been in-

The Round Table Meeting The Lao government (Chair) + The UNDP (Co-chair)

The 8th National Socio-Economic Development Plan (2016–2020) Goal: Be eligible to graduate from the LDC status by 2020 through continuous, inclusive, and sustainable growth		
Outcome 1: Continued, firm, and inclusive growth	Outcome 2: Human resources development, and upgrading public and private sectors	Outcome 3: Effectively protected and utilized natural resources

10 Sector Working groups (SWGs)		
Agriculture and Rural Development (ARD SWG)	Chair:	Ministry of Agriculture and Forestry
	Co-chair:	French Ambassador
Education (ESWG)	Chair:	Ministry of Education and Sport
	Co-chair:	Australian Ambassador and EU Ambassador
Health (HSWG)	Chair:	Ministry of Health
	Co-chair:	Japanese Ambassador and WHO
Illicit Drug Control (ILD SWG)	Chair:	The Lao National Commission for Drug Control and Supervision
	Co-chair:	Japanese Ambassador, Australian Ambassador, and UNODC
Infrastructure (ISWG)	Chair:	Ministry of Public Works and Transport
	Co-chair:	Japanese Ambassador, ADB and World Bank
Macro-Economic Working Group (MEWG)	Chair:	Ministry of Planning and Investment
	Co-chair:	ADB and World Bank
Natural Resources and Environmental (NRE SWG)	Chair:	Ministry of Natural Resource and Environment
	Co-chair:	German Ambassador and World Bank
Trade and Private Sector (TP SWG)	Chair:	Ministry of Industry and Commerce
	Co-chair:	German Ambassador and EU Ambassador
UXO (UXO SWG)	Chair:	The National Leading Committee for Rural Development and Poverty Eradication and the National Regulatory Authority for UXO
	Co-chair:	UNDP, Ambassador of the USA
Governance (GOVERNANCE SWG)	Chair:	Ministry of Home Affairs and Ministry of Justice
	Co-chair:	UNDP

Note: WHO = World Health Organization, UNODC = United Nations Office on Drugs and Crime, EU = European Union, ADB = Asian Development Bank, UNDP, United Nations Development Programme, UXO = Unexploded Ordnance
source: Author's compilation based on Ministry of Planning and Investment (MPI) (2016a) and ADB (2017)

DIAGRAM 2.1 Round Table Process and sector working groups in Laos creasing because of decentralization. Following Creak 's arguments, this book will shed additional light on the central-local relation and People's Provincial Assembly and Three Build Directive (Sam Sang—in Lao) to explore how decentralization in Laos is unique and could maintain the Party's power at the local level.

Given that development is another tool for regime legitimacy of the Party, this book will analyze how the Lao government maintains its guiding role (Sinam-Nampha—in Lao) in national-local development to obtain regime legitimacy. Unlike the development-related studies above, I particularly focus on the politics of development between the Lao government and the development partners by investigating the domestic institution and Lao development policy under the Sustainable Development Goals, which include the unmet Millennium Development Goals. Moreover, the question of how the Lao government copes with incompatible development norms for an undemocratic regime will be analyzed in order to provide insight in the Lao-style domestic institutions. In my opinion, this book will pave the way for examining Lao development in its political context, something currently absent from the Lao studies literature.

Concluding remarks

The Lao modernity has been constructed by external factors since the French colonial era that was localized by the Lao local elite. For this reason, the path to Lao modernity is the same as western modernity and has embedded in Lao people's mind-set in which the western one is more civilized, superior, and modern. Once this sort of modernity is widely accepted in the country's development, it is rather difficult for the country to be backward and undeveloped. After the country's independence in 1975, western modernity was less influential. Capitalism and western influence seemed to contradict the socialist regime and could be an obstacle to building the socialist utopia. The nationalist movement institutionalized itself into the political party adhering to the Marxist-Leninist ideology in political structure and national development. The centrally-planned economy was adopted to implement socialism in economic realms. However, the collapse of the Soviet Union and the economic downturn in the country were the turning points for the Party to open the country to capitalism. Western modernity reappeared in Lao development as the goal to legitimate the Party's leading role in development.

After all, the Party has been receptive to the international community or the development partners in Laos. They have been playing a role to support their development norms in the Official Development Assistance to the Lao government. Moreover, the development partners and the Lao government have a platform called the Round Table Process to shape Lao development plans and policies. After that, there is another process for the Party's members to make the final decision in Lao development. This process is called the Congress of the Lao People's Revolutionary Party or the Party Congress held every five years. The Party Congress is a crucial event in Lao politics as the Party's members in high-ranked positions always justify their leadership, achievement in the past five years, and challenges in the future. The outcomes after the Party's Congress is the national development plans, development strategy, and the development vision. With the interplay between the development partners and the Party, Lao development aspiration has recently followed the path to graduate from the Least Developed Country status with a strong commitment from the Party. This aspiration thus is worth analyzing why development from the western countries matters for the Party and how the Lao modernity is on the same path as the western one.

3

REGIME LEGITIMACY IN POST-SOCIALIST LAOS

"Long live Lao People's Democratic Republic.
Long live the glorious and dignified Lao People's Revolutionary Party.
Long live Marxism-Leninism."[17]

The above slogan continuously appeared on the billboard behind the Eleventh Congress of the Lao People's Revolutionary Party (LPRP or the Party) in 2016 (see PHOTO 3.1). The slogan simply implies that the sovereign power of Laos is in the hands of the Lao People's Revolutionary Party, which is steeped in Marxist-Leninist ideology. Since the Party is the primary actor in Lao politics, this chapter aims to investigate how the Party obtains and consolidates its political power, and the extent to which Lao state power has transformed under the international development norms. This information can provide insight into the interplay between the external-internal forces legitimizing the Party's power and which further shaped Lao domestic institutions and development policy.

This chapter is divided into three parts following the post-socialist approach. The first part will investigate regime legitimacy in post-socialist Laos. Saxonberg's (2013) post-socialist framework was employed (see chapter 1) here. The three variables identified by his framework support the argument of this chapter that the Party relies on ideological legitimacy, pragmatic acceptance of performance-based legitimation, and the suppression of revolutionary potential to maintain state power. These concepts can be utilized to help understand how the Party legitimized socialist ideology to serve its political purposes as new circumstances have arisen. In the second part, I will reveal how the Party seeks to maintain its political and institutional stability by consolidating socialism and the Party's power within the political structure of

[17] This slogan was translated in English by High and Petit (2013).

Laos, and by enhancing the elite cohesion. In the final part, I will investigate the state power, which is in the hands of the Party, under the international development norms. I argue that the Party has partly transformed itself to conform to the international development norms for its survival.

Process tracing and elite interviewing are the overarching tools I use to analyze the mechanisms sustaining the regime legitimacy of the Party and its power under the influx of international development norms. I conducted multiple interviews with high-status individuals including: A Party member, a National Assembly (NA) member, a Lao policymaker, and Lao government officers, representatives of the Lao Non-Profit Association (NPA), representatives of the development partners, Lao academics, Lao experts, and representatives of INGOs.

Process tracing was then used to trace historical events to explain why the Party, the independent variable, has a legitimate right to employ the state power, the dependent variable. It should be noted that the Party, regime legitimation, and state power are viewed singularly in this chapter. I categorize and divide second-hand data chronologically into three periods: 1) the nationalist movement's adoption of socialist ideology to national independence (1955–1975); 2) ideological legitimation following national independence (1975–1985); and the socialist ideology under the open economy (1986–present). Finally, first-hand and second-hand data are analyzed to provide insight into regime legitimacy and Lao state power in post-socialist Laos.

Ideological legitimacy

The Marxist-Leninist ideology is used to mobilize regime legitimacy in many socialist countries. When the communist party first seized political power, the ideology was the most important element, as Saxonberg (2013) notes, to make "a degree of voluntary compliance possible." In this sense, ideological legitimacy is the means of the communist party to gain legitimate right to rule with strong support from cadres, intellectuals, and the working class. He further contends that ideology plays "a major role in motivating their cadres to embark on a 'messianic' mission to change society" (Saxonberg, 2013, pp. 16–17). In the case of Laos, the Marxist-Leninist ideology is not only the political ideology of the country, but also used by the Party to prolong its political legitimacy to rule.

source: Bangkok Post, 2021

PHOTO 3.1 The Eleventh Congress of the Lao People's Revolutionary Party

This topic begins with a brief history of the Marxist-Leninist ideology in Laos and an examination of how this ideology is legitimized by the Party, which started as a nationalist movement in 1955. Socialist ideology in Laos formed in a manner unlike what Karl Marx predicted for this stage of communism, which he rooted in class struggle over the means of production. In Laos, evidence from many scholars, and a number of manuscripts and speeches given by political leaders,[18] shows that the ideology was established by the nationalist leaders who had a strong connection with the Vietnamese nationalist movement of the French colonial era (Langer and Zarloff, 1970; Christie, 1982; Brown, 1991; Stuart-Fox, 1997; Ivarsson; 2008; Creak, 2018).

Back in the colonial era, undesirable outcomes resulting from the French colonial administration served as an impetus for resistance groups in the Indochinese countries. Ho Chi Minh,[19] the Vietnamese nationalist leader who longed for national independence and admired the Marxist-Leninist ideology employed in the Russian revolution in 1917. He took Lenin, the ideology and the revolution as inspiration to find allies and establish the

18 For example, the Lao literature titled 'the Sixty Years of the LPRP' (Kana Kosana Aob Hom Soun Kang Pak, 2015, p. 4) notes that there are two contributing factors that came from the Indochinese Communist Party (ICP) relating to the formation of the Party. These factors include Marxist-Leninist ideology and the ICP's invaluable assistance to the Lao revolution.

19 Ho Chi Minh's revolutionary doctrine, according to his own writing, is based on Leninism (Ho Chi Minh, 1960 translated by Fall, 1960). He wrote in the cited article for the Soviet Review of Problems of the East, for the ninetieth anniversary of Lenin's birth, that when he was in France, he supported the October revolution and overwhelmingly admired Lenin as "the great patriot." He notes that "At first, patriotism, not yet communism, led to my confidence in Lenin…I gradually came upon the fact that only socialism can liberate oppressed nations, and working people throughout the world, from slavery" (pp. 5–7).

Indochinese Communist Party (ICP) in 1930. Its political mission mainly was to fight against French colonists, feudalism, and capitalism to obtain national independence and to establish a proletariat government (Ruane, 1995, p. 4). Thereafter, the ICP as an underground movement sought to establish the Marxist-Leninist ideology in Laos and Cambodia.

Although the nationalist movement[20] and the political consciousness of the Lao people grew slowly,[21] its pace to fight colonialism and imperialism was accelerated by nationalist leaders under Vietnamese supervision. In 1945, the Japanese occupation of Laos created an opportunity to empower the nationalist movement to be more cohesive. At that time, The Japanese occupation in Laos diminished French influence over Laos under the "*Meigo Sakusen*" operation to increase more troops in the fight against the Allied forces (Kikuchi, 2017). The leaders regarded as most influential and heroic were Kaysone Phomvihane and Prince Souphanouvong. They used their different backgrounds to build connections with the Viet Minh and Ho Chi Minh. Prince Souphanouvong, also known as the Red Prince, was one of the sons of Prince Bounkhong, the last vice-king of Luang Prabang and his half-brother was Prince Souvanna Phouma, the former Lao Prime Minister. Stuart-Fox (1997) describes him as an "energetic, headstrong and ambitious" person (p. 63). He became a radical nationalist because his wife was Vietnamese and a supporter of Vietminh. Unlike Prince Souphanouvong, Kaysone Phomevihane was half Lao and half Vietnamese, born in Savannakhet province. His father was a Vietnamese who worked in the French colonial service and his mother was a Lao peasant. He attended law school at university in Hanoi, Vietnam, where he first met Nouhak Phoumsavanh, another nationalist leader. Without a doubt, Kaysone was closely tied with Ho Chi Minh and Vietminh to fight against the French colonists as a small guerrilla army in southern and central Laos. He and other leaders, including Nouhak, were brought to a "Committee of Lao Resistance in the East" by the Vietminh in 1946. Both Prince Souphanouvong and Kaysone had worked with Vietminh for three years before establishing

20 After the Japanese surrendered in 1945, the French colony reestablished its occupation of the Indochinese countries. As a result of nationalist empowerment during Japanese occupation, Lao Issara (Free Lao) was established as an independent government that was an anti-French, non-communist nationalist movement. Prince Souphanouvong was Minister of Defense and Communication. However, I will particularly focus on the *Pathet Lao* as a communist movement to provide better understanding of the ideological movements toward Marxist-Leninism in Laos.

21 To address why the Lao people took to socialist ideology so gradually, many scholars have argued that Lao people at that time lacked awareness of political and economic affairs (Stuart-Fox, 1997; Rathie, 2017).

their own movement—the Lao Patriotic Front (LPF) and the *Pathet Lao*, respectively (Stuart-Fox, 1996, p. 75).[22]

In 1950, the *Pathet Lao* was established to unify and empower nationalist-communist factions to fight with the US troops during the Laotian civil war.[23] After that, the Lao People's Party (*Pak Pasason Lao*) was officially established in 1955. The Marxist-Leninist ideology first became manifest in "the Twelve Missions" of the Party, which were written in support of Marxism-Leninism (along with the nationalist ideology) and the liberation of the Lao people from imperialism. They united under the slogan: "We will unitize Lao people to achieve the national liberation mission and build Laos for peace, independence, democracy, unity and prosperity" (Kana Kosana Aob Hom Soun Kang Pak, 2015, pp. 10–11). From the French colonization to the civil war, the Party used emancipation discourse to encourage the Lao people to trust in its ideology and its capable leadership. After the thirty years struggle (1945–1975), in 1973, the Paris Peace Accords ordered the withdrawal of all foreign troops from Laos.[24] A few years later, the collapse of the anti-communist regimes in South Vietnam and Cambodia legitimized the communist victory in Indochina. In 1975, the Party proclaimed its victory over the country and the Lao People's Democratic Republic was first recognized as a communist one-party state.

Ideological legitimation for nation-building and the socialist transformation (1975–1985)

After gaining national independence in 1975, the Party seized state power. The Marxist-Leninist ideology was highly influential and became the dominant political ideology of the country. Since then, the Party sought to promote the ideology to its cadres and the Lao people. The Party's goal was to stabilize

[22] The Laotian civil war is considered a proxy war of the cold war (1960s—1970s). The fight between the *Pathet Lao* supported by the communist movement in North Vietnam and Royal Lao Army supported by the USA broke down a reconciliation government resulting from the 1962 Geneva Agreement of the Lao nationalist movement into political factions based on ideology (see Stuart-Fox, 1997a).

[23] Initially, as Stuart-Fox (1996, p. 75; 1997, p. 79) points out, the *Pathet Lao* was based on three factions: 1) Prince Souphanouvong and supporters of the traditional Lao elites 2) Kaysone Phomvihane and Nouhak Phoumsavanh and the ICP, or the Committee for Lao Resistance in the East, and 3) Faydang and Sithon who were chiefs of the dominant ethnic groups. These factions had become a single unit by the first Congress of the People's Representative in 1950. The *Pathet Lao* was then approved as the resistance government.

[24] Article 20(b) of the Paris Peace Accord issues, "Foreign countries shall put an end to all military activities in Cambodia and Laos, totally withdraw from and refrain from reintroducing into these two countries troops, military advisers, and military personnel, armaments, munitions and war material" (CVCE, 2015).

its regime to promote nation-building and socialist transformation.The path to the transformation at that time was introduced as "socialism without going through the stage of capitalist development" to reach the goal[25] in the Third Plenum of the Second Central Committee in 1975 (Stuart-Fox, 1997a, p.169).

A number of strategies were used to achieve the Party's mission in the socio-economic and political realms. The Party first implemented a Leninist political structure to institutionalize itself and other political organizations in the country that represented the Party's interests. The Politburo of the Lao People's Revolutionary Party, the main organization that keeps the political organizations organized under the principle of democratic centralism, (Stuart Fox; 1997a; Croissant & Lorenz, 2018), was a primary actor in designing the Lao development plan, which was based on the Soviet model. The collectivization of agriculture to support the formation of village cooperatives was first introduced in the Interim Three-Year Plan (1978–1980), and was considered "a pre-condition for a soviet-style, centrally planned economy" (Phraxayawong, 2009, p. 139). The collectivization of agriculture not only shaped the economic system, but also became a tool to control the Lao people at the local level. Pholsena (2006) supports this argument, stating that "Collectivization…was not only seen as a means to achieve economic security but also as an instrument for political consolidation… it was expected that collectivization would transform the people into 'new socialist men'" (p. 56). However, the outcome of collectivization was not as successful as the Party expected. The path to the socialist utopia through collectivization became stagnant due to a number of factors detailed in the next section.

The second strategy was to promote the ideology through the "Three Revolutions"[26] (see Dore, 1982; Zasloff, 1991; Stuart-Fox, 1997a; Pholsena, 2006) to propagandize a Marxist-Leninist ideology blended with nationalism in Lao social and cultural spheres. Particularly, the Party constructed a new Lao identity. Rehbein (2017, pp. 41–42) highlights the five ways the Party did this: idolizing the revolution, making Lao the national language, turning nationalist leaders into mythical figures, recruiting monks for political education to better reach the Lao people, and transforming the symbolic environment to convert Lao citizens into socialists. Regarding Lao cul-

[25] According to Kaysone Phomvihane's principle, Yamada (2018) notes the key Party goals for the social transition were "(i) eliminating traces of both colonialism and feudalism, while building a people's democratic regime by extending administrative power from the center to the 'grassroots'; and (ii) normalising people's lives by reconstructing the existing concept of production and establishing new relations of production" (p. 4).

[26] Stuart-Fox (1997) argues that the three revolutions included the overhaul of the relation of production, the scientific and technical revolution, and the cultural revolution.

ture, the Party replaced French colonial influences with socialist-inspired ones, which were combined with Buddhist principles,[27] and placed more emphasis on socialism in education. As I learned through my interviews, many nationalist leaders had previously been monks and were therefore able to influence the Party in that direction (Informant No. 16, 2017).

The third strategy the Party employed was to construct political rhetoric, within political speeches and press publications, to convince Lao people to believe in its leadership. Its members had always justified the socialist transformation, nation-building and the struggle of the Party under new difficulties to the public. It could be seen from the Party Secretary-General Kaysone Phomvihane's interview with the Vietnamese media. He emphasized the leadership of the Party is the most important factor to gain astonishing success in the revolution and socialist transformation based on Marxism-Leninism. He introduced the "two-line struggle" for the Party to tackle its enemy both within the Party and outside the country, according to Stuart-Fox's observation (1986). At the tenth anniversary of Lao's independence in 1985, moreover, he delivered a speech to justify economic achievement from the centrally-planned economy under the Party supervision that the first ten years of the establishment of Laos, the country's GDP had doubly increased, as well as the production per head increased by 60 percent (Stuart-Fox, 1986). Despite such notable outcomes, the Party announced that there were unfinished missions of the Party to facilitate "nation-building, the socialist transition, and the protection of national sovereignty" (Kaysone, 1985, pp. 16–18). Lao people, therefore, should have continually believed in the Party.

In conclusion, the socialist ideology in Laos is clearly a blend of Marxism-Leninism and nationalism. As a relatively new independent country, ideological legitimacy has served two political purposes: facilitating regime stability for nation-building and encouraging belief in the socialist transformation. The Party had served as the primary actor in socio-economic development almost completely without resistance by the Lao people. However, the Party did encounter difficulties with internal-external changes in 1986, which had become a challenge for the Party in its attempts to uphold socialist ideology. Thus, the Party had to re-legitimize itself by reinterpreting the former narrative to adapt.

27 Most of the Lao population is Buddhist. Lao social norms, beliefs, and culture are all based on Buddhist principles (see Rehbein, 2017). Their belief in Karma and charisma (*Baramee*) shape Lao social structure. Stuart-Fox (1996) argues, "this [Lao] social structure, and the exercise of authority within it, were legitimized through a combination of Lao mythology and Indian Buddhist notions" (p. 92). One of key informant stated that Buddhism in Laos is further blended with Animalism, Animism and Brahmanism (Informant No. 16, 2017)

The socialist dilemma: How the Party re-constructs the ideology to deal with capitalism and globalization (1986–present)

In the 1980s, there were three turning points that threatened to deteriorate socialist ideology in Laos. The first was the failure of collectivization since it did not meet the Party's expectations and encountered many difficulties. For example, the capacity of the government to provide technical and financial support to Lao farmers was limited, and natural disasters continued to pose a threat to agricultural production (Stuart-Fox, 1997; Soukamneuth, 2006). The second, and most important factor was the collapse of the Soviet Union, the major aid-donor to the country. Assistance thereafter to socialist fraternal countries, including Laos, was cut off (Phraxayavong, 2009; Rathie, 2017). From this unavoidable change, the Party had no choice left but to open the country to a new economic system, just like China and Vietnam. In 1986, the Lao government, in an unprecedented move, introduced to the country a market-oriented economic system known as the New Economic Mechanism (NEM).[28] As a result of opening itself up to non-Soviet development assistance and direct foreign investment, the country's economic performance improved; Specifically, Laos' Gross Domestic Product (GDP) and standard of living rose. The last turning point came with the end of the Cold War. The subsequent influence of globalization in the country created an inflow of information and technology from the West[29] directly affecting the Lao people's way of life and the socialist ideology.

These turning points put the Party in a difficult position of having to deal with capitalism and globalization, and to attempt to maintain their socialist stance simultaneously. This dilemma led to a fruitful discussion among Lao scholars, specifically regarding how the Party posits the socialist ideology to legitimize itself under capitalism and globalization to stay in power. Generally, these scholars have focused on the practical strategies employed by the Party through national symbols, political and religious ceremonies, representations of national heroes, international and national festivities, and political rhetoric (see Evans, 1998; Rehbein, 2007; Soukamneuth, 2006; Ivarsson, 2008; Creak, 2014; Rehbein, 2017; Tappe, 2017).

28 Yamada (2018) provides insights into the political context before the NEM. Specifically he notes that the failure of collectivization and pressure from the exogenous forces led to a two-line struggle between socialism and capitalism from those "aligned with Kaysone, the reformer or pragmatist, and the "ideologues and hardliners aligned with the LPRP… Nouhak Phoumsavanh, who adhered to a more orthodox socialism and an old-fashioned system of political patronage" (p. 8).

29 The "West" in his book includes rich countries in North America, Western Europe, some countries in non-Western Europe, and professionals who get involved with foreign aid (see Easterly, 2006).

Through my field research, I was able to gain additional insights into how the Party uses the ideology for its survival. From my interviews, I concluded that the Party currently plays three main roles: 1) the lead supporter of the socialist ideology; 2) the guardian of national interests; and 3) Each is able to pursue ideological legitimacy and maintain control of state power, even as circumstances change.

source: Author, 2018

PHOTO 3.2 The exhibition at the Lao National Museum

The first role of the Party is a lead supporter of socialist ideology throughout the country. In this role, the Party has initially applied Marxist-Leninist ideology as the political ideology in the country and idolized the nationalist heroes from the *Pathet Lao* in propaganda in the public sphere. This propaganda has explicitly aimed to convince the Lao people that the nationalist movement is dedicated to their interests for national independence. However, the way the Party presents these symbols in public is aesthetically less attractive and generally outdated in relation to the symbols of globalization, according to Rehbein (2007, pp. 77–84). This observation was affirmed when I visited the Lao National Museum in Vientiane, the capital city. Built in the semi-French colonial style, the exhibitions inside are composed of Lao historical documents, but some sentences in the documents are almost unreadable due to poor maintenance. The photos and weapons from the civil war are positioned in an unattractive manner (see PHOTO 3.2). For example, Kaysone Phomvihane, the nationalist hero and the former Prime Minister, is exhibited in the museum in a manner resembling that of a Buddhist altar (see PHOTO 3.3), his bust set up on a podium surrounded by plastic flowers in a vase. His brief biography below describes his legacy as a supporter of Marxist-Leninism and his dedication to the Lao people through national liberation and the socialist transformation.

Most importantly, the museum also exhibits photos of Karl Marx and Lenin with a quote from the nationalist movement of 1955 (see PHOTO 3.4). This quote is intended to encourage solidarity among the Lao people using national liberation symbols of peace, democracy, unity, and independence.

Additionally, propaganda used by the Party appears along the street in Vientiane, the capital city. The core of its content glorifies Kaysone Phomvihane (see PHOTO 3.5) and the Party's mission (see PHOTO 3.6). When I compare a commercial billboard with the propaganda sign in Vientiane capital city, it is obvious to see that the propaganda sign is much less attractive (see PHOTOS 3.7).

source: Author, 2018

PHOTO 3.3 Kaysone Phomvihane's burst at the Lao national museum

source: Author, 2018

PHOTO 3.4 Marx and Lenin photos in the national museum

source: Author, 2018

PHOTO 3.5 Kaysone Phomvihane billboard at the President Palace (Hor Kham)

source: Author, 2018

PHOTO 3.6 Propaganda billboard close to Thai-Lao border

source: Author, 2018

PHOTO 3.7 Commercial billboards at Vientiane Center

As the lead supporter of socialist ideology in Laos, the Party has emphasized socialist rhetoric through a number of speeches from its members. For instance, Saysy Santivong, a member of the Party Central Committee and the Minister of Justice, proclaimed in the Tenth Party Congress of the LPRP in 2015 that Party members are loyal to the Party and the socialist ideology and that they are attempting to improve their knowledge to bring democracy to the Lao people. His speech also implies that the Party's stance is to promote the socialist ideology to motivate the Lao people to protect national interest and bring prosperity to the country (see Pak Pasason Pativad Lao, 2015).

Moreover, at the Tenth Party Congress in 2016, introduced a political perspective called the Kaysone Phomvihand Thought (KPT). The five core concepts of the KPT, posted on the website of *Kongthap Pasason* news, emphasized the Kaysone Phomvihane's Thought as a development framework that includes: 1) national liberation and support for the Marxist-Leninist ideology; 2) Party solidarity; 3) adjustment of the country's strategy through new circumstances; 4) strengthening the Party and Marxist-Leninist ideology to protect national sovereignty as circumstances change; and 5) building friendly relations between Laos, its socialist fraternal countries, and the international community (Thang, 2018). Due to his heroic role in the Lao revolution, which was built upon these principles, the Party considered the use of Kaysone's thought as ideal for promoting the ideology and the Party's mission to emancipate the nation, society, and people. This information illustrates how the Party members continue to strive towards building a socialist utopia in Lao in parallel with capitalism and reassuring the Lao people of their competency to do so. This has further given rise to the other two roles of the Party.

The second role of the Party is "the guardian of national interests." This role arises from the fact that capitalism (and globalization for that matter) has become a double-edged sword for regime legitimacy—on one side it could both jeopardize the preservation of the socialist ideology within the country but, on the other side it provides an opportunity for the Party to play the hero in its dealings with backfires from capitalism. Yamada (2018) argues that the Party has brought the two-line struggle between capitalism and socialism back into its political rhetoric. The two-line struggle can be observed in a statement by one Party member I interviewed, who stated that:

> "Capitalism has both negative and positive impacts on the Lao people. The Party commits itself to the protection of the Lao people from the negative

> impacts of capitalism, and to bringing the country up to the socialist stage" (Informant No. 13, 2017).

In order to achieve that goal, the Party must strongly commit itself in narrowing the gap between the rich and the poor and in bringing equality to the country. His interview convinces me that the second role mentioned above should be considered along with the Party's third role as the builder of the socialist utopia.

It should be noted that the degree of ideological entrenchment among Party members is unmeasurable and complicated, and the socialist utopia itself is rather idealistic. From my interviews it is debatable whether the Party member and the National Assembly (NA) member I interviewed still believe in socialist ideology. Their opinions show that the Marxist-Leninist ideology can be practically employed to narrow the social inequality gap while the Party adjusts its ideological underpinnings to better mesh with the contemporary geopolitical context. As the Party member I interviewed stated:

> "The socialist ideology matters in Laos. As the Party is entrenched within Marxist-Leninist ideology, the Party believes that this ideology will bring equality to the Lao people by buffering the exploitative nature of the capitalist system. There is no concept of private property in socialist ideology. The Lao government currently tailors the ideology to a given situation by implementing it in a legal framework and with respect to Lao tradition...Party members have implemented and supported the Marxist-Leninist ideology because they believe in the Russian revolution and believe that capable leaders are important to maintain the ideology. The Party acknowledges itself as a group of capable leaders bringing the revolution to the Lao people, and I believe that the socialist ideology will be fully implemented in Laos eventually... socialism in Laos, means a one-Party system with an open mind to international and regional changes" (Informant No. 13, 2017).

The Party promotes socialist ideology to protect the Lao people; however, a member of the NA commented that, "There is no country that can reach a socialist level, as it takes time and will depend on many factors, one of which is the class struggle... I do not think that it will happen in my generation but I believe it will happen in the future". He also expressed his opinion that in order to reach such a level, a sense of equality among the people should first be established.

> "Laos decided to entrench itself in Marxist-Leninist ideology because the Lao government and the people wanted to. They believe that the ideology supports equality among the people and within the country. Consequently, the Lao government concedes that the socialist ideology matters for Lao development and they attempt to promote the ideology in government meetings" (Informant No. 16, 2017).

Maintaining the relevance of the ideological may further legitimize the Party's power in the aforementioned roles. In my view, socialist ideology in Laos has become "the spiritual anchor" for Party members to maintain cohesion and keep the trust of the Lao people. Moreover, the Party has turned the potential negative impacts of capitalism into an opportunity to manifest its leadership. As a result, the ideology will be reconstructed to serve the political purpose of prolonging the Party's political legitimacy and maintaining the status. Though the ideology can be used alone to justify the legitimacy of the current Lao government, it is unlikely that the Party will maintain its power without measurable, concrete achievements like those attained through the successful completion of socio-economic development milestones. Croissant and Lorenz (2018) refer to this as "performance-based legitimation," meaning that economic development and improvement of the standard of living "have become important new sources of legitimacy for the party" (p. 118). I will further emphasize this argument by considering developmental legitimation in national development.

Pragmatic acceptance: development legitimation in post-socialist Laos

In parallel with ideological legitimacy, pragmatic acceptance defines another dimension of regime legitimacy for the Party. According to Saxonberg's definition of pragmatic acceptance, if there are internal and external constraints on Laos, the Party members, as the delegates of the Lao people, will find an optimal means to deal with them. This leads to two questions on this topic: What internal and external constraints have been imposed on the Lao government so far? What has the Lao government done to cope with these constraints? In order to answer these questions, I will highlight the Party's aspirations and use of political rhetoric[30] to obtain more acceptance to sustain regime legitimacy to maintain power. Economic development, social stabil-

[30] Creak (2014) identifies a meaning of the political rhetoric that "political language and rhetoric are critical in any political setting but play an especially important role in revolutionary regimes, which use language to produce new cosmologies of rule, and in [the] one-party system... state rhetoric plays a key role in mobilizing legitimacy" (pp. 151–152).

ity, and the goal of graduating from the status of least developed country by 2020 under the Party's supervision will be taken into consideration. I hypothesize that this supervision plays a role in the "developmental legitimation" of the Party and the Lao government.

Developmental legitimation: economic development and graduation from the least developed country status under the Party's supervision

There are three general constraints to Lao development. First, Laos is a poor, land-locked country with a lack of state capacity to build human capacity or to accelerate development goals, and the economy is highly dependent on the international community. This is quite typical for countries that are classified as least developed. The second constraint is that the regime does not want to be perceived as lacking the necessary credibility in the public eye to run the country effectively. As a result, the Party is more receptive to international development assistance that helps Laos pursue international development standards to prove its development credibility and to trigger robust economic growth. For example, the Lao government introduced "fighting poverty with human resource development," "rural development," and "people's participation" to the Millennium Development Goals (MDGs) at the 7th Roundtable Meeting (RTM), supported by the development partners in November 2000 (Lao PDR, 2004). As a consequence of the RTM, the number of business sectors has increased considerably. These sectors include hydroelectric power construction, mining, construction materials, agriculture, and ecotourism. Almost 1,400 development projects which cost more than 76 trillion kips are included in the government's five-year plan (Howe and Park, 2015; Sengdara, 2015). In 2015, the Lao government worked with the development partners in implementing the SDGs in the national development plan.

Moreover, in 2017 the Party restated its ambitious goal to graduate from the status as a least developed country by 2020 and become an upper middle-income country by 2030. In order to reach these goals, the Lao government has emphasized its efforts on mega-development projects, particularly with regard to building a hydropower dam, increasing land connectivity to neighboring countries through the building of roads and an airport, and commercializing natural resources to foreign investors. Thus, the Lao government supports bilateral cooperation at the regional and the sub-regional levels, particularly in infrastructure development, as with railways, airports, roads, Special Economic Zones, human resource development, and tourism (Vaenkeo, 2017).

The outcomes of economic development in Laos have been impressive thus far according to the MDGs summary report in 2015. Laos has achieved universal access to primary education, gender equity in primary education, reduced maternal and child mortality, and safe water and sanitation (UN, 2015a). However, the Party and the Lao government have encountered difficulties in creating productive employment, eliminating malnutrition, increasing the literacy rate and gender equality in the education sector, empowering Lao women in employment and participation, reducing the mortality rate from disease, supporting environmental sustainability, and alleviating the Unexploded Ordnance (UXO) throughout the country. Another difficulty is that Laos was ranked 138 out of 188 countries in human development due in part to the fact that 23 percent of the population is living in poverty (UNDP, 2012). Although the development constraints stated above seem to jeopardize the regime's legitimacy, I argue that the Party has turned the development constraints into an opportunity to pursue its legitimacy, as the Party committedly becomes a leader in dealing with the challenge and bringing prosperity to the country. Thus, the Party is able to proclaim developmental achievements to maintain the status quo in the public eye.

The argument above is supported by the political rhetoric of the Party that blends the Party's mission to liberate the Lao people from poverty and backwardness with the socialist ideology to legitimize their role in development. Currently, the Party speaks of developmental achievements as the masterpieces of the Party's mission and development challenges as the threat of the country. Whenever socio-economic development is improved, the Party takes credit for the achievement. It is the same strategy that they used in the colonial era. At that time, as I mentioned, the Party produced socialist rhetoric to stabilize the new regime by taking full responsibility for the fight against imperialism and the liberation of the Lao people. Since then, the Party has shifted its mission statement from the liberation of the Lao people to liberating the country from poverty, backwardness, inequality, and capitalist exploitation. According to the Party, without the capable leadership of the Party, the Lao people would be stuck in a poverty trap. Accordingly, the Party members have manifested their full-fledged dedication and a strong commitment to tackling the threat and liberating the Lao people, a goal only possible as long as the Party stays in power. Such political rhetoric can be observed in a number of the Party members' speeches for national events like the national festivities in 2015 and the and the Party Congress in 2016.

The year 2015 was a memorable year for Laos. Two big events were particularly important: the 60th anniversary of the founding of the Lao People's Revolutionary Party and the 40th anniversary of its national independence. It is no surprise that the Party took advantage of these celebrations to demonstrate their trustworthiness by promoting its capability and dedication to socio-economic development and to tackling the development constraints.

In May 2015, Choummaly Sayasone, the former Secretary of the Lao People's Revolutionary Party and the former President of the State, proclaimed at the 60th Anniversary of the Founding of the Lao People's Revolutionary Party that developmental achievements depend on many factors. Among these factors, having capable leaders with strong abilities and the support of the Party was identified as the most important. His speech also emphasized the path to socialism under the Party's guidance, the development aspirations, and the cooperation between Laos and the international community. Regarding economic development, he ensured cadres and the Lao people that the Party would continually strive toward reducing the poverty rate and improving human capacity through effective implementation of development strategies from central to local levels (Sayasone as cited in Vientiane Times, 2015).

Developmental achievements were further stressed to the public at the 40th anniversary of Laos' national independence. On December 2nd, 2015, the grand parade began with the country's symbol and photos of nationalist heroes, such as Kaysone Phomvihane, Prince Souphanouvong, Khamtay Siphandone, and the President of the State, Choummaly Sayasone. National symbols like That Luang and Pratouxay[31] were asserted as reflecting Laos's national dignity. The marchers, who were soldiers, police officers, government officials, members of the private sector, youth, children, women, and local authorities were marching and waving Lao and communist flags with demonstrable pride and patriotism. This parade pervasively attempted to dignify the regime in the public eye via national television and online videos posted to the national and international websites.

During this event, Choummaly Sayasone proudly announced the achievements of the Lao government. As reported in the Vientiane Times,

> Mr. Choummaly described the development changes which have been made over the past 40 years, resulting in the continued growth of the Lao economy and the declining rate of poor families. The road network has been expanded.

[31] That Luang is a Buddhist stupa located in the center of Vientiane City. Phatouxay or the victory gate, located in the center of Vientiane city, was built between 1957 and 1968 as a national symbol to those who fought against the French colonists (see Evans, 1998).

> In addition, hydropower development and other mega projects have been realised (Vientiane Times as cited in Embassy of Lao People's Democratic Republic in the United States of America, 2015).

Economic growth itself has become one of the primary factors for proving the Party's legitimacy and reliability, which was reasserted at the Tenth Congress of the Lao Revolutionary Party in 2016. Thongsingh Thammavong, the former Prime Minister, proudly reported the accomplishments of the Party over the past 15 years, including the fact that Lao GDP rapidly grew from $319 in 2001 to $1,671 in 2014. In 2015, the growth rate likely reached $1,970. In 2011, Laos had shifted from a low-income country to a lower middle-income country, as ranked by the World Bank. The number of Foreign Direct Investments reached 236 billion kips in 2015 (Pak Pasason Pativad Lao, 2016, 78–79). The political rhetoric from the national events above demonstrates that the Party has shifted its effort to focus on narrowing social gaps. As the Party member interviewee stated, "The Party will reduce social inequality, which is an initial condition for reaching the socialist stage" (Informant No. 13, 2017).

In conclusion, it can be argued that development is another way for the Party to legitimize its regime and to maintain the one-party state. Socio-economic development, per se, contributes to the Party's regime legitimacy in the eyes of the Lao people. Most importantly, the Party acknowledges that political stability is a necessary condition to implement the development plan. In the following section, I will show how the Party employs development legitimation to maintain political stability.

Political stability in the one-state party

Political stability is a necessary condition for economic development, and political security is utilized in the Party's political rhetoric to legitimize its role in society. I argue here that the Party seeks to convince the Lao people that political stability under the one-Party state is the optimal means to implement the development plan effectively and bring the country out of its Least Developed Country status. Interview information from the Party member I spoke to affirm this argument. He asserts that the multi-party system is incompatible with the country's current situation as it may spark political conflict which could in turn become an obstacle to development. The informant believes that the one-party system, with capable leadership, can positively influence economic development and give rise to a socialist utopia in the country (Informant No.13, 2017). This is the apparent reason why the Party does not support a multi-party system. In this regard, the Party commits itself to bringing prosperity and equality by tightening its control throughout the country.

Due to the fact that Laos is democratically centralized, the hierarchy of command obviously appears horizontal in the organizational structure of the state at both central and local levels. Stuart-Fox (2005) describes the Lao state as "working and making decisions as a committee, while accepting individual responsibility, with the lower levels dependent on the higher levels" (p. 26). Considering the local administrations, the Party Committee has broadened its organ at provincial, district, and village levels to subordinate the Politburo of the Central Committee Lao People's Revolutionary Party. Its purpose is to monitor and manage the Lao government activities at local levels (Soukamneuth, 2006, p. 88).

At the Party Congress in 2016, Saysy Santivong, Party member and Minister of Justice, reported that the number of Party Committee members at the provincial level throughout the country has increased by 22.91% since 2011. Also, the current number of Party members is 252,879, which is a 50% increase since 2010. He proclaimed that Party members are well educated and have been indoctrinated to the Marxist-Leninist ideology. Thus, they are ready to become leaders in economic development, poverty reduction, and in monitoring the government's performance (Pak Pasason Pativad Lao, 2016, pp. 117–119). The increasing number of Party members at the local level reveals how the Party employs development legitimation to expand the Party's power thoroughly.

Another mechanism for the Party to build political stability is the Three Build (*Sam Sang*) Directive. The Three Builds directive has been strongly supported by the development partners under the National Governance and Public Administration Reform (GPAR) Programme. I will devote more time to examining how the development norms have shaped the Three Builds directive in the following chapter. For the Lao government, it has become another mechanism for them to spur development at the local level. As Choummaly affirms, the Three Builds directive aims "to build up provinces as strategy-making units, districts as comprehensively strengthened units and villages as development units" (Sayasone as cited in Vientiane Times, 2015). In addition, one of the Lao policy-makers I interviewed (Informant No.14, 2017) also acknowledged that the Three Builds directive serves the purpose "to implement the development goals and allocate natural resources at the local level… it is convenient to engage with, cooperate with, and to guide local people to help them to build an understanding of the development goals." In Choummaly Sayasone's speech, he commented on the role of the Three Builds directive:

Currently, our party stands ready to supervise organizations, leading officials at various levels, and party cadres are keen to work at the grassroots level to realize the four development-based contents and four development-based targets along with the implementation of the 'Three Builds' devolution initiative by paying attention to mobilizing the people, learning about local lives and circumstances, and absorbing people's opinions while protecting their economic, political, social and cultural interests in accordance with the rule of law (Sayasone as cited in Vientiane Times, 2015).

In practice, however, such efforts have strengthened state power in the hands of the cadres and justified state action with respect to the SDGs and MDGs achievements and progress on graduating from the Least Developed Country status. The Party has instead gained support from local sectors and further penetrated Lao society, and the effort to genuinely restructure central-local relations, unfortunately, were mostly just talk. One of the development partners said "the Three Builds directive has shown the political will of the Party to strongly control the local administrative sector (Informant No. 4, 2017). Her comment is consistent with Creak 's (2014) argument that:

> The 3 Builds pilot appears to represent both everything and nothing… Superficially, then, it may be tempting to view the directive as another word game—centralization masquerading as decentralization—or, more harshly, as all talk and no action (p. 162).

Thus the political rhetoric used by the Party, with regard to economic growth and particular developmental aspirations, can be used to legitimize the current regime. Through practical acceptance, or performance-based legitimation, the Party can use measurable growth to further support and strengthen the one-Party state, under the guise of conforming to international norms that support movement toward decentralization and democracy.

Revolutionary potential: the middle class, civil society and intellectuals in Laos

Another factor that influences regime survival is revolutionary potential. Uprisings and political turbulence can take place when the regime lacks sufficient legitimacy in the eyes of the people. Saxonberg (2014) proposes a revolutionary scenario that possibly "emerges if (a) there is an economic crisis or downturn; (b) expectations for wide-ranging reform of more radical change are arising (c) the regime does something to anger the population" (pp. 22–23). He further argues that revolutionary success depends on the (1) population's ability to find out what is happening; (2) communication skills and mass media; and most importantly (3) revolutionary leaders, who are generally intellectuals, and are capable of informing the public. His argument highlights the middle class, civil society, and intellectuals, which can organize into a civil society and threaten the undemocratic regime. Similarly, many political scientists believe that these actors, particularly well-educated people in the middle class, have the ability to bring democratization to the undemocratic regime (Huntington, 1991; Glassman, 1997).

In Laos, although economic development and urbanization contribute to social mobility, the middle class and the educated class remain relatively small, while there exists no channels for political participation. Social mobility in this sense is contingent upon the Lao peasantry shifting their positions to become Party members (Rehbein, 2016) and members of the middle-class working with international organizations. Regarding the demographic characteristic of the civil society, one of the development partners describes that, "the civil society is composed mainly of the youth—the third generation—and their parents— the second generation—who are no longer dependent nor practicing farming" (Informant No. 1, 2017). In reality, Lao civil society is considerably different from the civil society in the West. Therefore, the following information rather describes the characteristics of civil society in Laos and analyzes its limitations when comparing the civil society in Laos with that in the western democratic countries.

Firstly, the Lao government has defined civil society as a mass organization and, specifically, any quasi-governmental party organization[32] (Asian Development Bank [ADB], 2011, p. 2). It is obvious that the mass organizations in Laos were established for political purposes (see TABLE 3.1), and just as Kyaw (2006) argues, the Lao government "mainly used mass organizations to control societal groups... and that the Laotian people are still subject to numerous restrictions" (pp. 130–135). Likewise, Croissant and Lorenz (2018) noted that mass organizations are there to "serve as a transition belt for the LPRP party line into society" and are "meant to unify all 'patriot forces,' create

[32] Stuart-Fox (2005, 29) identified four sets of organizations that could be considered elements of a civil society. These include "religious associations; education support groups; sporting organizations; and economic and development support organizations."

'national solidarity,' and mobilize the masses" (p. 135). It is therefore evident that these organizations are subordinate to the Party.

To get the perspective of the university students—the third generation, I interviewed a student, who graduated from a university. He voiced concern that there exists is no public sphere for students to express their poliotical opinions and criticisms of the Party (Informant No. 25, 2017). Furthermore, students are left with no choice but to comply with the rules of the Lao People's Revolutionary Youth Union—a mass organization, largely controlling the activities inside the university—many of whom do so for the purpose of gaining membership within the youth organization, paving a way for their future entry into the Party.

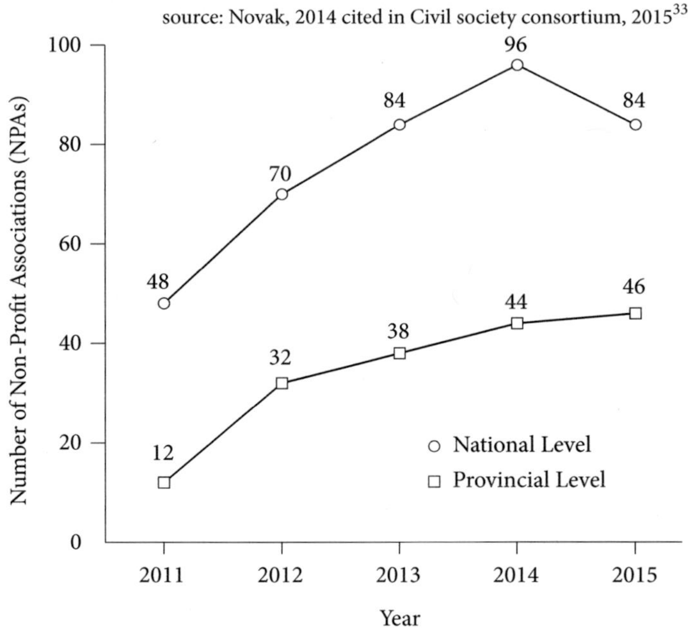

GRAPH 3.1 Lao NPAs at both national and provincial levels from 2011–2015

Secondly, as has been mentioned, the number of Civil Society Organizations (CSO),[34] such as the Non-Profit Association (NPA) in Laos, has been increas-

[33] The Civil Society Consortium (2015) notes "numbers are not always consistent even from MoHA themselves. Provincial figures tend to be less accurate than the national figures" (p. 9).

[34] According to the Decree on Association of 2017, article 2 states: "Associations that are established and operate under this Decree refer to non-profit civil society organization established on a voluntary basis that operate, provide mutual assistance, protect the rights and legitimate interests of the Associations, members of Associations or communities, and contribute to [the] country's socio-economic development" (National Assembly, 2017 translated by Civil Society Working Group, 2017).

ing over the past five years (see GRAPH 3.1). The Lao government concedes that the civil society is a crucial mechanism for implementing the development plan in remote areas where there is strong support from the development partners. The Lao government legalized the CSO under the CSO decree in 2009, acknowledging this role. The ADB (2011, p. 1) and the Civil Society Consortium (2015, p. 9) report that the number of INGOs in Laos was 160 in 2011 and fully registered NPAs (Non-Profit Association) in both national and provincial levels was 130 in 2015. These NPAs mostly work in social development, let alone the good governance that the Lao government is fully responsible for, at the provincial levels. GRAPH 3.1 illustrates the total number of Lao NPAs at both national and provincial levels between years 2011–2015. Shown in GRAPH 3.2 are the working sectors for the same NPAs during the same period.

source: Civil Society Consortium, 2015

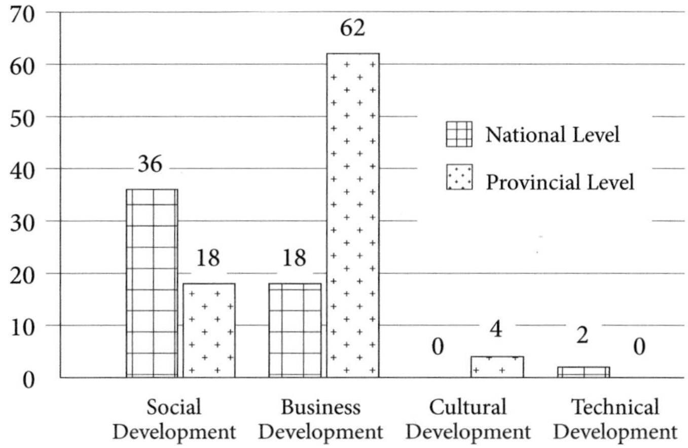

GRAPH 3.2 The number of registered Lao NPAs divided by working sectors

Members of the Lao NPAs interviewed commented that there are two big challenges to their operation. First, Lao NPAs have become a springboard for their volunteers to gain working experience and to get a better job in well-known INGOs or international organizations. Some will work with the NPA for a short-term period or until they get a new job, so a great deal of time is taken to recruit and train new volunteers. Secondly, the scope of an NPA's operations is limited by the Decree on Association, amended in 2017 to focus on social development, and is controlled by the Ministry of Home Affairs (Informant No. 25, 2017). The second problem has plunged Lao civil

TABLE 3.1 Lao mass organization

Mass organizations	Year Founded	Objectives
The Lao Front for National Construction (LFNC)	1979	This organization was founded in 1979. Its objectives are to build national solidarity and ensure the interests of ethnic groups. Moreover, this organization plays a role in coordinating mass organizations and other societal group for religious affairs.
The Lao Women's Union (LWU)	1955	This organization was established in 1955. Its objectives are to support women in community-level socio-economic development work in many sectors and increase the skills of women through vocational training and micro business development.
The Lao Federation of Trade Unions (LFTU)	1996	This organization was founded in 1996. Its main purpose is to support workers' right and education to serve the market economy.
The Lao People's Revolutionary Youth Union (LYU)	1955	This organization was founded in 1955. Its purpose is to support youth in vocational, development and marketing activities, and it is involved with youth activities in affiliation with the Association of Southeast Asian Nations (ASEAN).

SOURCE: ADB, 2011

society into turmoil. Instead of enhancing the role of civil society in Laos, the government controls CSO activities in accordance with the government's policy. Article 29 of the decree affirms that CSO operations must be in line with the government's policies, laws and regulations, and charters. In article 31 (2017), the decree issues Prohibitions for Associations so as to avoid conflict between the CSO and national security. It stresses:

The Associations are prohibited from actions that serve:

1. To abuse the right to freedom to establish an Association or to operate in conflict with the Lao Constitution, Laws, and Government's regulations;
2. To support or carry out activities that threaten national security, social order, individual freedom, or fine national, local, and ethnic traditions;
3. To carry out activities that will divide national or local solidarity, religions and ethnic groups;
4. To destroy national, collective and individual interests;
5. To falsify, transfer, rent or lend the approval to establish or register an Association in any form;
6. To borrow or lend money, or to secure a loan from a financial institution, legal person, and/or domestic or foreign individual;
7. To accept foreign experts and volunteers for permanent work in the Association

The Lao government thus uses these laws to assess CSO operations in the country. It takes many years to get government approval since the decree is so strict for the Lao NPA's members (Civil Society Consortium, 2015, p. 8). One of my informants observed that:

> The CSOs in Laos will continue to encounter difficulties because the law requires too many processes to receive an approval from the government. For instance, for approval, registration and renewal of an NPA, the NPA has to send an annual report to the Ministry of Home Affairs. As there are over 100 NPA working in Laos, it will take a very long time to gain approval. Moreover, the development funds from donor countries and other INGOs have to be approved by the Ministry of Foreign Affairs and that also takes time (Informant No. 26, 2017).

Many observers (Radio Free Asia, 2018; Hutt, 2018a) assume that the Party is rigid with regard to civil societies because they are perceived as a threat to the Party. This assumption is supported by Choummaly Sayasone's speech. He comments that the civil society should be restricted "because they could destroy our country through nonviolent means."[35] The Lao government has enshrined such restrictions in Article 4 of the decree, stating that, "the Government approves the official establishment of Associations and only the Government's agencies have the right to approve the establishment of Associations" (Read more in Article 4 of the Decree on Associations, Lao PDR, translated by Civil Society Working Group, 2017). It could be argued that the civil society in Laos is unique and different from the Western-style civil society. The Party is capable of depoliticizing civil society as a mechanism for Lao development and that there is no so-called "public sphere" for social and political movements. They are nearly voiceless in Lao politics unlike the development partners' expectations.

Particularly with regard to environmental degradation and the need for natural resources management involving the engagement of the people, the interview information secured during my field research shows that the development partners and INGOs have played a leading role in raising awareness of these issues in public. For example, one of my interviewees who works for an INGO that focuses on ecology, geo-cultural management, and natural resource management in the Mekong subregion, said that the "Mekong River is an international river that belongs to people whose daily lives rely on the natural resources in the river… the development projects of Laos, such as the building of hydroelectric dams on the river inevitably affect local people in a negative way" (Informant No. 11, 2016). Members of other INGOs also worry about the negative impacts of hydropower dams. The dams in Laos have caused ecological changes and fish extinctions, which affect locals who rely on them for subsistence. They have to adapt to survive, and some move to urban areas to find work (Informant No. 12, 2017). For these reasons, INGOs have worked to play a role in protecting natural resources and local ways of life. They express their concerns to the Lao government through relevant organizations and various channels. Their strategy is to attend public hearings arranged by the development partners and to empower local peoples that are part of the Mekong River ecosystem.

Social mobility has given rise to an increasing number of Lao intellectauls. Saxonberg (2013) believes that they will support democracy and mobilize

[35] In December 2012, Sombat Somphone, a well-known civil society leader, disappeared and is not yet to be found (see Hunt, 2017). His disappearance has been the center attention for some of the development partners. They have attempted to prompt the Lao government to investigate the case. One of the development partner representatives commented that "We have annual dialogue with the Lao government and we always ask the government about its progress in the investigation" (Informant No. 4, 2017). This issue raises grave suspicions about how the Lao government handles those perceived to be a threat to their power.

people when revolutionary conditions emerge. I interviewed some intellectuals and attended their lectures at the university. Their opinions on Lao development are mostly focused on economic growth and human development. Indeed, they seem to have full support for the government in tackling the development constraints, that they seldom mention the possible negative impact of development on the local population.

Contrary to the generally supportive and dismissing tone of these interviewees regarding the building of the dams, one Lao intellectual, who works at a university, discussed in a few words the possible negative impacts of the projects, but strongly pointed out the benefits from the dams. Economic growth, infrastructure development, electricity accessibility and urbanization are the bigger benefits the intellectual favor more, reason enough to overlook the possible negative impacts and thus he continually supports the hydropower dam's development in Laos. He then stated that:

> Economic performance will be improved… The dam can generate electricity and it can provide income for the government… There are positive and negative impacts on people's livelihood. Concerning resettlement issues, given that the Lao community is a distributed community; resettlement will help people gain access to infrastructure and public services like hospitals and schools… the people can get better jobs and learn better skills thereby increasing their income. It is normal to lose some traditional knowledge, ways of life, wildlife, and beliefs. There is a compensation policy that the investors and the government implemented to counter the possible impacts, by doing things like planting trees to create new forests areas and moving wildlife. They have tried their best to do so, but in reality, it's difficult to know what the outcome will be. (Informant No. 22, 2017).

His opinion alone does not imply that all Lao intellectuals politically side with the actions of the state. In fact, the scope of academic work in Laos is limited to serving the government's policies. According to my observation, in Laos, it is rather difficult to get approval for conducting research if researchers seem to be critical of the Lao government and the Party. It is no surprise that the average Lao university intellectual is likely to conduct research that supports the government's policies. Moreover, Rehbein (2016) highlights that the intellectual elite "hardly exists in Laos" as "the income for these groups is insufficient to secure their subsistence; therefore, they often have a second job, leaving little time for intellectual endeavours. Even if they had the time, they would not find a public sphere to engage in intellectual discussions" (p. 123).

Lao intellectuals are thus not likely to be able to jeopardize regime stability. They are generally on the side of the government and the Party for their own survival.

In conclusion, revolutionary potential in Laos appears weak and infeasible, even after considering that economic development could contribute to social mobility in Laos. This is especially due to the fact that there is no public sphere to express a political opinion. As for the civil society organizations, they became another mechanism for the country's development, a striking contrast from the civil society of western-democratic countries, which have strong tendencies of opposing their government. They act similar to Lao intellectuals, in that they would rather focus on their survival than support democracy, as it is likely too risky for them. It can be concluded that these actors would rarely rise up against the socialist regime. The Party can undoubtedly maintain its political power to play the leading role in socio-economic and political development. Viewed in this light, socialist consolidation has become a vital factor in maintaining the Party's status quo. In the following section, I will illustrate how the Party consolidates its power in the political structure of Laos, through the management of central-local relations and by fostering intra-Party cohesion among the elite.

Socialist consolidation in Lao political structure

In addition to maintaining the support of the Lao people through ideological legitimacy and pragmatic acceptance and oppression of the civil society, the Party has to continue to consolidate its state power to maintain the status quo of the one-party state and the socialist regime. In this section, I will analyze the consolidation of socialism within the political structure by the Party through central-local relations and elite cohesion. There are many reasons why these variables matter in any attempt to provide insight into the political and institutional stability of the Party. First, the political structure can reveal how the Party has embedded its power within. Influenced by Leninist principles, democratic centralism[36] affords favorable conditions for

[36] Croissant & Lorenz (2018) state that "democratic centralism" in Leninist thought, is "the ultimate organizational and leadership principle of party, state and mass organization in all communist states" (p. 120). He identifies six elements based on Schmidt (2010 as cited in Croissant & Lorenz, 2018). These include "(1) a centralist and hierarchical party and state structure; (2) the supremacy of the party over the state apparatus; (3) a system of hierarchical control from higher to lower echelons of party and state organizations; (4) firm party discipline and a ban on party factions; (5) party control over the selection of state officials; and (6) the principle of collective leadership in party and state."

the Party to design an institutional arrangement that embeds their power within thoroughly. Second, the political structure, as mentioned above may expose how elite cohesion is maintained and how it contributes to institutional stability. My stance here is to argue that elite cohesion in Laos can also be seen from the perspective of the patron-client relationship intra-Party as the legacy of the nationalist leaders.[37] I will show how the system works to unitize political factions inside the Party and how the Party acts as a mediator. Third, as the Party becomes more receptive to the exogenous forces, the political structure could reflect how the Party deals with the exogenous forces to construct the political structure to meet the international standard and disguise its power at the same time.

An account of socialist consolidation can provide a common understanding of how the Party and the Lao government exercise the state power to formulate and shape domestic institutions and development policy, which I will further analyze in chapter 4. To investigate the political structure, the 1991 Constitution and its amended version in 2015 will be taken into consideration to reveal the Party's power. As Croissant and Lorenz (2018) note, "The constitution is primarily a legal tool to consolidate the Party's claim on socio-political leadership" (p. 121).

Institutional overlap between the Parties, the Lao government, the National Assembly, and the People's Court

As a result of socio-economic and political transitions following the open economy in 1986, the first Constitution in 1991 was intended to guarantee social and political stability under the separation of powers principle. In the Constitution, power is separated into three branches: the legislative, the executive, and the judicial. Each branch has been encapsulated by the Party's power. The institutional overlap between the Party and these branches is noticeable in the Constitution via the dual structure arranged therein between the Party and the Lao government (see DIAGRAM 3.1). As the supreme law, the Constitution, in turn, has become a mechanism for consolidating the Party's power.

---

[37] Scott (1972) defined the patron-client relationship that is:

> an exchange between roles—may be defines as a special case of dyadic (two-persons) ties involving a largely instrument friendship in which an individual of higher socioeconomic status (patron) uses his own influence and resources to provide protection or benefits, or both, for a person of lower status (client) who, for his part, reciprocates by offering general support and assistance, including personal services, to the patron (p. 92).

Under the legislative branch, the National Assembly (NA, or *Sapha Heng Xat*—in Lao) developed from the Supreme People's Assembly is "the representative of the rights, powers, and interests of the multi-ethnic people" (see more Article 4 and Article 52 in the Constitution amended in 2015, National Assembly, 2015). Its members are elected by the Lao citizens who are eligible. The NA not only plays a role in preparing, considering, adopting, amending, and abrogating the constitution and the law, but also holds power that extends into the executive and judicial branches. According to Article 53 of the Constitution, the NA has the right to elect or remove the President and Vice-President of the State, the Prime Minister, other members of the government, the President of the People's Supreme Court, and the Supreme Public Prosecutor.

Despite the promise that the Party supports the people's rights in NA elections, the Party has ingeniously embedded its power inside this pivotal institution. Many scholars have seen the NA as "a rubber stamp" to endorse the Party's policies, which appear to be based more on the interests of Party members than those of the nation, and NA elections are often considered to be a sham (Stuart-Fox, 2005; Soukamneuth, 2006; International Federation for Human Rights & Lao Movement for Human Right [FIDH & LMHR], 2016). Most of the NA's responsibilities center around approving laws and monitoring government performance relative to the Constitution, however, Sayalath and Creak (2017) argue that the National Assembly is "an important component of the LPRP's pursuit of legitimacy" as it has raised concern on "development projects and other controversies" (p. 188) within the country. Although the Party has diminished its political role in the Constitution to meet good governance standards and to provide more room for the NA to operate, the space the Party gives the NA to exercise its own politics is not enough for being autonomous from the Party genuinely. I will elaborate this argument in the following points.

First, the Party has sought to consolidate its power through the elective process to create favorable conditions for Party members to become NA members. The NA election laws for candidates follow a criterion set out in article 8, such that a candidate must

1) be patriotic, be devoted to the people's democracy, be loyal to the New Economic Mechanism of the Party, be true to the nation, always serve the interests of the people, and have a strong, clear and absolute attitude towards friends and enemies;
2) have a sufficient level of knowledge of the Party's policies and strategic programs, and of State laws and regulations, and have the capacity to

> undertake propaganda and motivate people to be aware of and to participate in the implementation of Party policies and State laws (National Assembly, 2001).

This article creates favorable conditions for the Party to hold a monopoly over potential candidates which is unlike an election in a democratic country. Instead of being free, fair, and universalistic, Lao citizens have limited choices. They can either select a Party member, or an independent candidate that knows the Party's policies in-depth. Referring to the results of Lao elections since the open economy, Party members have won nearly every election and have overwhelmingly occupied most of the seats of the NA (see GRAPH 3.3). The election results, as Croissant and Lorenz (2018) argue, may "actually support the stability of the party rule in several ways" (p. 127) as there is no political opposition in Lao elections that allows the Party to monopolize its role in national development. Despite the fact that the NA ostensibly represents the Lao people and has a legitimate right to check and balance the Party's power, it seems apparent that the NA has become another political tool for the Party to pursue its legitimacy regarding the rule of law.

source: IPU, 2014; Thayer, 2003 (as cited in Croissant and Lorenz 2018, p. 127)

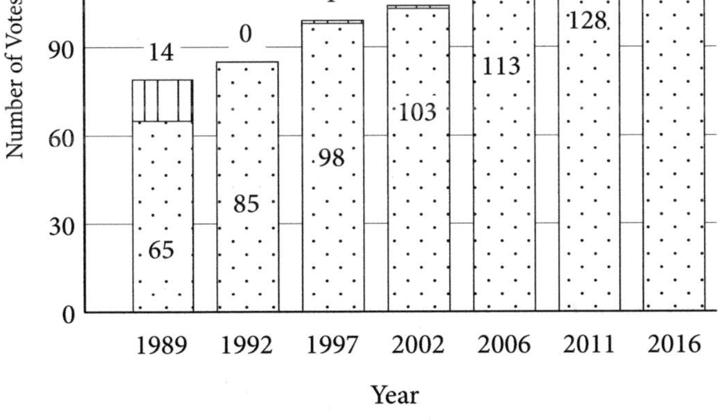

GRAPH 3.3 The election result in Laos from 1986–2016

Second, the NA plays a vital role in the election of the President of the State. It issued in Article 66 of the Constitution that "the President of the State is elected with a two-thirds majority in the NA." Since most of NA members are from the Party, they will almost certainly vote for the influential Party member. The President of the State then has the legitimate right to suggest the Prime Minister to the NA, as it issues in Article 53 "the Prime Minister is elected and removed by the NA under the President of the State's suggestion" (National Assembly, 2015). The Prime Minister of the country can be a Party member, who is in the same faction as the President of the State, or someone that has had a strong connection with the president.

Third, the NA has rights in the judicial branch. Article 53 of the Constitution, issues the rights and duties of the NA to "elect or remove the judges of the People's Supreme Courts, the Supreme People's Prosecutor, or the President of the State Audit Organization under the President of the State [sic] suggestion" (National Assembly, 2015). The laws enshrined in the Constitution show that the NA, whose members are mostly selected from Party members, is influential in three important branches of the state organ. As long as the Lao political structure creates favorable conditions for the Party to encapsulate its power, the separation of power in Laos is just nominal, and socialist consolidation of the one-party state and the political stability in the country are retained.

Central and local relations in the political structure of Laos

In 2015, the amended constitution first introduced the Provincial People Assembly (PPA or *Sapha Pasason* in Lao). This assembly is a subordinate of the NA. The development partners have placed a great deal of hope on the PPA delegates to support the interests of the multi-ethnic groups of Laos. For this hope to pay off, the PPA would have to genuinely contribute decentralization at the local administrative level. However, I argue that "decentralization" in Laos is just a disingenuous term for the Party to simply reorganize and consolidate its power at the local level. I will particularly focus on how the Party consolidates its power at the local level by controlling the local government and how the Party has distorted the term of "Decentralization" in local politics to support political stability. To investigate decentralization in Laos, some historical and background information regarding laws concerning local administrations will be examined.

Since 1986, decentralization has been employed in Laos to serve an economic purpose. In 2003, the Lao government promulgated laws on local administrations to authorize the local government in economic and political decisions to implement socio-economic development plans in line with democratic centralism.[38] This divided local administrations into three levels: provinces, districts, and villages horizontally (see DIAGRAM 3.1). The Lao government acknowledges that decentralization is an underlying principle supported by the development partners to pursue political legitimacy. After all, the Lao government initiated a number of authoritative bodies based on the decentralization principle to ensure this principle to the development partners and the Lao people. However, decentralization in Laos has been distorted to serve the Party's interests and the principle of democratic centralism (see Stuart-Fox, 2005; Soukamneuth, 2006; Creak, 2014; Croissant & Lorenz, 2018). Stuart-Fox (2005) coined the term "re-centralization," to refer to "Decentralization [that] caters to interests of regionally powerful figures in the party by providing them with resources to provide patronage to Party members... this merely reinforces the conclusion that decentralization is seen by the party as a means of increasing, not reducing, its power at the local level" (pp. 22–23).

Under the Party's control, local administration is not autonomous from the central government. More precisely, it is another subordinate of the Party at the local level. Archival data, including the Constitution and laws on elections and local administrations shows horizontal control from the central level to local levels. Article 5 of the laws on local administration implies that the local administration serves under the principle of democratic centralism, which divides responsibility among management levels (see more the Article 5 in the law on local administration, National Assembly, 2003). To maintain democratic centralism, therefore, the Party has controlled two pivotal actors in the local administration: the local governor and the Provincial People's Assembly. By examining how finances are distributed at the local level, this straitjacket around the local administration can be exposed.

Local governors,[39] are delegated by the Party rather than by the local people. Through the horizontal line of command (see DIAGRAM 3.1), the means to obtain

[38] Article 7 of the law on local administration notes that:
Provincial [administrations] and city administrations have the [following] roles, functions and operational procedures: to manage political, economic, [and] socio-cultural affairs and human resources; to protect, preserve and utilise natural resources, the environment and other resources; and to manage national and local defense and security, and foreign affairs as assigned by the government (National Assembly, 2003).

[39] Articles 13 and 14 of the laws on local administration note "Each governor or mayor is the chief of the [relevant] provincial or city administration and represents the province or city. He is responsible to the government for fulfilling his role, authority and duties of provincial or city administration" (see article 13 & 14 in the law on local administration, National Assembly, 2003).

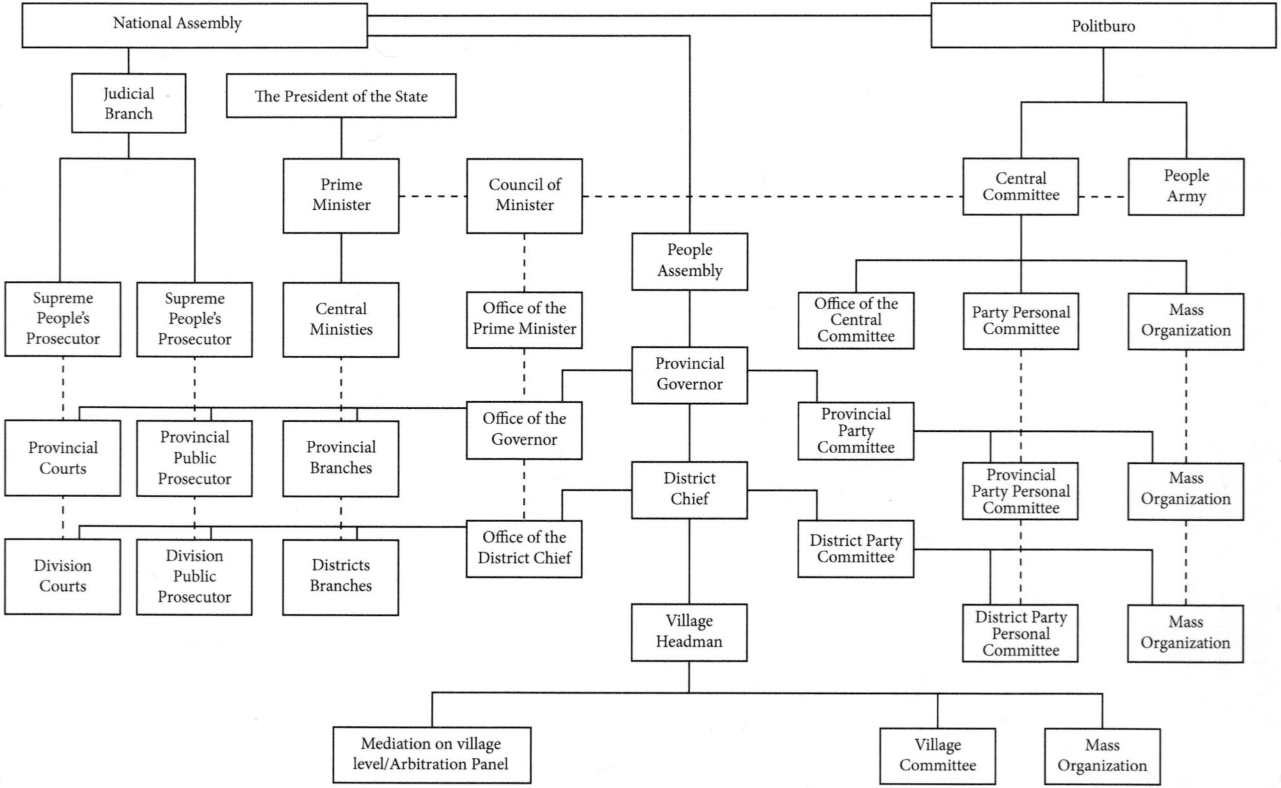

source Author's compilation based on UNDP (2015), Soukamneuth (2006, p. 84), Croissant and Lorenz (2018, p. 122)

DIAGRAM 3.1 Lao dual political structure

local governors have largely involved domination by the central government for decades. More precisely, the President of the State and the Prime Minister have the authority to appoint, transfer and remove local leaders at each level, as article 16 in the law on local administration clearly states. The chief district and municipality have the right to appoint or remove, under special circumstances, the village heads (see more Article 49 in the law on local administration, National Assembly, 2003). This law makes the village head, as Stuart-Fox comments (2005), "become less a representative of the villagers and more [a] representative of the district administration in the village (in other words, of the Party and the state)" (p. 21).

Furthermore, the Party overshadows the PPA both in candidate and election approval (Croissant & Lorenz, 2018). Despite the fact that the PPA is supposed to be a representative of local people, its role is also subordinate to the Party. According to an election law issued in 2015; the candidate's qualification requirements are the same as those of the National Assembly Candidate, who has to have insight into the Party's policies and has to be approved by the Party (see more Article 77 in the Constitution, National Assembly, 2015). Among the 360 seats of the People Assembly in 2016 (FIDH and LMHR, 2016), most of the PPA members are Party members at the local levels, according to the law on elections.

Another control from the central to local level relates to how finances are distributed. Local administrations have encountered difficulties in policy planning and implementation. Article 4 of the law on local administration issues that the local administration is authorized to "Prepare a strategic plan incorporating socio-economic development plans, state budget plans and defense and security plans based on national strategic plans" (National Assembly, 2003). This authority has to be approved by the central government since the Minister of Planning and Investment plays a role in formulating the national development plan. In addition, Article 59 issues local administrations to operate their budget in alignment with the development plan, the rules, and the laws that have been "approved by the government" (see more Article 59 of the laws on local administration). Thus it is no surprise that financial distribution at the local level is less than at the central level. According to the annual report on the fiscal budget in 2015–2016 (Ka Xouang Kan Ngeun, 2018), overall expenditures total 30,545,119 million Kip, which divides into central expenditure at 72.4 percent of this figure (22,123,706 million Kip) and local expenditure at 27.6 percent (8,421,413 Kip). It can be seen that the Party attempts to control the power of the local administration by limiting financial autonomy, peoples' participation, and governor and candidate endorsement. The local administrations in Laos are thus unique but different with regard to the orthodoxy of decentralization, and far from following the local self-governance policy that the development partners expect.

Elite cohesion and co-optation in the Party

According to Weiss (2003), the political structure of a nation may reveal elite cohesion, which contributes to institutional stability; this section will define how the patron-client relationship works in Laos and how it supports elite cohesion and intra-party co-optation. In Lao politics, political factions based on family clans are found in the high-ranking positions in the Party, the Lao government, and the National Assembly. For most of them, these positions are an outcome of political inheritance from nationalist leaders. I will therefore emphasize here the background information of current political leaders to support my argument. Prior to the background information, it is worth mentioning the patron-client relationship rooted in Lao political culture to understand why such the relationship stays in Laos, like many Southeast Asian countries, over decades.

The influence of the patron-client relationship in Laos is rooted in the political culture,[40] the social structure, and weak central power. Rehbein (2016) and Stuart-Fox (2006) shed light on the social structure by focusing on the *Baan*[41] and *Muang*,[42] the social organizations that create the conditions for the patron-client relationship between the Party members and Lao people. Lao people, particularly in remote areas, tend to focus on subsistence farming rather than capital accumulation, and often lack political awareness. Such a political culture allows the Party to create mass organizations and to assign Party members to positions in local areas, such that they are able to control Lao society at both Baan and Muang levels. With regard to weak central power, Croissant and Lorenz (2018, p. 128) identify three periods that strengthened the power of the regional elite. The first period occurred before

40 Almond & Verba (1963) refer to political culture as "specifically political orientations—attitudes toward the political system and its various parts, and attitudes toward the role of the self in the system…political system as internalized in the cognitions, feeling, and evaluations of its population" (p. 12).

41 *Baan* is a village, a small social organization, that believes in "subsistence ethics," in which "the villagers' interest is focused on having enough food until the next harvest, not on having as much as possible" (Rehbein, 2016, p. 118).

42 In the larger social organization, *Muang* represents a group of villages. The patterns of *Muang* favors the patron-client relationship in Laos, as Rehbein (2016) points out, through patrimonial or *Phu-Yai* culture.

the colonial era,[43] during which regional elites were quite powerful since "Laos did not have a strong central power." The second period came with the civil war in which "the weakness of the state and national government" resulted in the country being divided "into different zones controlled by the government forces, pro-government irregulars, and the *Pathet Lao*." The last period came after Lao national independence was attained in 1975. As he stresses, "the strength of regional party leaders and military commanders and the weak infrastructure linking the provinces to the capital allowed provincial governors to determine party policies at their own discretion." As a consequence of weak central power, local politics shaped national politics in Laos by the recruiting of political protégés of powerful family clans in each region to become Party members. The influence of pro-Vietnam and pro-China intra-party factions was also significant in influencing the selection process.

A strong argument can be made in support of the theory that political elites in the Party owe much to the patronage system of family networks (Informant No. 23, 2017). First, family clans can prolong their political lives by passing on power through their heirs and cross-family marriage among political clans. For example, Xaysomphone Phomvihane, the eldest son of Kaysone Phomvihane is now the President of the National Assembly. Another powerful political clan can be traced to Khamtay Siphandone, who is a nationalist leader, southerner and the most powerful person in both local and national politics. Viengthong Siphandone, Khamtay's daughter and former Deputy Finance Minister, was the former President of the State Audit Organization in 2016 and elected as the President of the People's Supreme Court in 2021. The case for cross-marriage entry could be made for Thongloun Sisoulith, who was born in the Hua Phan province and was educated in both Vietnam and the Soviet Union and a protégé of Khamtay Siphandone. He is married to Naly Sisoulith, the adopted daughter of Phoumi Vongvichit, the former statesman of Laos and the Acting President of the State. Due to his family background, his political path is promising. He is the former Deputy Prime Minister (2001), the former Minister of Foreign affairs (2006), the Prime Minister (from 2016–2021) and the current President of the State. His position as Prime Minister implicates both the influence of his clan's pro-Vietnam stance[44] and Siphandone's clan. All of these political successors

[43] At that time, Laos was divided into three kingdoms based on geographical factors: Luang Prabang in the north, Vientiane toward the center, and Champasak in the south. These kingdoms were later unified by French colonists.

[44] The influence of Vietnam and China in Lao elite can be seen from the case of Bouasone

above have both *de facto* and *de jure* relationships with the nationalist leaders, one way or the other.

However, these clan-based relationships are insufficient for explaining elite cohesion. One of the Lao scholars argues that nepotistic political reciprocation (as opposed to familial reciprocation) between new political leaders and former ones should be taken into consideration as well (Informant No. 23, 2017). The value of gratitude matters in Lao politics because political leaders would lack credibility and be stigmatized if they left their political backers behind. This has led to political factions that are based on strong connections and close working relationships with former leaders. In fact, some political successors in the second generation[45] started their political careers as secretariats of their political backers, which were the leaders of the first generation. As soon as the new political successors took power, they would reciprocate their backers by appointing family members of the first generation to positions in the Party, the government, the National Assembly, and mass organizations. This kind of power rotation has been ongoing.

Lintner (2008) provides an analysis of the nepotism in Lao politics using the results of the Lao election of 2006, starting that the new appointments are "a clear indication of the desire for continuity on part of old leadership" (p. 173). For instance, Choummaly Sayasone, the President of the State, and Bouasone Bouphavanh, the Prime Minister, are southerners. Their position in Lao politics implies the power of Siphandone's clan, particularly Bouasone Bouphavanh. He is recognized as the protégé of Khamtay Siphandone. Another example is Somsavat Lengsavat, a protégé of Kaysone Phomvihane, who was appointed Deputy Prime Minister in 2011 and was elected as an advisor to the Party Central Committee in 2016 (see Sayalath and Creak, 2017). These examples expose family networks and the regional patronage system, and they chart the political transitions that occurred from the first generation to the second one in the Party Congress. As Sayalath and Creak (2017) argue "the patron-client relations extend from local party committee, identifying and putting forward their own 'targets for building,' to the most

Bouphavong, who is the former Prime Minister and the protégé of Khamtay Siphandone. In 2010, he resigned from his position due to his "family problems." Many observers, for example Stuart-Fox (2009) and Creak (2011), noticed that the close relationship between Bouasone and the Chinese government is unsatisfying for the pro-Vietnam individuals in the Party. As Creak (2011) affirms "This is possible but other observers discount the idea that Politburo is divided so clearly into China and Vietnam camps" (p. 123).

45 The first generation mainly consists of nationalist leaders in the *Pathet Lao* such as Kaysone Phomvihane, Prince Suphanouvong, and Khamtay Siphandone, yet the second one consists of their princeling and political successors (see Sayalath & Creak, 2017).

powerful families of the party leadership, including the new generation of princelings that are now strongly positioned to move further up the ranks" (p. 196). Any resemblance of a merit system or professionalization in the Lao political environment also remains to be seen.

The co-optation of the Party's factions can also be considered from the point of view of the Party as a policy-maker organization. The Party has a capacity to proffer national development positions and resources preferentially to elite political clans. Viewing the Party as policy-maker, it is obvious to see that intra-party policy decisions would somehow have to be based on the interests of Party members in each region that could serve the national interests. One Lao expert I interviewed perceives mega-project development in Laos a result of such policy decisions. She believes Siphandone's clan is attempting to obtain their political and economic interests through development projects:

> "The Lao government supports the dams, particularly the Don Sahong dam, in the southern part of Laos because of the influence of Khamtay Siphandone. He is the most powerful leader and the megaproject would bring prosperity to his clan and the southern part of Laos. After all, he will obtain support from the Lao people since he will provide them with electricity from dam" (Informant No. 20, 2017).

The Party thus becomes the mediator of economic and political interests from development projects to political clans. Avoiding such conflict sustains the survival of the Party.[46] As long as members of powerful clans can use the Party for their own interests, they will continue to support the Party reciprocally.

In Laos, it can be concluded that although Marxist-Leninist ideology as an economic system has been dead since the Lao government introduced the open economy in 1986, the Lao government or, more precisely, the Lao People's Revolutionary Party, which includes many political clans within, remains capable of reviving the ideology in the political realm. After all, the Party has legitimized itself and consolidated its political power in the political structure and through domestic institutions, and has weakened the possibility of a civil society through law. Finally, the institutional overlapping that blurs the line between the Party, the Lao government, and the

[46] Currently, many scholars regularly highlight the political successors of Kaysone Phomvihane and Khamtay Siphandone since their successors still play an important role in high-level positions of the Party and state organizations (see Soukamneuth, 2006; Litner, 2008; Sayalath & Creak, 2017).

National Assembly reveals that separation of power in Lao political structure is nominal and, unlike the democratic regimes, the institutional overlap between the Party and the legislative, executive, juridical branches is present at both the central and local levels.

Concluding remarks

Regime survival in Laos is dependent on a number of factors. The first is ideological legitimacy. The Party has legitimized the blended ideology of Marxism-Leninism and nationalism to maintain its control over the state. Since the open economy, the Party has re-legitimize itself through two roles it has played: the lead supporter of socialist ideology and the guardian of national interests. Second, the pragmatic acceptance, or the performance-based legitimation are crucial for the Party to obtain popular support. Recently, the Party set a development goal to graduate from the LDC status by 2020. The Party claims to be a "leading nucleus" and actively creates its subordinates through, for instance, the local Party Committees and the three builds directive. These subordinates serve to justify the Party's actions toward an improved economy and standard of living, and in its work to bring the country out of its current LDC status. Third, the Party has limited the scope of the civil society through the Decree on Association adopted in 2017. This decree has allowed the Party to tighten its control over the civil society. The Party has thus become the leading actor in socio-economic and political development in Laos. Moreover, the Party seeks to consolidate socialism and its power in the political structure in accordance with the tenets of democratic centralism. Socialist consolidation in the political structure of Laos may contribute to institutional stability in its political institutions, central-local relations, and intra-party elite cohesion. For example, Party members play a big role in important political institutions such as the National Assembly, the Lao government, and in mass organizations leading to institutional overlap. In addition, the Party also extends to local authorities, as it appoints and approves local governors and local elections. Likewise, elite cohesion can be seen through the patron-client relationship, as the Party mediates the interest of family clans.

4

THE POLITICS OF DEVELOPMENT IN LAOS UNDER THE SUSTAINABLE DEVELOPMENT GOALS

Do you think the time has come? That we need to change the way we perceive and imagine development to simplify our lives to the nature-based livelihood that consumes whatever we receive.

—Thongloun Sisoulith, 17 July 2018[46]

This chapter focuses on the politics of development in Laos. It particularly examines how the Sustainable Development Goals, as promoted by the development partners, have shaped the Lao domestic institution's development policies, strategic plans, and visions under the Party-led development efforts discussed in chapter 2. Four arguments were presented to analyze the SDGs vis-à-vis Lao development. The first argument contends that Lao development has relied on Official Development Assistance (ODA) from the development partners for over the half a century. Without a doubt, the development partners, especially western countries and international organizations, have encapsulated western modernization and democratization encapsulated in their contributions to ODA. It could maintain the status quo of western modernity in Lao development. This argument requires an investigation into how the development partners support the Lao government to implement the SDGs in the country and how they have encapsulated into their development discourse, terms related to modernization and democratization.

The second argument is that the Party and the Lao government have shaped domestic institutions and development policies to initially reflect

[46] Thongloun Sisoulith delivered this speech during the meeting for Decree 348 implementation on 16–17 July 2018 (Santi, 2018).

the SDGs while simultaneously upholding the Party's power. Viewed in this light, the Party has obtained the regime legitimacy analyzed in the previous chapter. The Party employed this right to power to design domestic institutions and a development policy at the Party Congress, through what I call the Party-led development. In the second part of the chapter, I will focus on how the Party has reframed and interpreted the SDGs in the context of national development.

In this chapter, I employ process tracing and elite interviewing to obtain first-hand and second-hand data. Process tracing is used here to trace crucial events, speeches, policies, strategic plans, and visions on Lao development since the implementation of the SDGs in the country's development in 2015. This has led to the final argument that the Party is capable of interpreting the SDGs to serve the Party's legitimation in Lao development. No matter whether the development partners remain supporting the democratic process, the Lao state power in the hands of the Party is intact. Eventually, the Party could shape Lao-style development to meet the SDGs and maintain its political power, at the same time. The SDGs are thus another source of the regime's legitimacy for the Party.

The controversy of the international development norms: from the Millennium Development Goals to the Sustainable Development Goals

Over the past 15 years, issues related to poverty, hunger, disease, literacy, gender equality, and environmental degradation have been raised as global challenges for member states of the United Nations. In an effort to tackle these challenges, the Millennium Development Goals (MDGs) were set to promote global awareness, political accountability, improved development metrics, social feedback, and public pressure (Sachs, 2012). The trajectory of the MDGs was completed in 2015, and the results showed a notable outcome. Extreme poverty had declined significantly over the preceding two decades and the number of people living in extreme poverty had been reduced by more than half, falling from 1.9 billion in 1990 to 836 million in 2015. Despite this outcome, there are several challenges that remain to address inequality, climate change, and extreme poverty in particular (see Sachs, 2012; UN, 2015a). These issues have remained in the post-2015 development agenda, dubbed "Sustainable Development Goals."

Ban Ki-Moon, the UN Secretary-General said in the summary report of the MDGs that "2015 is a milestone year. We will complete the Millennium

Development Goals. We are forging a bold version for sustainable development, including a set of Sustainable Development Goals" (UN, 2015a). Sachs (2015) has argued in support of the SDGs by stating that:

> The world economy is not only remarkably unequal but also remarkably threatening to the Earth itself. Like all living species, humanity depends on nature for food and water, materials for survival, and safety from dire environmental threats... Thus we arrive at the [sic] sustainable development (p. 23).

The Brundtland report (1987), identifies sustainable development as "development that meets the needs of the present without compromising the ability of future generations to meet their own needs" (p. 5). Sustainable development ostensibly takes into consideration the Rio+20 summit, which set the new global development goals with 17 goals: And end to poverty, an end to world hunger, improved health and well-being, quality education, gender equality, clean water and sanitation, affordable and clean energy, decent work and economic growth, industry, innovation and infrastructure, reduced inequality, sustainable cities and communities, responsible consumption and production, climate action, life below water, life on land, peace, justice and strong institutions, and partnership in attaining these goals (UN, 2015d).

A normative approach to the SDGs emphasizes, as Sachs (2012) argues, a holistic version of what a good society should be. He believes this boils down to five types of concerns about the social distribution of wellbeing: extreme poverty; inequality; social mobility; discrimination; and social cohesion. This development approach is called the triple line approach to human wellbeing with its combined focus on economic development, environmental sustainability, and social inclusion, and which depends on good governance at all levels (local, national, regional, and global) between government and the private sector. In order to bring sustainability to society, he strongly believes in the partnership between governments, the private sector, and civil society to achieve the development goals. In his perspective, the private sector is the most productive sector of the world economy and the holder of advanced technologies and management systems that will be crucial for the success of the SDGs.

There are 17 goals that comprise the SDGs, which include the unmet MDGs. It is obviously difficult for third-world countries to implement these goals in a national development plan effectively since these countries lack a development budget, and the human capacity and technical knowledge to eradicate national poverty. As a consequence, rich countries, international organizations and financial institutions, international non-governmental organizations, and non-state actors have already committed themselves in providing developmental assistance to help the poor countries in the UN's Finance for Development (FFD) summit in 2002.

Hulme (2015) further clarifies regarding the FFD summit that "the summit in 2002 produced the Monterrey Consensus, with rich countries committing themselves to increased funding to achieve the MDGs and developing countries promising to improve national governance" (p. 100). He refers collectively to this effort as "the international landscape for global poverty" in the fight to eradicate extreme poverty. With an optimistic perspective, Sachs (2005) has further suggested that because rich countries are wealthier, the cost of the assistance is likely to be small compared to their income and tax revenue. In his book "The End of Poverty: How We Can Make It Happen in Our Life Time" he states,

> The rich world today is so vastly rich… part of the solution of getting donors to honor their commitment to the world's extreme poor is to assign more responsibilities… direct foreign assistance should be used for investment in infrastructure and human capital (through public services in health, nutrition, and education), thereby empowering the poor to be more productive on their account, and putting the poor countries on a path of self-sustaining growth (pp. 289–291).

However, transferring a development budget and the necessary materials and resources is problematic since corruption remains a worrying issue in poor countries. To mitigate the issue, moreover, Sachs (2005) suggests, "the actual transfer of funds must be based on rigorous, country-specific plans that are developed through an open and consultative process, backed by the good governance in the recipient countries, as well as careful monitoring and evaluation" (p. 292). As Hunt (2012) reaffirms, "the development targets have caused donors to focus more closely on quality and effectiveness of aid, particularly its impact on poverty reduction, rather than on more general measures of growth and development" (p. 82). Good governance is thus a primary condition for underdeveloped countries to become aid recipients.

Since international development assistance has been pervasively provided to third-world countries, the number of critics has risen in recent years due to the continuing economic vulnerability of these countries. Many scholars have broadened the debate on the impacts of international development assistance. For instance, Hulme (2012, pp. 190–195) points to the paradox of the institutional framework in tackling global poverty, particularly the way in which the governments, leaders, civil societies, and non-state actors of the global north, consisting of mostly rich countries, take action to promote and mobilize the development goals. These actors have greater resources, multilateral institutions, and international media accessibility and thus their voices are louder and more effectively disseminated across the world than the southern voices. Hulme argues that the global south instead should be tackling poverty.

Likewise, Easterly (2006) divides the world into the West and the Rest in his book "The White Man's Burden: Why the West's Efforts to Aid the Rest Have Done So Much Ill and So Little Good." The poor countries or "the rest" are currently in a poverty trap. Conversely, the West has fantasized itself as the chosen one to save the Rest by playing the heroic role of pushing its Big Plan. He stresses that,

> At first, these agencies called for the planning of poor countries' economies. Later they shifted toward an advocacy for establishing free market for these countries, yet in many ways the agencies themselves continued to operate as Planners … the aid agencies cannot end world poverty, but they can do many useful things to meet the desperate needs of the poor and give them new opportunities… The foreign aid, the diplomatic relations and military intervention become a part of the crusade to transform the Rest (pp. 426).

In 2013, Easterly argued that the cause of poverty "is the absence of political and economic rights, the absence of a free political and economic system that would find the technical solutions to the poor's [sic] problems" (Easterly, 2013, p. 7). He argues that the expert, who can improve economic growth through technical knowledge and can bring prosperity to the country, in turn has employed authoritarian development to deprive individual rights and freedom. In Easterly's view, this is a reason why some poor countries remain poor and vulnerable.

Taking Schumpeter and Paine's approaches, Reinert (2008, pp. 255–256) attempts to discover why poverty reduction is an erroneous approach and why the MDGs do not represent good social policy in the long run. He proposed the use of the terms "cronyism" and "welfare colonials" to frame how the international community legalizes its role in poor countries. With regard to cronyism, he concludes, the rent-seeking institutions, which consist of international organizations, create the process of development in order to protect knowledge and to produce more for themselves in new geographic areas. He further contends,

> Welfare colonialism creates parlaying dependencies on the center of a peripheral population, a center exerting control through incentives that create total economic dependency… welfare colonialism will develop into a system where the rich countries will always be able to cut off aid, food and livelihood sources from the poor countries if they disapprove of their national policies… rather than promoting global democracy, such policies will lead towards global plutocracy (pp. 263–266).

Ziai (2015) defines the structures of SDGs as the same structures that were used after World War II that set the common development practices widely accepted among capitalist countries. Among the arguments presented, little has been said about the influence of the international development norms on socialist countries or how socialist countries have attempted to cope with the practice of good governance and the implementation of SDGs in their respective efforts for national development. With regard to Laos, it is obvious that the international community and the Lao government had to work in a partnership to implement the SDGs throughout the country. However, the Lao government can indeed offer significant evidence to support the possibility of blending socialist ideology and the practice of sustainable development. Before making any evaluation on the outcome of the implementation of SDGs on Lao development, a look into how western countries use the SDGs to influence and shape the state through the guise of development must be explored. This closer look could expose the possibility that these development assistance might have an attached self-serving agenda favoring these development partners.

The standardization of the state: The development assistance from the development partners under the SDGs

The strategic plans formulated by the development partners are not only based on international development norms, but also on their self-interests vis-à-vis Lao development. In this section, I will discuss the current development norms under the SDGs framework. According to my information obtained from representatives of the development partners, there are four focal areas emphasized in the development partnership framework. These include: poverty reduction, capacity building, environmental protection and climate change resilience, and good governance.

Regarding poverty reduction, in 2013, about 80 percent of the Lao people lived on less than $2.5 per day (World Bank, 2015, p. 9). One of my informants working for a development partner concerned with poverty reduction commented, “Our big goal is to help Laos bring all its people up above this” (Informant No. 2, 2017). Although the ongoing Lao development plan has promisingly improved GDP growth, this is insufficient to bring people out of poverty. An interviewee who works at a financial institution asserted that the reason why poverty reduction remains a burden for both the development partners and the Lao government is that Lao economic diversification, human and infrastructure developments do not meet the new demand in the global market. There is a surplus of unskilled laborers that often relocate to Thailand for work (Informant No. 8, 2017).

The development partners provide financial and technical support to the Lao government to reduce extreme poverty and contribute to sustained and inclusive economic growth, particularly with regard to developing infrastructure for connecting regional and sub-regional levels, improving financial management, creating investment-friendly environments, developing the private sector, diversifying economic activities for employment, improving agricultural processes and income generation, and including gender equality in economic activities. Another emphasis is to reduce Unexploded Ordnance (UXO) throughout the country. Laos is heavily carpeted by unexploded bombs from the Second Indochina War and the Lao civil war. Both the Lao government and the development partners concede that the UXO is a primary obstacle to exploring Laos’ economic development potential. Thus explosive eradication in Laos has become an additional goal named “Lives Safe from UXO.”

The second focal point is capacity building to ensure inclusive growth. They believe that economic development will be more efficient and sustainable if the country is capable of enhancing its own development strategy. However, such capacity is problematic in Laos. As one development partner interviewee commented that the capacity of the Lao government is limited and outside experts are in need (Informant No. 2, 2017). The country thus needs to improve on human development, its legal framework, and its political institutions to meet the international development standards. The development partners address these needs by supporting education, health, food security, and nutrition, supplying technical experts, and arranging training and workshops with the Lao government. The Village Bank project could be an example of the development partners' effort to provide small funds for the village and help Lao people save money and secure small loans.

The third focal point is environmental protection and climate change resilience. This strategy is based on notions of environmental sustainability enshrined in the Sustainable Development Goals. The development partners have thus initiated an environment-friendly development strategy for Laos. For example, the development partners promote sustainable natural resources management and utilization by providing technical assistance for climate change resilience and forest protection, surveying land to modernize its use and encouraging Lao people to have awareness of environmental degradation.

The last focal point is good governance. The development partners believe that good governance contributes to effectiveness in the implementation of their development strategy in Lao development. Efforts are currently underway to enhance the effectiveness of the Public Service Improvement under the National Governance and Public Administration Reform Programme (NGPAR). Its purposes are to improve the capacity of public administration in order to deliver efficient, effective, transparent and accountable services to citizens and to ensure better implementation of government policies (Larrabure, 2014). For example, One Door Service Centers was designated to serve multiple needs for basic public services to local people in 17 provinces. This reform has been supported by a number of development partners that work together to bring good governance to the country. TABLE 4.1 represents the major development partners, project names and durations under the public sector management reform.

It can be seen that the strategy of the development partners concerns four focal areas: poverty reduction, capacity building, environmental protection, climate change resilience, and good governance. The purpose is to achieve the SDGs and to bring Laos out of the least developed country status. However, Laos has a long way to go to meet international development standards since development per se is a dynamic process, and it will be difficult to narrow the development gap between Laos and other countries. As one interviewee commented "If there is a development gap, you cannot tell other countries to stop developing for this country to fill the development gap" (Informant No. 10, 2017).

TABLE 4.1 Selected the major development partners in public sector management

Development partners	Project name	Duration
Asian Development Bank	1. Governance and Capacity Development in Public Sector Management Program	2010–2014
	2. Governance and Capacity Development in Public Sector Management Project	2013–2016
	3. Technical Assistant for Strengthening the Capacity of the State Audit Organization	2012–2014
	4. Regional Technical Assistant to Public Administration and Civil Service Authority (Ministry of Home Affairs) Public Policy Training Project	2009–2011
EU	Poverty Reduction Support Operation 8 (with the World Bank)	2002–2012
GIZ	Land Management and Registration Project	2009–2011
UNDP	1. Community Participation and Communication Support Project (in partnership with Oxfam Novib)	2011–2014
	2. GPAR: Strengthening Capacity and Service Delivery of Local Administration (in partnership with UNCDR, SDC, GEF, and the Republic of Korea)	2012–2015
	3. Support to an Effective Lao National Assembly (in partnership with Finland and EU)	2009–2012
	4. Civil Society Support Program	2011–2014
The World Bank	1. Poverty Reduction Support Operation 8 (in partnership with EU)	2012–2015
	2. Public Finance and Management Strengthening Project (Multi donor trust fund, AusAID, EU, SIDA, SDC)	2011–2015

Note: ADB — Asian Development Bank, AusAID — Australia Government Overseas Aid Program, EU — European Union, GIZ — German Agency for International Cooperation, GEF — Global Environment Facility, GPAR — Governance and Public Administration Reforms, Oxfam Novib — 14 national affiliates of Oxfam International Confederation, SDC — Swiss Agency for Development and Cooperation, SIDA — Swedish International Development Cooperation Agency, UNDP — United Nations Development Programme

source: ADB, 2016

The development agendas of the development partners in Lao development

The development agendas of the development partners ultimately both positively and negatively affect Laos. I analyze the agendas of the development partners by inquiring how the SDGs could serve their interests, or at least, how they could promote their development norms to maintain their status quo on Lao development. The general agenda is simple: they genuinely promote the Sustainable Development Goals in socio-economic development. As one interviewee states that "we are right now working with the Lao government because there are things that you have to do in every country. So more emphasis with regard to national goals and national targets in Laos is into helping them implement the SDGs" (Informant No. 4, 2017).

I further analyzed the development partners' plans in Lao development and connected with the SDGs to show how the plan could help the Lao government achieve the SDGs. For example, the three strategies enshrined in the World Bank Partnership Strategy (2017b) notes that the World Bank's main points of focus are: to support inclusive growth, protect the environment, invest in people, and strengthen institutions to establish a ruled-based environment. Similarly, the developmental strategies of UNDP in Lao development consist of: inclusive growth, human livelihood and resilience, human development, and governance based on dignity, equity, and inclusiveness (UNDP, 2016). Moreover, some of the development partners promote natural resource management, sustainable infrastructure development, and environmental sustainability (see TABLE 4.2).

However, the second general agenda item consists of developmental aid with conditions attached, so that they can profit from Laos. They become brokers with the power to approve development projects and mediate profit and the use of natural resources to generate income for their organizations. The case of the Nam Theun 2 dam, supported by the World Bank, provides a sufficient example. This dam has been proclaimed by the World Bank to have been built using the best monitoring and assessing processes, and compensation policy.[47] A great deal of criticism, in turn, has been directed at the dam for causing changes in the ecological system and local people's ways of life. Baird, Shoemaker, and Manorom (2015, pp. 1083–1093) contend that the negative impacts of the dam in Laos consist of "fishery

[47] The World Bank issued a report called "Doing a Dam is Better: The Lao People's Democratic Republic and the Story of Nam Theun 2," that claims that hydropower projects contribute to poverty reduction in the country and the World Bank can design and implement sustainable outcomes through "state-of-the-art environmental and social practices and strengthened public financial management systems, but this takes a long time" (Porter and Shivakumer, 2010, pp. 12).

TABLE 4.2 The selected partnership framework of the development partners in Laos

European Commission (EU)		
Partnership framework	Objectives /Strategic plan	SDGs relevance
1. Agriculture and Rural Development	1. Improve agricultural practices 2. Strengthen the role of family farming 3. Improve economic efficiency 4. Improve service delivery in rural areas	—SDGs Goal 13 —SDGs Goal 2 —SDGs Goal 12 —SDGs Goal 3 —SDGs Goal 6 —SDGs Goal 8
2. Education	1. Support to ensure equitable access to and completion of basic education (with focus on disadvantaged groups) 2. Support to improvement of education quality and relevance 3. Support to improved governance of the education system	—SDGs Goal 4 —SDGs Goal 5 —SDGs Goal 10
3. Environment and Natural Resources	1. Protect, restore and promote sustainable use of terrestrial ecosystems, sustainably manage forests, combat desertification, halt and reverse land degradation and halt biodiversity loss 2. End poverty; end hunger, achieve food security, improve nutrition and promote sustainable agriculture 3. Ensure government takes urgent action to combat climate change and its impact	—SDGs Goal 15 —SDGs Goal 2 —SDGs Goal 1 —SDGs Goal 13
4. Governance	1. Support improvements in government services 2. Contribute to an environment that promotes citizens' engagement for sustainable development and good governance 3. Support the consolidation of the rule of law	—SDGs Goal 16
5. Health	1. Strengthen public health systems in Laos 2. Improve access to and quality of maternal and child health	—SDGs Goal 3

6. Nutrition	1. Support strengthened nutrition governance 2. Contribute to scaled-up nutrition-specific support 3. Contribute to scaled-up nutrition-sensitive support	—SDGs Goal 2 —SDGs Goal 6
7. Private Sector Development	1. Enable Laos to make use of its potential and reduce the economic risks of the ASEAN Economic Community (AEC) 2. Improve quality, relevance and inclusiveness of the Technical and Vocational Education and Training (TVET) system 3. Facilitate financial sector development: Access to finance for MSMEs	—SDGs Goal 1 —SDGs Goal 8 —SDGs Goal 10
United Nation Development Programme (UNDP)		
Pillar 1: Focusing inclusive growth, livelihood and resilience	Outcome 1: All women and men have increased opportunities for decent livelihoods and jobs Outcome 2: More people have access to social protection benefits, in particular vulnerable groups and the poor Outcome 3: Forests and other ecosystems are protected and enhanced, and people are less vulnerable to climate-related events and disasters	—SDGs Goal 1 —SDGs Goal 5 —SDGs Goal 10 —SDGs Goal 13 —SDGs Goal 14 —SDGs Goal 15 —SDGs Goal 18
Pillar 2: Focusing on human development	Outcome 4: Children and youth enjoy better access to inclusive and equitable quality basic education and vocational skills Outcome 5: People enjoy improved access to quality health services, and water, sanitation and hygiene Outcome 6: The most vulnerable people benefit from improved food security and nutrition	—SDGs Goal 2 —SDGs Goal 3 —SDGs Goal 4 —SDGs Goal 4 —SDGs Goal 6 —SDGs Goal 10
Pillar 3: Focusing on governance	Outcome 7: Institutions and policies at the national and local levels support the delivery of quality services that better respond to people's needs Outcome 8: People enjoy improved access to justice and fulfillment of their human rights	—SDGs Goal 16

The World Bank		
Focus Area 1: Supporting inclusive growth	1. Put public finance on a sustainable path and support financial sector stability 2. Make it easier to do business 3. Invest in infrastructure for growth and inclusion	—SDGs Goal 1 —SDGs Goal 8 —SDGs Goal 9
Focus Area 2: Investing in people	1. Reduce the prevalence of malnutrition 2. Improve the quality of primary and pre-primary education and keep girls in school 3. Improve access to and quality of health services 4. Reduce vulnerability and inclusive access to social services	—SDGs Goal 2 —SDGs Goal 3 —SDGs Goal 4 —SDGs Goal 10
Focus Area 3: Protecting the environment	1. Promote environmental protection and sustainable natural resources management 2. Put in place enhanced disaster risk management and climate and disaster resilience	—SDGs Goal 13 —SDGs Goal 14 —SDGs Goal 15
Asian Development Bank (ADB)		
Strategic Priority 1: Infrastructure and private sector development to support employment and income generation	1. Develop infrastructure and the private sector to support employment and income generation 2. Strengthen private enterprise development 3. Increase productivity and promote agriculture commercialization 4. Improve access to sustainable water supply and sanitation	—SDGs Goal 1 —SDGs Goal 9 —SDGs Goal 8 —SDGs Goal 3 —SDGs Goal 2 —SDGs Goal 6 —SDGs Goal 12
Strategic Priority 2: Enhanced human development	1. Build resilient human capital with relevant skills 2. Improve health services delivery	—SDGs Goal 3 —SDGs Goal 4

Strategic Priority 3: Sustainable natural resource management and climate resilience	1. Mainstream climate change and disaster risk assessment and response 2. Improve urban environment services 3. Sustain agriculture gains without diminishing natural resource endowment	—SDGs Goal 13 —SDGs Goal 12 —SDGs Goal 11
Crosscutting theme	Increase gender equality and good governance	—SDGs Goal 16 —SDGs Goal 17
Japan International Cooperation Agency (JICA)		
Pillar 1: Strengthen connectivity with countries in the region on tangible and intangible fronts	—Develop infrastructure for making Lao PDR a transportation hub of the Mekong region —Develop the systems and infrastructure (improve customs clearances, international border check-point etc.) for making Lao PDR a distribution network base of the Mekong region —Develop and operate Vientiane International Airport in order to strengthen the connectivity of the sky —Develop safe operating structures at theregional airport —Develop power sources and the electricity transmission network in Lao PDR, which is being counted on to become the "*battery*" of the Mekong region	—SDGs Goal 1 —SDGs Goal 9 —SDGs Goal 11 —SDGs Goal 7 —SDGs Goal 16
Pillar 2: Develop the industrial human resources in order to diversify Lao PDR's industries and enhance their competitiveness	—Strengthen basic education in such areas as science and mathematics, enhance higher education and develop vocational training —Develop the investment environment, enhance the capacity for formulating industrial policy, and promote public-private sector dialogues —Improve access to the funding needed to establish and nourish SMEs —Promote areas such as irrigation agriculture in order to encourage commercial crops, and clean agriculture that offers safety and peace of mind. —Build a food value chain that meets the standard for the markets of neighboring countries	—SDGs Goal 1 —SDGs Goal 2 —SDGs Goal 3 —SDGs Goal 4 —SDGs Goal 12

Pillar 3: Rectify disparity through balanced urban and regional development that takes environmental and cultural preservation into account	—Develop public transportation modes such as buses, including formulating strategies for transport development in the capital. —Develop basic public infrastructure, such as waterworks —Pursue sustainable development in regional cities, including Luang Prabang, a World Heritage City —Conserve the environment and develop it sustainably, including by preserving the forests of the Mekong River basin. —Improve the quality of healthcare, education and other sectors, and rectify domestic disparity	—SDGs Goal 3 —SDGs Goal 9 —SDGs Goal 11 —SDGs Goal 13 —SDGs Goal 14 —SDGs Goal 15

Note: SDGs Goal 1 — No Poverty; SDGs Goal 2 — Zero Hunger; SDGs Goal 3 — Good Health and Well-Being; SDGs Goal 4: Quality Education; SDGs Goal 5 — Gender Equality, SDGs Goal 6 — Clean Water and Sanitation; SDGs Goal 7 — Affordable and Clean Energy; SDGs Goal 8 — Decent Work and Economic Growth; SDGs Goal 9 — Industry, Innovation and Infrastructure; SDGs Goal 10 — Reduced Inequalities; SDGs Goal 11 — Sustainable Cities and Communities; SDGs Goal 12 — Responsible Consumption and Production; SDGs Goal 13 — Climate Action; SDGs Goal 14 — Life Below Water; SDGs Goal 15 — Life on Land; SDGs Goal 16 — Peace, Justice and Strong Institutions; SDGs Goal 17 — Partnership for the Goals; SDGs Goal 18 — Lives Safe from UXO

source: Author's analysis and compilation based on UNDP, 2017b; World Bank, 2017; Ministry of Foreign Affairs of Japan, 2017; ADB, 2017; EU, 2017 losses, the loss of rain-fed rice fields, and the loss of riverbank gardens appear to have led to severe declines in the villager well-being" (p. 1093). They argue that the World Bank has become "the deal maker" since "the Nam Theun 2 Power Company (NTPC) is 40 percent owned by Electricite de France, 35 percent by Electricity Generating Public Company in Thailand and 25 percent by the GoL [Government of Laos]." The dam will be transferred to the Lao government after the 25 years concession agreement has come to term, a duration long enough to generate big profit for the development partners before the dam is handed over to the Lao government.

The third agenda item is the standardization of state matters to improve the connectivity of the global, regional and sub-regional levels to bring mutual prosperity to those countries. Thus massive development projects related to establishing roads and bridges in remote regions have been increasing in recent decades. The ADB is one of the development partners specializing in this effort via increasing connectivity and economic integration in the Greater Mekong Sub-region (GMS). The GMS, according to the ADB's (2006, p. 1) report, is now designated to become a "prosperous, integrated, and harmonious sub-region," privileged due to its being built around the Mekong River. To strengthen the connectivity, the ADB initiated an economic corridor to utilize the geographic potential of six countries that rely on the Mekong River: Thailand, Laos, Cambodia, Myanmar, China (Yunnan and Guangxi provinces), and Vietnam. Since 1992, the ADB has supported the issuing of loans and grants to improve infrastructure to connect the North-South, East-West, and Southern economic corridors (see PHOTO 4.1). It aims to develop infrastructure and the private sector to support employment and income generation and regional cooperation and integration. The ADB provides financial assistance for 2017–2020 to the Lao government at $421 million to improve the infrastructure development of the country (ADB, 2017, p. 12).

In order to harmonize Laos with other countries in the region, some development partners provide technical assistance to the Lao government to increase trade and investment in food and agriculture, improve the capacity to facilitate trade and investment of the region (e.g., Association of Southeast Asian Nations [ASEAN]) and sub-regional levels (e.g., the GMS), deregulate the custom procedure, support Small and Medium Enterprises, develop human capital through education, and provide assistance on health and well-being to the country. For example, the ASEAN Free Trade Area (AFTA) promotes the trade and investment of intra-ASEAN countries, including Laos

(Asia Regional Integration Center, 1992). By doing so, the legal framework of the 10 countries will be simplified and harmonized to decrease customs procedures at the borders, and to facilitate trade and investment in these countries–including Laos.

The fourth agenda of the development partners in Laos is to provide humanitarian aid. This agenda item is based on the fact that many Lao people are living in extreme poverty and some of them have lost their land due to these megaproject developments, especially in the case of the hydropower dam. Humanitarian assistance was seen in the assistance provided to flood victims of the Xe-Pian Xe-Namnoy dam in 2018.[48] Hundreds of people are missing and more than one thousand families were endangered due to the dam's collapse. The development partners and neighboring countries sought to provide rescue and medical teams, donate money, and send emergency supplies to the Attapeu province to mitigate the impact of the dam collapse, according to the reporter of the Vientiane Times (Vilaysack, 2018).

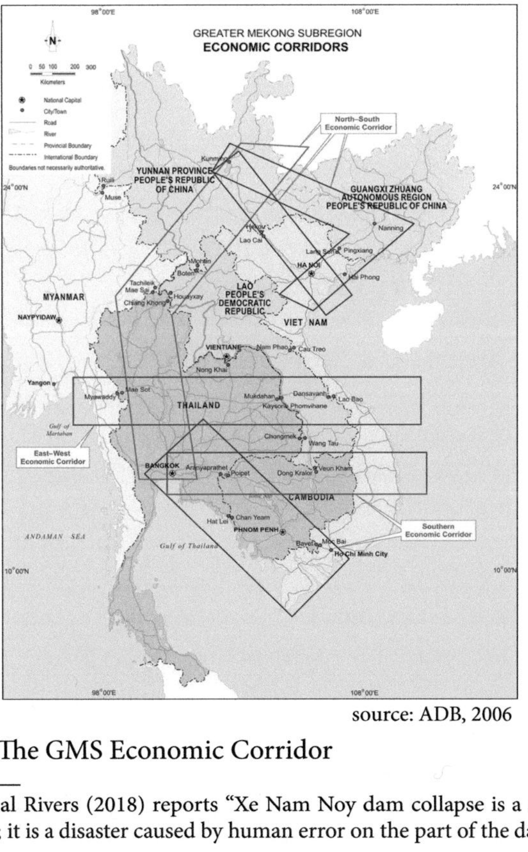

source: ADB, 2006

PHOTO 4.1 The GMS Economic Corridor

---

48 The International Rivers (2018) reports "Xe Nam Noy dam collapse is a disaster, but not a natural disaster; it is a disaster caused by human error on the part of the dam-builders."

The last agenda item is that the development partners attempt to advocate their national interest through Lao development. The most important national interests for the development partners are to maintain hegemonic power in the Mekong sub-region and Southeast Asian region. My argument can be observed through hegemonic competition in Lao development. This is specifically true with regard to development assistance that comes from the USA, China, and Japan. Although these countries have prioritized different aspects of development, their agenda is ultimately to maintain the status quo as superpower countries.

The policy of the US government towards Laos, recently, is built on economic development, health, education, energy, and the environment under the Lower Mekong Initiative (LMI)[49] and later the Mekong-U.S. Partnership launched in 2020. Additionally, in 2016, the former U.S. President Barack Obama visited Laos to express his apology about unexploded Ordnance in Laos, and proclaimed, "Today, the United States is more deeply engaged across the Asia Pacific than it had been in decades. Our position is stronger. We have sent a clear message that, as a Pacific nation, we are here to stay" (The New York Time, 2016). As a result, the US government provided extra assistance in clearing the Unexploded Ordnance in Laos and established a Comprehensive Partnership dubbed the "Joint Declaration between the United States of America and the Lao People's Democratic Republic" (see the White House President Barack Obama, 2016). Many analysts believe that the main purpose of US diplomacy in Southeast Asia is to outmaneuver China's influence while maintaining its global hegemonic stability (Radio Free Asia, 2016), which in this case, is evidently seen by the exclusion of China and Myanmar in the Mekong-U.S. Partnership.

Another powerful country in Lao development is China, which has been providing development assistance to Laos since the Asian economic crisis in 1997. Tan (2014) argues that, "China has no political ambitions in Laos. Its intentions are primarily economic, and its leaders are willing to provide economic aid and political support for the Lao government" (p. 13). I argue that the political goals of China are as significant as its economic goals in Laos. Along with the fact that the developmental agenda of the Chinese government in Laos includes accumulating wealth for its people and government, it supports the national interest of China and provides regime legitimacy that favors the Chinese government. It aims to become the "Big Brother" of the Mekong sub-region and Southeast Asian region.

[49] The LMI consists of four countries in the lower Mekong–Cambodia, Laos, Thailand, and Vietnam.

Since the reconciliation between the Chinese and the Lao governments in 1997,[50] the bilateral and multilateral cooperation between the two countries has been increasing. The Chinese influence in Laos is obvious when one examines Foreign Direct Investment (FDI) in Laos as the result of the "go-out" strategy[51] of the Chinese government. Furthermore, infrastructure development under the GMS has closely connected the two countries through the road in the North-South Economic Corridor. The economic fruit of Chinese investments should not come as much of a surprise considering the Chinese FDI has become the main driver of the Lao economy, through 830 development projects costing over $5 billion between 1989–2014 (see GRAPH 4.1). My development partner interviewee commented that the rise of Chinese influence in Laos is due to the fact that loan and assistance conditions attached to agreements with the Chinese government are accessible and fewer in number than those negotiated by development partners with different countries of origin (Informant No. 5, 2017). As a consequence, Chinese investments in mining, hydropower dams, agriculture, transportation, and tourism are booming.

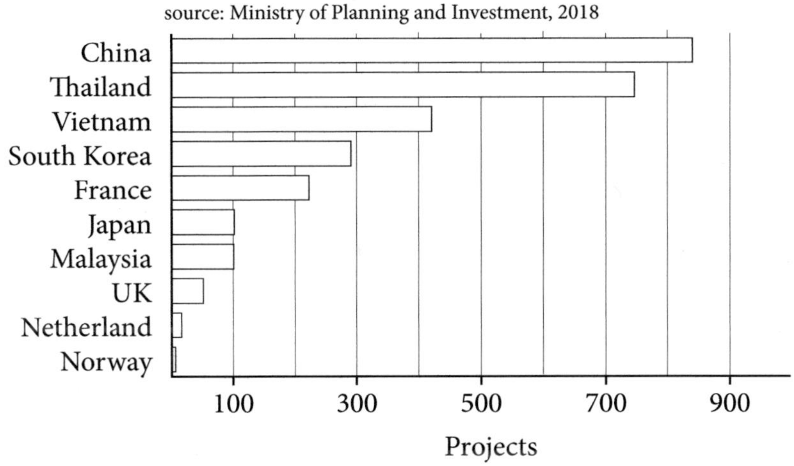

GRAPH 4.2 The value of Foreign Direct Investment (FDI) in Laos from 1989–2014.

Tan, for example, points out that Chinese investors are involved in 14 hydropower projects under the Build-Operate-Transfer (BOT) model, which

50 Phaxayavong (2009) highlights one the reason for the reconciliation between the Chinese and Lao governments in 1997. The Asian Financial crisis hit the Laos economy via Thailand. The Chinese government provided financial assistance to the Lao government to recover from this.

51 The going-out strategy of Chinese government refers to encouraging "domestic enterprises to invest overseas" (Tan, 2014, p. 4).

states that the dams will transfer to the Lao government after a 25–30 year-concession period (Tan, 2014, p. 6). Another example is Chinese contract farming in Laos. Contract farming is used to improve the rural economy by supporting the agricultural sector in Laos to access the market and by diversifying agricultural products with modern technology from China. According to Onphalanda and Suruga (2013), the Chinese have invested in rubber, maize, tobacco, vegetables and fruits, and herbal and crude drugs. Chinese investments in contract farming have both positive and negative effects on Lao farmers. Positively, Lao agricultural products, such as maize, exported to China increased to $8,305 million in 2011, the total investment value of which amounted to more than four times that of 2007. However, contract farming has had a negative impact on local people as well. For example, chemical pesticide overuse has given rise to land degradation in Bokeo province located in northern Laos. In Bokeo province, there are a plethora of banana plantations of Chinese investors that use chemicals on more than 10,000 hectares in the province. Khamphang Pheuyavong, the Governor of the Bokeo province, said that "Impact on the environment and nearby communities partly results from the fact that relevant government authorities failed to carry out proper management and monitoring… As a result, chemical fertilizers and harmful herbicides and pesticides have been used by foreign investors" (Pheuyavong as cited in Ghosh, 2016). Thus, the establishment of a more large-scale banana plantation in Laos has been recently prohibited, according to the Nations (2016b).

Chinese investment in Laos amounts to a financial win-win situation, as the profits can support economic growth in both countries. In 2017, the Chinese President Xi Jin-Ping visited Laos and signed an article entitled "China and Laos: Working Together for a Shared Future with Strategic Significance" to reiterate the friendship between China and Laos. Moreover, he delivered a speech to reinforce political trust between these two socialist countries and the developmental direction in Laos of the Chinese government, stating:

> We should continue to support each other on issues involving each other's core interests and major concerns…We need to expand practical cooperation and build a community of shared future for mutual benefit… Laos enjoys good natural endowments and fast economic development… China has a rich experience and strength in capital, technology and equipment. The two sides should tap cooperation potential and explore new ways of cooperation (Xinhua, 2017).

Japan provides the largest number of development grants in Lao development (see GRAPH 4.3), and has occupied the highest-level position of the ADB since 1966 (Wan, 1995, p. 509). Fauer (2010) contends, "In fact, Japan's influence in this multilateral bank was perceived as a tool at the service of Japanese diplomacy" (p. 163). The official development cooperation agency of the Japanese government is the Japan International Cooperation Agency (JICA). This agency has been working on Lao development since 1958 and is "recognized as the leading bilateral development organization to the Lao PDR providing assistance across various sectors to aid socio-economic development in partnership and friendship with the Lao people" (Ministry of Foreign Affairs of Japan, 2017, p. 1). Currently, the main foci of JICA are to: 1) strengthen connectivity with countries in the region on the tangible and intangible fronts; 2) Develop industrial human resources in order to diversify Lao PDR industries and enhance and rectify disparity through balanced urban and regional development that takes environmental and cultural preservation into account. In the Japanese fiscal year of 2015, 2.77 Billion Yen had been approved to implement Lao development. Such connectivity supports the economic corridor approach of the ADB as mentioned above. In 2000, for instance, the Japanese government granted 5.46 billion Yen to build a bridge named the Lao-Nippon Bridge (Japan Times, 2000). This bridge was built in Champasak, the capital city of the Pakse province.

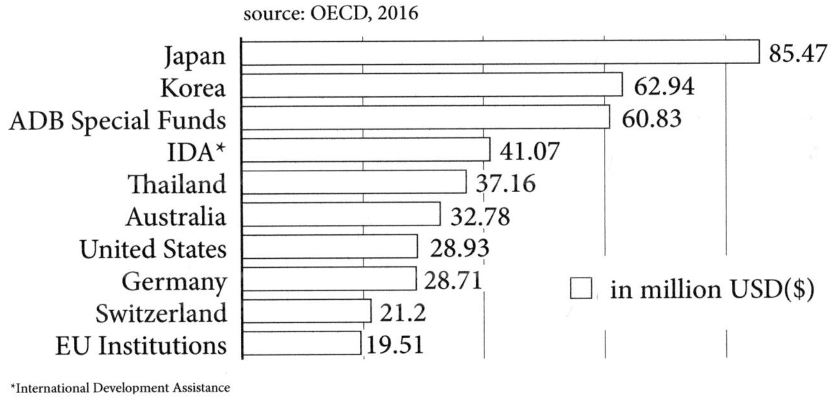

GRAPH 4.3 Top Ten Donors of Gross ODA for Lao People's Democratic Republic (2015–2016) in USD

Japanese assistance to Laos has led to a fruitful discussion about the Japanese government's development agenda. This dispute falls on the notion that another vital motivation of the Japanese government is to balance its power with China in Asia.[52] The development norms supported by the Japanese government are unlike those of the US government and the Chinese government. Recently, the Japanese government has mostly emphasized the quality of infrastructure development with respect to building more environmentally-friendly and sustainable infrastructures for the Lao people and the environment. At the Mekong-Japan Summit in 2018 the Japanese Government promoted the three-year strategy in improving the connectivity of the Mekong sub-regional countries with 'quality infrastructure' and set a new development direction named the 'Green Mekong' to promote the environmental protection, water resource management, disaster risk reduction, and protective measures against climate change in the Mekong sub-region (Vientiane Time, 2018a).

This information on the development assistance provided by the USA, China, and Japan reveals a hegemonic power competition to promote national interests through development norms in Laos. Yoshimatsu (2015, pp. 176–190) summarizes that the development norms of the USA are based on the "ideal-oriented policies" to support "good governance, sustainability and human security." Contrary to China, its development policies are based on the "pragmatic approach" to "pursue realistic and concrete consequences with reality." Among the development agendas stated above, however, the most important agenda item of the development partners, particularly from the western countries and international organizations, is to bring democracy, or at least to advocate for democratic process in Laos. In the next section, I will analyze democratization inside the SDGs with respect to how the development partners build democracy in Lao development indirectly.

Are principles of democracy hidden in the SDGs?

The interplay between the SDGs and principles of democracy remains controversial. SDGs, in general, have been criticized by many observers for simultaneously supporting and overlooking democratic principles (see Penumetcha, 2016; Smith & Gladstein, 2018). Optimistically, the UN Secretary-General Ban Ki-Moon (as cited in Penumetcha, 2016) pointed out the democratic principle in the SDGs that,

[52] Fauer (2010) proposes "Today the Chinese economic emergence may appear threatening by its sheer size and speed but one must not quickly discount the fact that in the past decades it was Japan that held this place of an aggressive and predatory economic power" (p. 177). Likewise, Hartley (2015) argues "Japan's ODA also interacts with institutional power and attempts to reform Laos's state bodies away from their ties with China and Vietnam… Japan's hegemony in Laos is a picture of two halves, with the trend being for Japan's economic power to be focused sub-nationally in Laos's southern province" (Hartley, 2015, pp. 15–17).

> Democratic principles run through the Agenda like a golden thread, from universal access to public goods, health care and education, as well as safe places to live and decent work opportunities for all. Goal 16 addresses democracy directly: it calls for inclusive societies and accountable institutions.

To implement the SDGs in many countries effectively, some observers believe it is necessary to bring the principles of democratic governance to undemocratic countries. However, some analysts question whether the SDGs themselves are in fact democratic. For example, Smith and Gladstein (2018) argues that the SDGs undermine democracy. Only SDG 16 (Peace, Justice and Strong Institutions) is related to democratization. He argues that the mention of democratization is superficial, especially considering participatory undemocratic governments in the SDGs (like China, Vietnam, Belarus, and Egypt) continue to engage in human rights violations and civil repression, both of which contradict democratic principles.

My interviews with representatives of the development partners demonstrate that the development partners still attempt to advocate democracy in Laos, but they have to depoliticize their approach to do so. They instead use terms like modernization, good governance, rule of law, and decentralization. These terms are integral aspects of democratization, as they relate to creating more participatory channels for people in many countries. According to political scientists, they believe that economic development, industrialization, urbanization, and enhanced social mobility are the foundations of democracy. Inglehart and Welzel (2009) contend that such outcomes of modernization create "a self-reinforcing process that transforms social life and political institutions, bringing rising mass participation in politics. The expectation is that with economic development comes social mobility, raising the middle-class bracket and thus the number of people who are well educated and specialized. There is no doubt that the development partners would like to see this take place in Laos.

The Governance Sector Working Group (GWSG) is an outcome of their advocacy, and the development strategies of the working group are compatible with democratization, as I will illustrate in the three following points. First, the Lao government and the development partners have taken an important step to improve the checks and balances in their system by updating their administrative framework. This updated framework clarifies and upgrades the roles and responsibilities of the government, local administrations, the

National Assembly (NA), mass organizations, the Provincial People's Assembly (PPA) and the civil society at all levels. The National Assembly and Provincial People Assembly, for instance, now have more rights to appoint, remove, and monitor the governor at central and local levels (see chapter 3).

Second, the Lao government has created various channels and forums for people's participation in the National Assembly, Provincial People's Assembly, mass organizations and Non-Profit Associations. For instance, the Lao people can participate in the decision-making process of the NA and PPA through hotlines, petitions, and public hearings supported by the Lao government. Third, the Lao government has become more receptive to people's participation in improving the legal framework and rule of laws under the 'Legal Sector Master Plan (LSMP).' Presently, the NA has adopted approximately 109 laws and the Lao government has improved the justice service delivery to guarantee the rule of laws (Ministry of Planning and Investment, 2016b, p. 19). With regard to human rights issues in the country, the development partners recommend that the Lao government improve its approach to human rights. The Lao government has thus far adopted 116 recommendations out of the 196 recommendations received.

The rule of law and the democratic processes mentioned above are interlinked with the accountability and transparency of the government to protect citizen rights, which signifies the boundary between citizens and government authority (Tommasoli, 2012). It is clear that the development projects under the GSWG allow the Lao people to monitor the Lao government's performance and enhance the checks and balances system of the country. Moreover, it can create political awareness for the Lao people to gain knowledge of their rights and duties. This awareness encourages people to participate, which is an essential principle for democracy.

Another principle of democracy is decentralization. For the third point, the Three Build directive and the Provincial People's Assembly have obtained the full support of the development partners for enhancing local authority in public management, service delivery, and implementation of the national development plan. If the local authorities can implement the development plan to meet the needs of local peoples, the development will be more effective and sustainable in given areas. Another channel for local engagement is community-based tourism in the tourist sector. The Lao government recognizes that the service sector matters for economic growth, as this sector contributes the most to the country's GDP. In 2018, the Lao government introduced "Visit Laos Year" to promote natural attractions and cultural diversity in Laos to foreigners and to increase the participation of local groups in tourism management. In this way, local groups could increase their revenue while preserving their traditional culture.

Although the development partners have disguised democratization within the SDGs, the Lao government still has absolute power to suppress democratization within the country (see chapter 3). Nevertheless, their effort is not worthless. When asking my development partner informants about their opinions regarding democratization in Laos, they had both positive and negative things to say. For the positive analysis, one representative argued "Democracy is already here in Laos, but socialism still matters... socialism and democracy can go hand in hand... Even in a socialist state you have elections" (Informant No. 2, 2017). Another believes that the democratic process is more important than democracy as a political system, stating "We don't want to change the political system in Laos, but we do try to support the democratic process by increasing people's participation to improve state and citizen relations... We try to professionalize the role of the National Assembly... and build trust relations between the CSO and the Lao government (Informant No. 4, 2017). In contrast, another delegate voiced her concern that "At least, we can see the Provincial People's Assembly election in Laos, but it is not democracy because the communist system controls the whole of the government and the government fully controls Lao society... the nature of the Lao people is to always be under the control of the government" (Informant No. 5, 2017).

From these selected opinions of the development partners on democratization in Laos, it could be concluded that they respect the socialist ideology in the political system of Laos. Instead of changing the political regime through the power relationship between the development partners and the Lao government, they initiate the democratic process to bring political awareness to the Lao people through the election process and other participatory channels. Some interviewees believe that the most important factor necessary for bringing democracy to the country is strong political leadership combined with persuasive appeal to the Party to accept democratic principles (Informant No. 6, 2017).

Is Lao state power being transformed under the international development norms?

One of the Lao development partners interviewed stated, "State power in Laos is consolidated by the Party, which dominates the Lao government. However, it could be weakened by exogenous forces, particularly, by direct foreign investment" (Informant No. 5, 2017). I contend that the Party employs state power to alter domestic institutions and development policy under the SDGs. If the development partners can weaken Lao state power, the domestic institutions and development policy will reflect the development partners' development norms rather than those of Laos. To support my hypothesis, in this section, I analyze Laos state power under the international development norms, questioning the extent to which the Party has transformed state power to deal with them.

The results from my interviews imply that the development partners have some influence in Laos, but cannot force the Party to absolutely comply with their norms. The development partners, in turn, have depoliticized their role in Lao development. Recently, they have focused on capacity building in economics, human development, environmental sustainability, human rights, good governance and rule of law, and mitigating other worrying issues related to Lao development. Additionally, they do not attempt to pressure the Lao government to have more concern for human rights issues and democratization. Rather, they have talked with the Lao government privately as they attempt to build a trusting relationship with the Lao government. For example, one representative of the development partners said that her organization has arranged an annual meeting on human rights with the Lao government to follow up on previous discussions. The main purpose of the meeting is to express concerns about human rights in Laos and the meeting is confidential. Our organization has voiced our concerns about human rights, the environment, and freedom of expression because there is no space in Laos to address such things (Informant No. 4, 2017).

Viewing of the Party, it has initially complied with the international development norms and implemented the norms in the national development. This could help the Party bring modernity into Lao development and receive external acceptance. As mentioned earlier, it could be argued that the Lao state power is rather constrained by the FDI. The Lao government has loosened upon its laws and regulations and has increased incentives to support direct foreign investment because economic growth will help legitimize the Party's regime. Therefore, the Lao government seeks to commercialize and promote natural resources to foreign investors based on the potential for the development of each province. The Lao government has considered the developmental potential with regard to natural resources, geographical advantages, and human capital, to formulate its five-year national socio-economic development plan, which is created by the Ministry of Planning and Investment. The development plan is used to support the development policy in each province based on the government's decisions. Special Economic Zones (SEZs) provide a useful example of this.

An SEZ is an exceptional zone in that the state devolves power over them to committees to endorse specific laws and regulations in order to facilitate investment in each area.[53] The Lao expert I interviewed confirms that, "investment promotion in Laos is much better than other countries" (Informant No. 19, 2017). One of the incentives from the Lao government is that more than 10,000 hectares of the land were provided to the investor for 99 years (Maierbrugger, 2013). Indeed, the committees of the SEZ are seen as a rubber stamp for foreign investors, because the investors can design rules and regulations inside their SEZ. For instance, a casino in the Bokeo Province (or *King Roman*—translated from Lao) built by a Chinese investor rests in a designated SEZ. In 2013, the casino officially opened. When I visited the casino, I noticed many Chinese restaurants and shops employing Chinese laborers. This region has essentially become a Lao Chinatown.

This same kind of situation has had an unavoidable impact on locals. The Lao expert commented on SEZs that relocation and losing the lands are the main problem for the local people as they moved their homes and land to the compensation areas from the investors. Even though an investor builds a new house, develops infrastructure, and provides jobs at the SEZ to compensate for it, this is still insufficient because it creates a struggle for local people to find new jobs, and only 10 percent of Lao people can work inside SEZs. Infrastructure development, as with an airport, remains incomplete. The worst-case scenario for this situation is that local people will have no land for food production, and are simply used and exploited by the government and investors. Such a condition does not support capital accumulation for the people, but deprives them of their property rights. Moreover, the Lao government itself could not contribute to a long-term plan to support local entrepreneurs and workers, unlike China (Informant No. 19, 2017).

View in this light, economic development, and local people's rights, at some point, are contradicting. With the global competitiveness, it seems like the Lao government has not had so many options to improve their economy by trading with the local people's interests. However, this sort of situation is a clear example of "crony capitalism"[54] happening in many countries. For Laos,

[53] According to the laws on the SEZ issued in 2010, developers of the SEZ have legitimate right to manage the activity inside the SEZ and to import labor from their countries (see more the article 24 and 25 in the laws on the SEZ, Prime Minister's Office, 2010).

[54] The Committee for Economic Development (2015) defines crony capitalism as a deal

crony capitalism is resulting from the patronage system fostered by a strong connection between the Lao government, Party members, and their business partners. In conclusion, the state power in Laos is strengthening in domestic realms, and diminishing under global competitiveness. Economic development that exploits natural resources and people does not mesh well with the intentions of the Marxist-Leninist framework. As one of the Lao experts said,

> "When socialism meets capitalism, the outcome is more worrying than capitalism itself. Indeed, it marginalizes people more than in the capitalist society because at least in the capitalist society, people can express their feelings and debate with the government. But this has never happened in Laos" (Informant No. 20, 2017).

Her observation rings true since Lao-style capitalism has simply broadened the gap between the rich and the poor, as a consequence of capitalism, in which the rich stay rich, but the poor remain poor and insecure.

Lao-style development

In this section, I will analyze Lao-style development, arguing that the Lao government initially agreed to implement the development norms to obtain regime legitimacy. Development in Laos is dubbed the "Party-led development," because the Party has employed state power to tackle and reframe the Sustainable Development Goals. Understanding the Party Congress is essential to understand how the Party influences the direction of national development, so this is where I will begin.

According to the interview with the member of NA, he mentioned that the term sustainability (*Yuenyong*–in Lao) is not a new concept in Lao development. Indeed, this term was already mentioned in the Ninth Party Congress in 2011, at which the Party included it as a priority in the Millennium Development Goals (MDGs). At the Tenth Party Congress in 2016, moreover, sustainability was used in the Party slogan '*to enhance the Party's capability and leading role, increase the unity of the people, adhere to new developmental directions and initiate principles of change necessary to sustainably develop the country while continuing to strive toward the socialist utopia*' (Pak

"between some private interests (business, anti-business interests, professions, social groups) and government to "pick winners" and there by also pick "losers" that is based on "political influence rather than merit" (p. 5). Similarly, Haber (2002) states that crony capitalism is a system in which "those close to the political authorities who make and enforce policies receive favors that have large economic value" (p. xii).

Pasason Pativad Lao, 2016, p. VI). The result of the Tenth Party Congress not only revealed the leadership transition from the first generation to their descendants, but also the new direction in Lao development under the SDGs framework. The Party set the four pillars as the Party's development norms, which include economic development, environment sustainability (or Green growth development), social inclusion, and, the most important for the Party, security. The Party member I interviewed proclaimed that "In the next five years, our Party will have adhered to and enhanced the new changes, continuing the principles of the Four Breakthroughs (*Boukthalou* in Lao),[55] and improving the Party's capability in politics and leadership" (Informant No. 13, 2017).

The current direction of the Party-led development is laid out in the 8th five-year NSEDP (2016–2020), the Socio-Economic Development Strategy for 2016–2025, and the Vision 2030 report. The slogan for this period is: '*fighting to graduate from LDC status by 2020 and becoming a middle-income developing country under the direction of green development and sustainability by 2030.*' Aside from this example, additional efforts have been made to promote "sustainability" in political, socio-economic and environmental aspects, as well as in regional and international integration. It has also been noted in the main objectives of the development plan, which include:

1. Ensure that continued economic growth, with quality and macro-stability, is achieved; ensure budgeting goes hand in hand with development targets and is consistent with the new environment of industrialization and modernization;
2. Ensure sustainable development in harmony with economic development, socio-cultural development and environmental protection; be prepared to handle natural disasters in a timely manner; ensure integrated rural development has a strong link to poverty reduction through the implementation of the 3-builds directive;
3. Strengthen human resource capacity by improving workforce skills, encourage workers to be more disciplined and tolerant; increase the number of technical experts and specialists; enhance the technical and professional capacity of civil servants, members of the private sector, and entrepreneurs to enable them to compete within the country and abroad;

[55] The four breakthroughs included: 1) the breakthrough in thinking; 2) the breakthrough in human resource development; 3) the breakthrough in reforming governance and management systems; and 4) the breakthrough in poverty eradication. The breakthroughs initiated by the Lao government and the development partners to promote.

4. Maintain political stability, peace and social order; embed solidarity, democracy, justice and civilization in society; and
5. Actively continue widening international cooperation with ownership in various forms oriented towards benefit for all, enhancing favorable conditions for regional and international integration (The Ministry of Planning and Investment, 2016a, p. 87).

The SDGs in Laos, in general, may seem compatible with the principle of sustainable development that the Lao government focuses on environmental sustainability. Nevertheless, the fourth pillar, security, I contend is likely to contribute the greatest to regime legitimacy for the Party due to the fact that sustainability has been interpreted as political security under the one-Party state.

The fourth pillar of the SDGs in Laos

The SDGs are supposed to be implemented sustainably through environmentally-friendly and inclusive developmental practices. Indeed, the SDGs in Laos are special, relative to those implemented in other countries, due to the security pillar. Under the Party-led development, the Party has reinterpreted the SDGs to serve its socio-economic and, most importantly, political aims. In this section, I will examine the security pillar of the SDGs in Laos. I argue that the Party uses the SDGs as another source of political legitimacy to maintain the status quo of the Party-led development.

The Party member I interviewed pointed out how the security pillar is connected to sustainability in which it is about stability and unity in the country. If there is conflict, the country cannot develop or become more modern. In Laos, sustainability means bringing people across different ethnic and religious groups. Therefore, the Party strongly believes that the SDGs could contribute to that sustainability by playing the main role to bring stability and unity to the Lao people (Informant No. 13, 2017). Furthermore, the member of the NA mentioned that sustainability is the most important mechanism for bringing the country up to the socialist stage of development and that it is necessary in order to implement the rest of the three pillars in the country effectively. As he said, "If there is no political stability due to things like political conflict or war, the development process and the movement toward socialism will be slow" (Informant No. 15, 2017). To ensure political stability and social order, therefore, the Party has to play the leading role in ensuring social justice for the Lao people, narrowing the gap between the rich and the poor, and bringing social equality to the country. The guise of security has thus allowed the Party to concentrate its power inside domestic institutions and its development policy.

The terms political stability, unity, peace and social order have also been employed to index political sustainability. The 8th five-year NSEDP (2016–2020) emphasizes that through the pillars of security, "political stability, social peace and order, justice and transparency, are maintained" (Ministry of Planning and Investment, 2016a, p. 89). Aside from this, Vision 2030 emphasizes that the security pillar is necessary "to ensure social order, political development, and the rule of law" and to increase the scope of responsibility to the local administrations, particularly through the Three Build directive, to consolidate, strengthen, and sustain (Ministry of Planning and Investment, 2016b, p. 16). The security pillar, as emphasized in the development plans and strategies, is a crucial part of the Party-led development, particularly in the way in which the term sustainability extends beyond the principles of the SDGs therein. It becomes an underlying condition for the Party-led development to bring the country out of the LDC status and reach the socialist stage.

Thus the SDGs become another source of the Party's legitimacy as the Party emphasizes its role in contributing the political security in the 8th NSEDP as follows:

> "[The targets and expected outcomes of the 2025 development strategy are] to strengthen political stability based on democratic principles to support the leading role of the LPRP to become more enhanced, consolidated, and democratic. There should be national unity, social order, and justice in the country." (Ministry of Planning and Investment, 2016b, p. 17).

Furthermore, by claiming that the Party's subsidiary body is fully responsible for the political sustainability of the country, the security pillar creates more rights and duties for the Party and government authority at central and local levels to control Lao society. The Party member I interviewed claimed that "The Party has a duty to bring sustainability to Lao people by building peace through mass organizations." In this sense, the role of the mass organization as a quasi-governmental organization is to improve the efficiency of the SDGs by supporting the idea of sustainability at the local level (Information No. 13, 2017).

In summary, Party members and Lao policy-makers have politically reinterpreted sustainability in the SDGs as political stability and social order under the one-Party state. The security pillar is the means to maintain that status quo. Domestic institutions and the development policy under the SDGs have thus been shaped to meet the international standards and conceal the Party's power concurrently.

Restructuring Lao domestic institutions under the SDGs in Laos

The SDGs advance the global development agenda, which normalizes the development standards of many countries. In Laos, the SDGs not only serve a socio-economic and an environmental purpose, but also a political purpose. The Party has set up the four pillars of the SDGs to reshape and restructure Lao domestic institutions and development policy. In this section, I will analyze this restructuring of domestic institutions and development policy using Sach's framework (2012; 2015) which includes: 1) economic development; 2) environmental sustainability; 3) social inclusion, and 4) good governance.

Economic development: sustainable and inclusive growth to bring the country out of LDC status

Before turning to an analysis of the SDGs and economic development in Laos, it is worth mentioning that Lao economic development has been shaped from the outside since 1986. The historical evidence suggests that there were three major external-internal changes that must be understood to fully grasp the restructuring of domestic institutions and development policy for economic development in Laos.

The first major change was, as already mentioned, the economic reform of the USSR that pervasively, and unavoidably, affected the economic and political development of many socialist countries. In Laos, the USSR was the main aid-donor country. The failure of the USSR led to the Party's decision to open the country to the global economy, following the Vietnamese model, by announcing the New Economic Mechanism (NEM) at the Fourth Party Congress in 1986. The purpose of the NEM was to loosen economic control by the Party to adopt a more liberal approach to the private sector, and to integrate the country with the regional and global economy (Phimphanthavong, 2012). Thereafter, the Lao government restructured domestic institutions and the development policy to support direct foreign investment, trade, and privatization and to improve the bank system by modernizing its legal framework. For an example of the latter, the Lao government issued the first Foreign

Investment Law in 1988 to facilitate direct foreign investment and the first Constitution to ensure the political stability of the country in 1991.

Since economic development has come to the fore in Lao development, the second major change in Lao economic policy was the Lao government's shift to bilateral and multilateral economic integration. In 1992, Laos became a member of the Greater Mekong Sub-region (GMS) initiated by ADB. Under the GMS framework, the Lao government prioritized land connectivity to other GMS countries using the economic corridor approach, as mentioned earlier. The Lao government announced its 'landlocked to land-linked policy' that would link Laos up to the sub-regional economy. In 1997, Laos became a member of ASEAN. The fruit of this membership, in regional and sub-regional economic integration, was both the boost to infrastructure development that linked Laos to the borders of the other GMS countries and the additional support in trade and investment among the GMS and ASEAN countries.

More importantly, the Lao government shaped its development plan and strategies to follow the trend of regional integration. In 2000, the Lao government passed a policy that created investment incentives for land usage. As a result, contract farming and SEZs have been promoted to foreign investors, a move that has not come without criticism. The Lao government also moved forward with its 'battery of Asia' policy to utilize the potential of its natural resources by building a hydropower dam to generate electricity for domestic consumption and foreign sale.

The third major change came just before 2000. The Party set the ultimate development goals to bring the country out of the LDC status by 2020 at the Sixth Party Congress in 1996. To achieve these goals, the Lao government and the development partners set the five years goal based on the criteria that determines LDC status[56] at the Round Table Meeting in November 2000. At around that same time, the Brussels Programme of Action was endorsed by the United Nations Office of the High Representative for Least Developed Countries, Landlocked Developing Countries, and Small Island Developing States (UN-OHRLLS) to assist the 50 LDC countries. The main goal of the program is "to make substantial progress toward halving the proportion of people living in extreme poverty and suffering from hunger by 2015, and promoting sustainable development of the LDCs" (UN-OHRLLS, 2006, p.6) by providing a framework and partnership to those LDC countries. As a conse-

[56] The criteria for the LDC graduation is comprised of three development thresholds including Gross National Income (GNI) per capita at $1,230 or above, income-only at $2,460 or above; Human Assets Index (HAI) at 66 or above; and Economic Vulnerability Index (EVI) at 32 or below (UN-OHRLLS, 2018).

quence, the Lao government issued the 5th five-year NSEDP in 2001 introducing "sustainable development" to meet the LDC graduation criteria.

Since 2001, the economic development norms in Laos have mostly focused on graduating from the LDC status by 2020. The Lao government has strived toward reducing poverty by implementing the Millennium Development Goals (MDGs) as the development norms to fight poverty and meet international development standards. There were goals emphasized under the MDGs in the national development plan and development strategy. These 9 goals can be divided into two main focal points: poverty reduction and graduation from LDC status by 2020.

For economic development under the SDGs, according to Sach's framework, it is not only economic growth but also the ability to meet basic needs in poorer countries that counts. This framework was implemented at the 8th five-year NSEDP (2016–2020) issued by the Ministry of Planning and Investment under the resolution of the Party Congress. In the plan, the Lao government set target figures to be achieved within five years including reducing the poverty rate to 10 percent by 2020, ensuring the real GDP growth rate is not less than 7.5 percent on average and that GNI per capita is higher than $1,574 by 2028 and $1,810 by 2021 (see more the Ministry of Planning and Investment, 2016a, p. 88). Another ultimate goal of the Party is to become a middle-income country by 2030. Additionally, in the development plan, the Lao government seeks to reduce the Economic Vulnerability Index (EVI) from 36.2 in 2015 to 32. TABLE 4.3 presents the indicators and targets set to achieve Outcome 1.

In addition to the indicators listed to achieve the Outcome 1, the Lao government set the seven outputs[57] as development subcategories. Under the seven outputs for economic development, the expectation for the current development plan is that the Lao government will support sustainable economic growth in each sector. For example, the Lao government will support the industrial and service sectors to develop qualitatively and quantitatively, diversify commercial goods to meet domestic consumptive needs, export in proportion to international demands, and create jobs for the Lao people.

The Lao government set the development policy to meet the basic needs of the Lao people equally throughout the country. I take food security as an example. Despite the fact that the proportion of undernourished individuals

[57] Those outputs include: 1) sustained and inclusive economic growth; 2) macroeconomic stability; 3) alignment of development planning and budgeting; 4) balanced regional and local development; 5) improved public/private labor force capacity; 6) entrepreneurs, technical experts and professionals; and 7) regional and international cooperation and integration.

TABLE 4.3 Indicators and Targets set to achieve the outcome 1

8th NSEDP Design Summary	Performance indicators and targets
Outcome 1: Sustained inclusive economic growth with economic vulnerability (EVI) reduced to the level required for LDC graduation and consolidated financial, legal and human resources to support growth	**Economic vulnerability index: Final Index Improved** ▷ Population increased over 2015 (baseline: 2015 population sub-index for size 41.4) ▷ Location exposure index reduced over 2015 (baseline: exposure index = 58.5) ▷ Export Concentration reduced over 2015 (baseline: Export Concentration 22.4) ▷ Share of Agriculture/Forestry reduced over 2015 (baseline: 2015 Share of Agriculture and Forestry Index 41.9) ▷ Instability of Exports (Trade Shock–Shock Index) reduced over 2015 (baseline: Shock index = 24.2)
	Investment and financial management resources ▷ Investment will be achieved at approximately 30% of GDP (approximately 223 trillion kips) ▷ Development planning and budgeting integrated through operationalization of MTEF ▷ Development planning and budgeting aligned through PIP rolling programme
	Legal Framework and Human Resource Development ▷ Enhance entrepreneur management capacity/competitiveness ▷ Enhance the use of science and technology ▷ Micro-enterprise/SME/management capacity/competitiveness improved–Ease of Doing Business rating improves

source: Ministry of Planning and Investment, 2016a, pp. 9091 in the population was reduced from 42.8 percent in 1990 to around 18.2 percent in 2015, that approximately 76 percent of the population has access to an improved source of drinking water, that sanitation appears to have improved by 71 percent, and that the maternal mortality rate declined to 206 per 100,000 live births in 2015 (United Nations, 2015a), challenges in food security remain with regard in particular to accessibility of some remote areas. Under the principle of "leave no one behind," the Lao government issued the Agriculture Development Strategy and the National Nutrition Strategy to fight hunger and malnutrition. The vision of the Agriculture Development Strategy issued in 2015 put a spotlight on food security and the development of clean, safe and sustainable agricultural commodities (Ministry of Agriculture and Forestry, 2015). For the National Nutrition Strategy, the strategic directions and objectives have focused on achieving sufficient food consumption, improving the safety and diversity of food consumed, improving maternal and child health practices, and providing clean water and sanitation, a healthy living environment, and access to health care services (Government of Lao PDR, 2015).

Another example is industry, innovation, and infrastructure in Laos. The government highlights green growth and green industry. The Ministry of Industry and Commerce plays the main role in promoting participation by both the public and private sectors in the green and growth industry and supporting this kind of industry to other ministries. The Lao government also restructured legal instruments and policies to support development projects in each sector. For example, the Lao government set targets to "increase the industry sector's processing and handicraft as well as trade and services growth rates to approximately 15 percent per annum on average" (Ministry of Planning and Investment, 2016a, p. 95). More precisely, the industry sector has to increase the ratio of the GDP to more than 70. To accelerate those targets, there are five main sectors that have been supported: the industrial processing sector; the handicraft sector; the energy sector; the mining sector; and the construction (infrastructure) sector. As a result of such development promotion, the Lao government has created a favorable environment for processing industries and handicrafts through policy and legislation.

Social Inclusion: Narrowing the development and gender inequality gaps

Social inclusion, as Sach (2012; 2015) describes, is the commitment to future economic and technological progress under the conditions of fairness and equitable access to public services, and with the government counteracting social discrimination on the basis of gender, ethnic origin, religion, and race. In the SDGs, these values have been contained. In Laos, despite the fact that the poverty rate significantly declined from 46 percent to 17 percent in 2015, social inequality remains unchanged from the 1992/93 levels (Warr, Rasphone, and Menon, 2015). The inequality issues in Laos, according to the UNDP reports, are demonstrated through the gap between rural and urban areas, which sits at 18.6 percent. More precisely, the poverty rate in rural areas is 2.9 times that in urban areas, but the rising socioeconomic gap in urban areas is also a cause of worry. The report further stresses that the rural poverty rates from 2007/08 to 2012/13 declined much slower (by 9.8 percent) than in urban areas (by 42.5 percent). Even though the national poverty rate was reduced by 23 percent, one-third of the population in the mountainous areas remain below the poverty line, while approximately one-fifth of the population in the lowland areas is poor (UNDP, 2018h).

In order to reduce the inequality gap, the Lao government has linked social inclusion to economic development in its approach to narrowing the gap. Their main approach centers on reducing gender inequality, because the number of women enrolled in educational programs and employed in both private and governmental organizations is lower than for men. According to the UNDP website (2018d), the Gender Disparity Index shows that 66 girls attend secondary school for every 100 boys. In employment, women's wages are lower in every sector by 35 percent. Although women make up 27.5 percent of the National Assembly, the proportion of women in the decision-making institutions of the Lao government was sitting at 5 percent, in 2012. According to a study by the National Commission for the Advancement of Women that sampled 3,000 Lao women, one in seven women have experienced physical or sexual violence perpetrated by an intimate partner at least once in their lifetime. Only one in five women reported it to the local authorities, with 4% reporting to the police and 3% to a health service provider (National Commission for Advancement Women, 2014). Reducing gender inequality has been a developmental target for the Lao government since the MDGs (2000–2015).

In 2004, the Law on Development and Protection of Women was passed by the Lao government. This law aims to guarantee and promote the roles of women, identify the responsibility of the state, society, and family to women, eliminate discrimination against women, tackle the human trafficking of women and children, and address domestic violence. (Lao PDR, 2004, p.1). Likewise, the target of women's protection is ongoing to shape the desired outcomes in the 8th five-year NSEDP. It states, "All ethnic groups and both genders [should] have access to quality education and health services" (Ministry of Planning and Investment, 2016a, p. 89). In outcome 2, the Lao government has set up the development policies and the legal framework to promote the roles of women, juveniles, and children.

The primary focus of women's development in Laos is to improve skill acquisition by encouraging access to education, increasing awareness to engage in socio-economic development, conserving national culture, and empowering the Lao Women's Union (LWU) as a delegate to protect women's and children's rights and interests at every level. Gender equality in politics, economics, socio-cultural affairs and the family, along with concern for reducing discrimination and violence against women and children have also been taken into consideration (Ministry of Planning and Investment, 2016a, p. 153).

The results of all of this include the promulgation of the law on the Lao Women's Union, the Law on Women's Development and Protection, the Law on Non-Violence Against Women and Children, the Vision 2030 on Women's Development, the 10-year Women's Development Strategy (2017–2025), the First-year Lao PDR Women Development Plan (2016–2020), the National Plan of Action on Protection and Elimination of Violence Against Women and Children of Lao PDR (2014–2020), the Vision 2030 and 10-year National Strategy on Gender Equality (2016–2025), and the 3rd Five-Year National Plan of Action on Gender Equality. In 2017, the Lao government and the World Bank issued the Country Gender Action Plan for the Lao PDR 2017 along with the 8th Five Year NSEDP. The action plan aims to "contribute to inclusive development and poverty reduction by reducing gaps between men, women, and ethnic groups and promoting human development and economic opportunities" (World Bank, 2017a, p. 1). In summary, social inclusion in Lao development, in the eyes of the Lao government, means narrowing the inequality gap and distributing public services to people across the country.

The development partner representatives I interviewed have a different interpretation of social inclusion that is associated with good governance. To them, social inclusion means to include the role of civil society in the country's development. In 2009, the Lao government promulgated the decree in order to legalize Non-Profit Associations (NPA) in Laos and provide room for these organizations to work with the Lao government and the development partners. The Lao government welcomes NPAs that work in accordance with the government's policy because the Lao government concedes that they employ developmental mechanisms in remote areas effectively. Though the decree can increase the number of registered NPAs in Laos, the Lao government revised the decree in 2017 to control the scope of their work in economic, human, social, environmental, and political areas (see chapter 3).

Environmental Sustainability: Green-growth development

"The temperature in northern Laos now hits below zero in the winter, which never happened in the past" (Informant No. 2, 2017). Climate change in Laos signifies environmental degradation. The country has been facing the consequences of climate change and natural disasters, such as floods and storms, for decades. The report of the UNDP notes that Laos had 21 severe floods and storms that affected 500,000 people from 1990 to 2015 (UNDP, 2018g; 2018f). Thus, development partners promote environmental sustainability and climate change resilience in Laos in order to alleviate its effects on the Lao people, prepare them to handle unexpected outcomes of natural disasters, and improve their ability to maintain the qualities that are valued in their physical environment.

In 2007, the Water Resources and Environmental Administration was established to supervise the country to work toward more sustainable development. In 2008, the National Steering Committee on Climate Change, Disaster Management Offices at provincial and district levels, the Climate Change Office under the Department of Environment, and the Environment and Social Impact Assessment Department of WREA were established. In the following years, the Lao government issued the Strategy on Climate Change of the Lao PDR, which is a strategic plan that aims to enhance the quality of Laos's natural environment whilst advancing the quality of life of the Lao people. This strategy consists of seven priority areas: 1) Agriculture and Food Security; 2) Forestry and Land Use Change; 3) Water Resources; 4) Energy and Transport; 5) Industry; 6) Urban Development; and 7) Public Health. Furthermore, the Lao government stated that it aims to prevent slash and burn agriculture, increasing forest cover to 65 percent by 2015, and 70 percent by 2020 (Food and Agriculture Organization of the United Nations [FAO], 2016). In 2017, however, the forest cover was at 58 percent, or 13.73 million Hectares (UNDP, 2018f).

For the SDGs, there are four development goals concerned with environmental sustainability, which are: affordable and clean energy; climate action; life below water; and life on land in Lao development. The Lao government has continually supported environmental sustainability based on these goals.

The 8th NSEDP archives in outcome 3 of the 8th Five Year NSEDP that,

> Natural resources and the environment are effectively protected and utilized according to green-growth and sustainable principles; there is a readiness to cope with natural disasters and the effects of climate change and for reconstruction following natural disasters (Ministry of Planning and Investment, 2016a, p. 89).

Outcome 3 further reflects the commitment of the Lao government to support environmental sustainability and "ensured continued quality, green and sustainable economic growth, development and natural resource management... planned in a practical, sustainable, fair and most effective manner" (Ministry of Planning and Investment, 2016a, p. 138). The Lao government has thus been proactive at tackling climate change by promoting climate action and reducing greenhouse gas emissions, signing the Paris Agreement[58] on 22 April 2016 (The US Embassy in Laos, 2016). The Lao government has also linked environmental sustainability with Green-Growth development to utilize natural resources and achieve green, clean, and sustainable development in urban and rural areas. As Kikeo Chanthabouly, the Vice Minister of Planning and Investment for Lao PDR justified,

> "Green growth is cleaner, more resource-efficient, and more resilient to risks like climate change... This development policy operation is closely linked with the strategic priorities of the Government of Lao PDR's 8th National Socio Economic Development Plan and can help to sustain strong economic growth while also protecting the environment and human health" (World Bank, 2017e).

In practice, the informant from the government sector explained that the Lao government complies with the Environmental Impact Assessment (EIA)[59] in the development project at the national level. Regarding the EIA for building the hydropower dams in Laos, the informant remarks that the government made a deal with the project developers to protect the environment and in the process compensated the land of local peoples, relocating them off of the land. The local administration has played a role in assessing the compensa-

58 The Paris Agreement, issued in 2015, is the outcome of the Convention on Climate Change which met on 12 December 2015. This convention brought all nations together to discuss how to combat climate change and take action for a sustainable low carbon future. Its purpose is to strengthen the global response to the climate change, and the ability of countries to cope with the impacts of climate change (see United Nations, 2015).

59 The EIA directive refers to the European Union (2017, p. 10), the assessment process for public and private projects that may have had notable effects on the environment prior to when consent from the authorities was established.

tion to the local people and enforcing developers to compensate them reasonably (Informant No. 23, 2017). Although the EIA is supposed to protect local peoples from unfair treatment, INGOs and Lao scholars have pointed out that the compensation from developers is often unfair in the way it marginalizes people, forcing them to become landless laborers (Informant No. 12, 19 and 20, 2017). This controversy will be more emphasized in the next chapter.

With regard to preparation for natural disasters and risk mitigation, the Lao government has committed itself to minimize greenhouse gas emissions and improving and increasing the country's ability to adapt to and prepare for climate change by integrating climate change and risk mitigation into strategic and operational plans of the SWGs. The Lao government also supports sustainable development by promoting stable jobs for farmers and ensuring stable supplies, markets, and prices for agriculture products. The Lao government set the policy and strategy on disaster and natural disaster emergency at the provincial and the district levels, as well as the policy promoting pilot projects on climate change in the agriculture and forestry sectors, with local community participation (Minister of Planning and Investment, 2016a, pp. 138–142). This effort was introduced in the Disaster Management and Climate Change Law, which was expected to be passed in 2017 but this process is ongoing in 2019.

Good Governance: rule of law, people's participation, and tackling corruption in nominal democratic institutions

After the SDGs have been adopted in many countries, good governance is viewed as the key to determining the success or failure of implementation. The development partners believe that each country will implement the SDGs successfully if their government practices support good governance. In general, good governance consists of accountability, transparency, participation, and responsibility. In this sense, SDG 16 (the goal related to Peace, Justice and Strong Institutions) is the only goal that promotes good governance. Its focus is on peaceful and inclusive societies, sustainable development, providing access to justice for all, and building effective, accountable, and inclusive institutions at all levels.

In Laos, the desired outcomes of SDG 16 are: 1) systems and services that protect children from violence and discrimination established and maintained; and 2) good governance that ensures the balanced and sustainable development of Lao society and administration, with a focus on (a) clean government, (b) effective accountable and transparent institutions, and (c) responsive, inclusive, participatory and representative decision-making at all levels (The United Nations, 2015b, p. 16). These outcomes have enhanced the role of the development partners to continually include supporting good governance in Lao development.

Evidence from the development policy of the development partners shows that the development partners have promoted good governance since the first Constitution in 1991. As a newly independent country, Laos encountered difficulties in governance and administration systems that worsened fiscal and administrative management in the 1980s. The Party had to improve in management using the rule of law. The first Constitution in 1991 was the result of such an effort. The Party employed the separation of powers system between the legislative, executive, and judiciary branches. The National Assembly was officially established as the legislative branch. In the following years, the UNDP and the Lao government started the first Public Administration Reform (PAR) as a resolution to their discussion on public administration reform, which was ultimately an attempt to modernize the legal and administrative systems, and increase the effectiveness, transparency, and accountability, while decreasing the cost of public delivery of the Lao government (Larrabure et al., 2014, p. 7; SIDA, 2003, p. 36). The Department of Administration and Civil Society (DACS) under the Prime Minister Office (PMO) was also established in 1992 to contribute to political reform under the PAR. It should be noted that the DACS was the first important step toward political reform in Lao politics under the good governance principle.

Following this, the PAR gradually developed a new political reform framework, since the Party required more reform in the Sixth Party Congress in 1996. The Governance and Public Administration Reform (GPAR) from 1997–2012 and National Governance and Public Administration Reform (NGPAR) in 2012 reshaped domestic institutions to implement good governance in the country's development plan. The core ideas in administrative reform under the GPAR and the NGAR programs cycle around strengthening public administration, people's participation, rule of law and financial management at national, provincial, and district levels, so as to support policy formulation and implementation, institutional and legal frameworks, organization and development, civil service management, training and capacity development.

The GPAR and NGPAR ultimately led to the establishment of the Ministry of Home Affairs (MoHA) in 2011. Prior to the MoHA, government organizations were under the control of the Prime Minister's Office (PMO), including the Department of Public Administration (DPA), the Department of

Public Administration and Civil Society (DPACS), and the Public Administration and Civil Service Authority (PACSA), all organizations that were developed from the DACS mentioned earlier. The mission of MoHA is "to strengthen the capacity of the public administration to deliver efficient, effective and accountable services to citizens through high-level oversight and leadership, strategic management and support to the government of Lao PDR" (Ministry of Home Affairs, 2018). Good governance matters for the Lao government in order to modernize the administrative, fiscal, and public delivery systems to be more effective, accountable, transparent, cost-efficient and, most importantly, to maintain the Party-led development. If the Lao government fails to implement good governance in the country, the developmental policy will become stagnant.

According to the interview and development policy information collected, the Governance Sector Working Group (GSWG) founded in 2008 has worked on increasing good governance in the country. Before this the SDGs, the GSWG focused on the MDGs and the 7th Five Year NSEDP, which consisted of public service improvement, people's participation, rule of law, and public financial management (MoHA, 2018). As a result of the Round Table Implementation Meeting in 2016, the additional focal points of the GWSG include the National Assembly and Provincial People's Assemblies. I will divide these points into four primary issues related to the international development norms, which include: fighting corruption, increasing people's participation and rule of law, decentralization, and human right.

First, corruption in the country is still unalterable at both at central and local levels. This ranking threatens to deteriorate the government's credibility. Accordingly, the Lao government has to commit itself to fight corruption by addressing the issue in its development policy and through its domestic institutions. This has been attempted through the State Audit Organization (SAO), which was established in 1998. This organization plays the role of government auditor to the President of the State, the National Assembly, and the Prime Minister, and enhances public financial management in the country. Aside from this, the National Assembly promulgated the Anti-Corruption law in 2012 to strictly enforce the law via national and local authorities.

Despite these attempts to address corruption, the corruption rate has worsened. Laos fell from 123rd to 135th in 2017, according to the Annual Corruption Index. Moreover, so-called "ghost projects" were written into the budget, but never built (hence the name), and were exposed by the State Audit Organization (SAO) (ASEAN Today, 2018). In 2017, the SAO claimed that over one trillion kips ($123 million) worth of unauthorized spending was uncovered. This money was spent without the approval of the National Assembly (The Laotian Times, 2017).

To enhance the government's credibility, the former Prime Minister and the current President of the State, Thoungloun Sisoulith, has been pro-active about the anti-corruption campaign and has aimed to foster a 'clean government.' According to Hutt (2017a), the State Inspection Authority (SIA), a government watchdog agency, recently investigated 71 officials and made 25 corruption-related arrests. Nevertheless, corruption remains a major obstacle to Lao development. Moreover, he concluded that there are three events that justified the Prime Minister's action in tackling the corruption issues. The first came with the arrest of Phouphet Khamphounvong, the former finance minister, and four ministry officials. They are suspected of involvement with the ghost project investigated by the SIA. The second was the arrest of major drug traffickers like Khonepasong Soukkaseum who have connections with Xaysana Keopimpha, also known as the ASEAN drug lord. Third, the Lao government now bans timber export and considers mining contracts in more detail in order to promote environmental sustainability.

However, his impetus is inadequate to fully alleviate Laos of its corruption issues and clean up the government, as he apparently wishes. Compared to other ASEAN countries, Laos is the second most corrupt country, as can be seen from TABLE 4.4 below. This rating, along with the human rights issues in Laos, threatens his credibility and legitimacy

TABLE 4.4 The corruption index of ASEAN countries in 2017 (Lower numbers reflect higher corruption).

Country	Score
Singapore	84
Brunei	62
Malaysia	47
Thailand	37
Indonesia	37
Vietnam	35
Philippines	34
Myanmar	30
Laos	29
Cambodia	21

source: Author's compilation based on Transparency International, 2018

Lastly, the political will of the Prime Minister is in synch with the Party's vision. Strong leadership in Laos overrides the line between liberal and conservative, and a strong leader in Laos has the capacity to move the state in either direction. Strong leadership is vital in convincing the Party to be progressive or conservative. As the corruption issue is a chronic problem in Laos, it could be concluded that big change takes a lot of time and effort, and political reform is no exception.

In view of people's participation and rule of law, the second issue, the Lao government increased participatory channels for the Lao people in the National Assembly and People's Provincial Assembly. For example, Lao people can now make a petition to the Lao government and the National Assembly through a hotline. The Lao government has also altered the development policy to support people's participation in monitoring and promoting development policies and orders of the Party and government. It also allows them to report their needs to governmental authorities. This policy is aimed at reducing the inequality gap in the country. The development partners, through workshops and training, have attempted to push the National Assembly to represent the Lao people and the legislative branch. On the other hand, many Lao scholars believe that the NA is a rubber stamp due to the fact that there is an ongoing power rotation between the Party and the NA (see chapter 3).

Among these contradictory points of view, I argue that the NA matters in Lao politics for promoting good governance and the rule of law in Laos, but that cannot help balance power as is expected by development partners. It is just a nominal democratic institution. The interviewee from the NA stated, "We have to follow up on the government's policies and make suggestions to the government about the sustainability of their proposals… The government listens to and understands our points. But it takes time for them to work on our suggestions. Now the government has the three-opens policy which consists of openness of mind, openness to the international community, and openness to correcting obstructions to socio-economic development" (Informant No. 16, 2017).

As for the third issue, the Lao government and the development partners have promoted decentralization as the needed mechanism to implement the development policies and strategies effectively. In 2001, the Lao government issued a law for local administrators to narrow their scope of duties and responsibilities. According to the budget distribution, however, local authorities could not fully implement the development plan, particularly in remote areas. As a consequence, resolution No. 03/PCP resulting of the Party Congress in 2011 introduced the Three-Build Directive (Samsang) with the slogan "Building province as a strategic unit, district as a strong comprehensive unit, and village as a development unit" (Ministry of Planning and Investment, 2016a, p. 67). The overall objective is to promote local ownership and to implement the development plan at the local level in order to achieve the poverty reduction goals. Between 2012–2013, the pilot project of the Three Build directive began with 15 ministries, 51 districts, and 108 villages. The selected 15 ministries have sent their officials to visit their local administrations to build stronger localities with administrative, judicial, district, and village level fund management, to build a stronger socio-economic development plan and to manage government invested-projects at the village level. This pilot project led to an extension of the Three-Build directive at local levels in the 8th NSDEP.

The last area of focus with regard to good governance is human rights. Human rights issues in Laos are always in the public eye due to the fact that local people suffer from the development projects, as in the cases of the hydropower dam, Special Economic Zones, and most importantly the disappearance of Sombat Somphone in 2012 (see chapter 3). These issues provoked the development partners and the INGOs to raise their concerns to the Lao government in public. They spoke particularly to restrictions on civil and political rights, the lack of freedom of speech and fair trials for criminal suspects, and on human rights violations raised by Human Right Watch (2017). To prove its credibility with regard to human rights issues, in 2015, the Lao government conceded to 116 of 196 recommendations made by the Working Group on the Universal Periodic Review. The current Prime Minister accepted the right, on the environmental issues, to provide reasonable and effective compensation for land expropriations and to protect land rights. However, with regard to human rights issues related to political freedom, the Prime Minister has remained silent.

The SDGs as a source of regime legitimacy: How do the SDGs work in Laos?

Sustainable development has been a priority in Laos since the 9th Congress in 2011 and was implemented on a massive scale following the Tenth Party Congress in 2016. The Lao government set up the four pillars of the SDGs, noted earlier, to serve socio-economic and, of course, political purposes. In this section I will analyze how the SDGs have become another source of regime legitimacy for the Party in Lao development. The post-socialist approach will be used to examine the role of domestic institutions and development policy in the age of the SDGs.

The three main areas the SDGs cover include economic development, environmental sustainability, and social inclusion. There is one cross-cutting area however, good governance. In Laos, the three main areas (including good governance) present in the 8th NSEDP (2016-2020) are intended to reduce the poverty rate with sustained inclusive economic growth and to mitigate environmental degradation by supporting green growth development. It can be seen that the Party welcomes the civil society to act as an integral part of development implementation, except with regard to good governance. DIAGRAM 4.1 illustrates the model of the SDGs in Lao-style development.

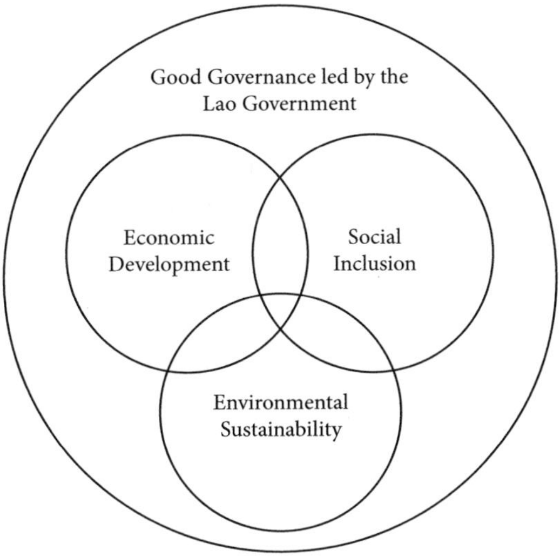

DIAGRAM 4.1 The model of the SDGs in Lao-style development

The Lao government and the Party have thus monopolized this leading role to legitimize the ability of governmental organizations to control society and justify this via the promotion of good governance. For example, the Lao government and the Party have given more power to the National Assembly, the Provincial People's Assembly, and the Three Builds directive to ensure the four principles of good governance (i.e. accountability, transparency, rule of law, and people's participation) are applied. Data analyzed in chapter 3 shows that the NA, PPA, and Three Builds directives, in turn, are nominal democratic institutions that conceal the Party's power. Good governance in Laos rather reflects the Party's power in political development which unlikely falls in line with the expectations of the development partners.

As I pointed out, the Party, as the supreme organ in Lao development, added the security pillar to the SDGs to maintain the Party-led development of the country. As already noted, the security pillar emphasizes sustainability in the political arena, which means stabilization of social order in the country by the one-Party state. There is no doubt that the Party plays the leading role in bringing political stability to the country by controlling the Lao people, civil society, and the press. Domestic institutions conceal the Party's power, particularly with regard to the power of intra-Party clans. This power rotation can ruin the Party's creditability in the eyes of the development partners and the Lao people. Developmental goals and challenges are thus used optimally as a means to distract their attention from the reality of this undemocratic.

Though the SDGs are not being addressed flawlessly in Laos, the domestic institutions and the development policy have at least been altered to achieve the SDGs and to bring the country out of the LDC status. This effort reveals two characteristics of the Lao domestic institutions: 1) governmental organizations take action with regard to inclusive economic growth, green growth development, social inclusion and good governance based on the development policy in the 8th five-year NSEDP; and 2) nominal democratic organizations, such as the National Assembly and the Provincial People's Assembly and the Three Build Directive, which aims to meet the good governance standards, maintain the so-called Party-led development in the country. The Party could thus gain external support and to help the country's development reach.

In the next chapter, the consequences of the international development norms in Laos, and the Lao state's capacity to achieve the development goals will be analyzed. As I will argue, the development partners and the Lao government have different expectations and desired outcomes in Lao development, and put in the effort to make their expectations come true. However, when the reality of Laos state capacity is reinvestigated, the expectations of the development partners may be found to be out of reach.

Concluding remarks

The main objective of this chapter was to describe the concept behind the SDGs and analyze how the SDGs shaped Lao domestic institutions and the development goals. The data analyzed shows that the 17 goals of the SDGs place emphasis on economic development, environmental sustainability, social inclusion and good governance. To achieve the SDGs, the international community believes that the development assistance is crucial for third-world countries to reach the development goals. This has led to fruitful debate among many scholars who agree and disagree with such beliefs. In Laos, the SDGs were first introduced in the RTP in 2015.

The data analyzed show that two events have shaped Lao's developmental direction. As a result, the 17 goals of the Sustainable Development Goals, and one additional goal, have been introduced in Lao development which consists of three main areas (economic development, environmental sustainability and social inclusion) and one cross-cutting theme (the good governance) enshrined in the 18 goals of the SDGs in Laos. Even the development partners have played a role in Lao development over the decade, it could be argued that they cannot constrain the Lao state power. This argument is from the fact that the final decision-making in Lao development is in the Party Congress, another important event of Lao development. The Party, which is the supreme organ in Lao development, sets the development direction and the targets of the country in the five-year national development plan, the development strategy, and the 15 year-vision. At the Tenth Party Congress in 2016, the Party set up the four pillars of the SDGs as the framework for Lao development, which comprises economic development, environmental sustainability, social inclusion, and security. The concrete outcomes have been the creation of the 8th NSEDP and the additional norm for the existing domestic institutions. For example, governmental organizations now support green-growth development in their development strategy. However, my conclusion of this chapter shows that although the Party and the Lao government promote the SDGs in the domestic institutions and the development policy, the Party has concealed its power within to maintain the status quo of the one-Party state. It can be concluded that SDGs are another source of regime legitimacy.

5

WHEN EXPECTATIONS MEET REALITY: LAO STATE CAPACITY TO GRADUATE FROM THE LDC STATUS

Graduation from the Least Developed Country status means a lot for the government. The government commits itself because the government wants to change and do something for its own sake.

—Informant No. 15, 2017

The year 2018 was tragic for Laos. The collapse of the Xe-Pian Xe-Namnoy dam, a kind of tragedy unheard of in the country, overwhelmed the Lao people without warning; over a hundred people died, and more than five thousand people in its wake had no place to go. They lost land, home, and family all at once. This tragedy reveals another side of development. Though the Lao government and the dam developer attempted to compensate victims with temporary accommodations and food, nothing can replace what they had. Recently, news reports reveal that local people, still in temporary camps, suffer to have their basic needs met. Likewise, hundreds of families still live in tents and have only their small monthly subsidy of 100,000 Kip per victim. One of the victims complained that "We do not know how to survive. We do not have jobs or anywhere to go. The allowance from the government is too small to survive on and we only get rice with nothing to eat with it" (Vieng as cited in the Strait Times, 2019). The Lao government does not seem to be able to live up to its promise to compensate the victims. This issue gets at the question of Lao state's capacity to deal with worrying issues resulting from development and to graduate from the least developed country status.

In this chapter, I analyze the Lao state's capacity to accomplish the development goals (i.e. the SDGs), and graduate from the LDC status as these goals are the supreme development aspirations of the Lao government. As mentioned in chapter 2, the country's modernity has followed the path of the Western one, but the reality of the least developed country status has not left many choices for the Party to pursue such modernity. The development assistance from the development partners remains essential for the country. Moreover, this chapter argues that the path to reach the country's modernity and communist utopia remain the unfinished missions for the Party. This could serve the Party's legitimacy to maintain the status quo as the leading nucleus to tackle obstacles of the development goals. The analysis of the Lao state capacity could provide insight into what the Lao government has done to improve its capacity to achieve the goal and the challenges based on the international development standards, how the capacity improvement works in a socialist country context, and how the Party and the Lao government have justified the challenges as the unfinished missions in public to maintain their role to emancipate Lao people from poverty and bring equality to the country.

In the first part of the chapter, I shed light on the state capacity in Laos and demonstrate that the Lao government has put its effort into strengthening the effectiveness of its domestic institutions to reach the development thresholds set by the development partners. The state capacity of the country is currently insufficient to do so. However, I argue Laos is only effectively succeeding at addressing the potential security issues of the nation. In Laos, certain domestic institutions are subsidiary apparatuses of the Party. They can contribute to political stability and social order in the country. As a result, the Lao state capacity is rather practical and consists of maintaining the power of the one-Party state and regime legitimacy through the Party-led development rather than truly striving to achieve the development goals.

The effort of the Lao government and the development partners to improve state capacity is the subject of the second part of the chapter. Whether Laos can meet the expectations of the development partners is questionable. In this section, a reflection of the realities of the Lao model for development will be presented. Despite falling behind development partners' expectations, this section aims to prove that Lao development is unique in its own way, and that there is something beyond what can be seen through western perspective. This could provide a better understanding of how the Party deals with the worrying issues raised by the development partners, many scholars, observers, and civil society. I extracted two debatable development issues in the Lao pertinent literature which are: 1) hydropower dams development; 2) the global pandemic and the graduation from the LDC status. For the last part of the chapter, I emphasize current issues in Laos and the likely consequences if Laos graduates from the LDC status. Specifically, I will reflect on the subsequent cost and benefits, from various perspectives, likely to be experienced by the Lao government and consider its readiness to address these consequences.

How to investigate Lao state capacity

To investigate the state's capacity, it should be noted that the debate on the measurement of state capacity is ongoing (see Mann, 1984; Skocpol, 1985; Fukuyama, 2013; Vu, 2010; Holt and Manning, 2014). This part begins with Fukuyama's framework (2013), which considers state capacity as sufficiently good governance to carry out its vision and the quality of the government as an organization to perform its various functions for better or worse. State capacity, in his framework, consists of resource extraction, degree of professionalization of bureaucratic staff, and bureaucratic autonomy. He believes that "the quality of governance is ultimately a function of [an] interaction [between] capacity and autonomy and that either one independently is inadequate as a measure of government quality" (Fukuyama, 2013, p. 360).

Analysts from the development partners broadly accept Fukuyama's framework on state capacity. For example, Holt and Manning (2014) from the World Bank employ the framework to clarify how to measure the quality of government. They pay particular attention to the organization of the governmental body, processes related to policy implementation, and specific statistical outcomes of these policies as variables for measuring state capacity. They further divide their analysis into upstream and downstream bodies.[60] Upstream refers to central agencies, and downstream the local ones. A breakdown of their analytical model can be seen in TABLE 5.1, which shows that the main task of the central agency is public management.

I employ this framework to analyze Lao state capacity because the development assistance from the development partners can support the Party to reach its modernity (see chapter 2). Moreover, the Party commits itself to meeting the development standards and goals set by the development partners. To analyze the Lao state capacity to do so, the framework used by the development partners are needed. I develop this framework, by reducing it to

[60] The upstream bodies, or the central agencies, are comprises of "core ministries and agencies at the center of government… that support the head of government, with functions that cut cross sectors." The downstream delivery bodies are comprised of "sector ministries and agencies that deliver, commission, or fund services under the policy direction of government" (Holt and Manning, 2014, p. 719).

three categories. The first category is financial capacity, which is the ability of the government to manage state finances through public finance management systems and tax extraction. Human capital capacity, which refers to human development to carry out the development goals effectively, is the second category. I contend that assessments of the degree of professionalization of bureaucratic staff should factor into human resource development and the patronage system. The last category is institutional capacity. As this institutional capacity reflects bureaucratic autonomy, the ability of the domestic institutions to implement the development plans and policies to achieve the development goals and political stability throughout the country. To provide useful insight into Lao state capacity, it will be analyzed with the interview information, along with supplemental statistics related to the Lao government's performance.

TABLE 5.1 The public management system of the central agencies

Public Management Systems	
Fiscal And Financial Management System	▹ Planning and budgeting ▹ Financial management ▹ Accounting, fiscal reporting, and auditing
Procurement System	▹ Quality management in legislation and regulation ▹ Capacity development ▹ Operations and market practices
Revenue Mobilization System	▹ Tax policy ▹ Tax administration
Public Administration and Civil Service System	▹ Management of operations within the core administration ▹ Quality management in policy and regulatory management ▹ Coordination of public sector HRM regime outside the administration
"Public information system"	▹ Citizen access to information ▹ Record management ▹ Framework for monitoring and evaluating for sector ministries

source: Holt and Manning, 2014, p. 720

Financial management capacity: Centralized fiscal management and an unbalanced distribution

Financial is crucial for the state to actionably implement the development plan, provide services to its people, decrease its debt, and improve the country's standard of living. The state needs to accumulate capital by taxing industrial uses of natural resources and by more effectively managing its finances. In this sense, public financial management is one of the most important duties of the government.

The PEFA report[61] has identified seven pillars for effective public financial management that have become noteworthy indicators for measuring this aspect of governance. These pillars include: budget reliability, transparency of public finances, management of assets and liabilities, policy-based fiscal strategies and budgeting, predictability and control in execution, accounting and reporting, and external scrutiny and auditing. It is arguable whether or not effective public finance management alone is sufficient for an in-depth analysis of financial capacity. Indeed, it should be considered along with institutional arrangements.

Due to the fact that Laos is poor, its economic performance, in general, is vulnerable and heavily relies on Official Development Assistance (ODA) from the development partners. Their performance is typical of countries classified as Least Developed. According to statistical information reported by the World Bank, Laos' GDP was slightly reduced from 7.0 percent to 6.9 percent in 2016. The power sector, due to manufacturing in Special Economic Zones (SEZs), has increased the country's GDP, whereas the tourist and mining sectors[62] have contributed to the decline. Apart from the GDP as an economic indicator, examining the government's revenue, expenditures,[63] deficits,

[61] PEFA is a measurement standard used to assess public finance management in many counties. It was set in 2001 by the European Commission, the International Monetary Fund, the World Bank, and the governments of France, Norway, the United Kingdom, and Switzerland. It aims to improve national fiscal policies by harmonizing country-level assessments of public financial management (PFM) between the governments and their development partners, providing standard methodologies and reference tools for assessing the PFM, and developing a common, shared analytical tool. It has become the standard for the PFM as it has been used more than 500 times in 150 countries in 2005 (PEFA, 2016).

[62] In Xinhua (2018), the National Economic Research Institute (NERI) reported that the mining sector has declined due to lowered productivity. The Sepon mine will be closed in 2020, which will further affect mining productivity.

[63] The Law on State Budget states that government revenue comes from taxes and state wages, development assistance grants, and other revenue (see more Article 15–19 in Kot May Va Douay Ngop Paman Heng Lat, Sapha Heng Xat, 2015b), whereas government expenditure is roughly divided into two categories: normal expenditure and state investment expenditure (see more Article 20–23 in Kot May Va Douay Ngop Paman Heng Lat, Sapha Heng Xat 2015b).

and public debts allows for a much deeper analysis. GRAPH 5.1 below exhibits the economic performance of Laos over the past five fiscal years.

source: Ministry of Finance in the World Bank, 2017c

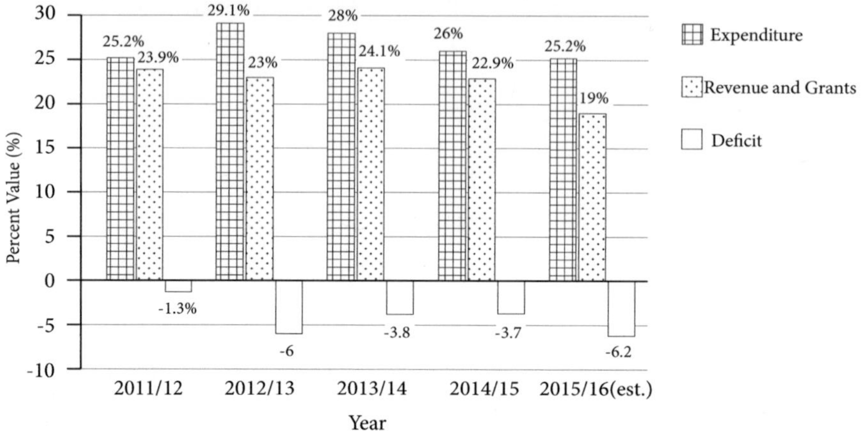

GRAPH 5.1 The Lao government's revenue and grant, and expenditure per GDP in Lao fiscal years (2012–2016)

The figure shows an imbalance with respect to the government's expenditures and revenue and the estimated −6.2 percent GDP deficit in the 2015/16 fiscal year. On average, the GDP deficit in Laos was −6.13 percent between 2000 and 2017 (Trading Economy, 2017). In the 2015/16 fiscal year, government expenditures amounted to 30,535,119.40 million Kips, which was mostly spent on the current expenditure[64] at 18,173,866.42 million Kips. Capital expenditures[65] however amounted to 9,631,921.98 million Kips. Capital expenditure is thus still less than the current expenditure. In terms of development, if capital expenditure is high, it implies that the government will turn the development into a substantial development project.

Public debt in Laos is also worrying. Over this past decade, public debt in Laos increased to 68 percent, as of 2016, according to the World Bank's report. Indeed, over 80 percent of that public debt is from external debt. High external debt reflects the limitations of the country to generate government revenue. GRAPH 5.2 illustrates this rising external debt in Laos, indicating that more external financial sources (e.g. development partners and aid-donor

64 Current expenditures include wages and salaries, benefits and allowances, materials and supplies, subsidies and transfers, financial expenditures, miscellaneous and contingencies expenditures, and debt payment.

65 Capital expenditure includes foreign and local investments.

countries) are necessary for revenue generation. It also reflects the influence of donors in Lao development. This debt situation has prompted the Lao government to become more proactive in economic development in order to reduce external debt and pay interest to the organizations and countries represented in figure 14, and thus avoid an economic downturn.

source: World Bank, 2017c

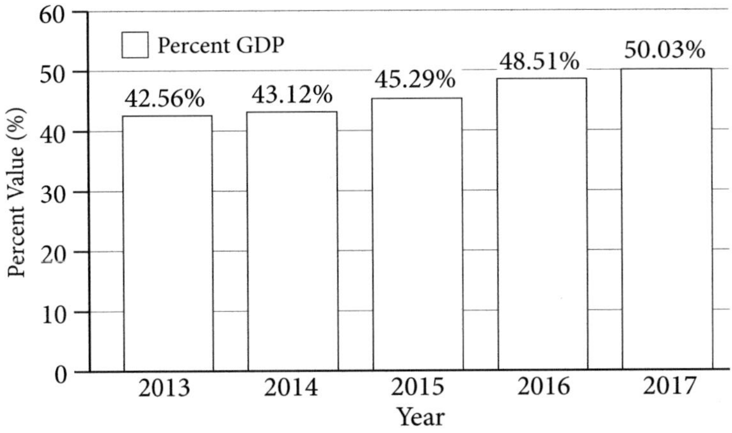

GRAPH 5.2 Lao External Debt (Percent of GDP)

The representative of the development partners expressed his concern in this situation that the income of the Lao government has been reducing which is hard to balance. The government has had to borrow more money from some development partners (such as, the financial institutions) to reduce its external debt. Once the country has more money, it is feasible to make a plan to implement the SDGs in the country's development (Informant No. 2, 2017). It could be seen that the development partners have provided the financial assistance to improve the Lao economy, particularly at the local level to generate more income. Whereas, the development partners could gain profit from their assistance to Laos, at least the interest from the loan. It is arguable that the financial assistance seems like the debt trap for the Lao government to repetitively rely on the development partners in order to meet the international development standards and pay off the country's debt.

From GRAPH 5.3, the greatest portion of public debt in Laos is owed to China, largely as the result of the high-speed railway launched through the Belt and Road Initiative.[66] The high-speed rail linking Southern China to the Vientiane

[66] The Belt and Road Initiative (BRI) was initiated by President Xi Jinping as "the 21st century silk road" to connect China with some 65 countries (some sources estimate 71 countries). Its objective is to improve connectivity and regional cooperation on a trans-continental scale with through infrastructure, trade, and investment (see more World Bank, 2018a; Kuo & Kommenda, 2018).

capital cost the country $5.8 billion, almost half of Lao's GDP. Thongloun Sisoulith, the former Lao Prime Minister, commented to the Nikkei reporter:

> I am not concerned much about the burden of debt or the construction of the high-speed railway… I can see that provisions in the construction agreement are favorable… we hope that the construction of the railway will encourage and promote investment and cooperation and bring benefits to the country (Tani, 2018).

Though his reaction reflects opportunities taken to diversify the economy, other observers have criticized the rising public debt as a reflection of mismanagement of funds by the Lao government. As Hutt (2018b), the reporter from the Diplomat, argues "What the Lao government is betting on… is that by indebting itself today future revenue will grow quicker than future outgoings, in term of debt repayment… The problem for Laos, however, is that the odds of success are slim."

source: World Bank, 2017c

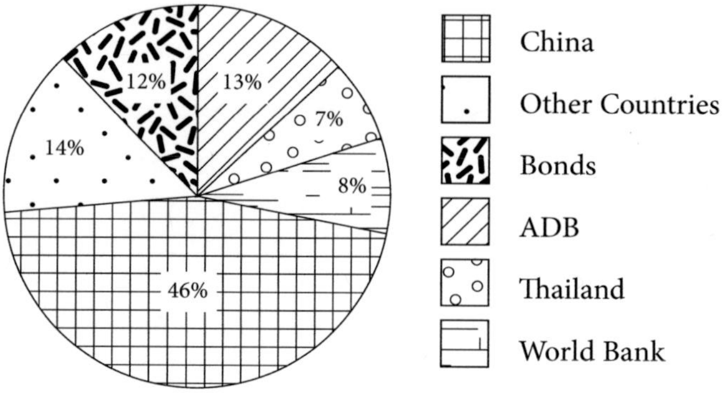

GRAPH 5.3 Lao external debt at the end of 2015 (percent share)

As long as the Lao government fails to reduce public debt, while being committed to reaching 55 percent of the GDP by 2022, Laos' economic performance will be highly dependent on outside sources for income. This shows that support from the development partners will be necessary for Lao economic development. The Public Finance Management Reform promoted by the development partners therefore has become an optimal means for improving macroeconomic stability and public debt sustainability.

As a socialist country, in reality, finance management in Laos is usually dominated by central agencies—the National Assembly, the Ministry of Finance, the Ministry of Planning and Investment and the Lao government, according to the Law on State Budget revised in 2015. These government organizations play the leading roles in approving and planning fiscal policy, distributing the state budget to the central and local organization, and collecting government revenue based on the Law on the State Budget and the five-year national development plan. Under the SDGs framework, the Lao government has set its macroeconomic financial stabilization targets to achieve GDP growth of no less than 7.5 percent per annum, with total revenue at 19–20 percent of the GDP and budget revenue at 16–17 percent of the GDP, and maintaining a total budget expenditure within 25 percent of the GDP, with expenditures on wages no more than 45 percent of budget revenue and a budget deficit no more than 5 percent of the GDP per annum (Ministry of Planning and Investment, 2016a, 104). Moreover, the state budget should be correlated with the development plan as it notes the 8th five-year NSEDP (2016–2020) that:

> Development and funding should be consistent and synchronized and interlinked from the outset, i.e., funding should be in line with the country's overall development policies. For instance, it should focus on achieving growth standards, allowing the country to graduate from LDC status; development investment should be based on the budget funding capacity for each period in collaboration with the raising of foreign loans and grant aid as well as efforts to attract funds from domestic and foreign private sectors, procurement of bank credits and the general population contribution for production and service business investment (Ministry of Planning and Investment, 2016a, p. 105).

The Lao government also issued the Vision 2030 in 2018 and the development strategy on the financial management with the slogan "The [Vision 3030 is the] road towards a strong, transparent, modern and fair Public Finance Management System". The development targets and strategies reflect the efforts of the Lao government to strengthen public finance management and mitigate challenges.[67] According to the PEFA report in 2010,[68] however, Laos

[67] Regarding the Vision 2030 (2018, p. 8) on financial management, the Lao government acknowledges the problems of the public finance management in general. For instance, fiscal planning is not informative in term of risk management and the lack of adequate law enforcement. Moreover, the Lao government lacks the capacity to tighten the monitoring process of the governmental budget, and the scope of financial management at central and local levels is not in step with situations being faced (see more Ministry of Finance, 2018).

[68] In the report, the PEFA employed an indicator used for the year of 2010, which is unlike that used in the 2016 framework. Its assessment comprises the credibility of the budget, comprehensiveness and transparency, policy-based budgeting, accounting, recording and reporting, external scrutiny and auditing, and donor practices (see World Bank, 2010). The PEFA report of Lao public finance management based on the 2016 framework is inaccessible.

faced difficulties in public finance management; in particular Laos struggled to implement transparency in policy, adequate accounting and reporting, and external auditing. The report notes:

> The development of public services in Lao PDR continues to experience numerous constraints. They are the lack of resources, weak policy-based budgeting, mediocre procurement practices, lack of information to frontline service providers and the general public about resources provided for service delivery, and a general lack of information about or scrutiny of the results achieved… However, due to limited implementation capacities and capabilities… the government agencies often appear to find it difficult to take a detailed follow-up actions to ensure that new legislation or Prime Ministerial decrees are implemented in the intended timetable… As a result, progress on some reform aspects has been slower than hoped (World Bank, 2010, pp. x–xi).

These problems seem to remain in the Lao public financial management system, no matter how hard the Lao government tries to mitigate them. In 2010, the same report stressed that the Lao government sought to improve central control by ensuring that improvements in health, education, and transportation were made in each province. Furthermore, the Lao government justifies state budget expenditures in the fiscal year report and devotes more power to the NA and the PPA to approve government expenditures at both central and local levels. Such improvements are the fruit of the Public Finance Management Strengthening Program Project supported by the World Bank, ADB, and other development partners. They provided technical assistance and expertise to the Lao government to regain financial management and debt sustainability. As a consequence, public financial management seems to be more progressive than in previous years.

However, analysis of public finance management always overlooks the fact that decision power and external auditing go hand-in-hand with the Party's power over nominal democratic institutions. The Vision 2030, points out "Leadership of Party Committee at all levels should provide close guidance on the performance of the duties of public finance personnel and ensure strict fiscal discipline" (Ministry of Finance, 2018, p. 56). As mentioned earlier, the National Assembly has the legitimate right to approve the budget. The Law on the State Budget, revised in 2015, endorses the scope of the responsibility of the NA and PPA and, in Articles 27 and 28, states that the NA is responsible for approving the fiscal policy, the financial development strategy, and the fiscal development budget, revising the state budget, and distributing the development budget based on the government balance, and debt. The PPA, in contrast, is obliged to approve the development plan and strategy and the state development budget, and report proposals by the provincial governor at the local level. More importantly, both the NA and PPA have the legitimate right to approve state capital investments based on the level of their operation (Sapha Heng Xat, 2015b, p. 9). Since most NA and PPA members are also Party members, it begs the question on how the NA can approve development projects without considering the Party's interests.

The Party's power also embeds in the State Audit Organization (SAO) plays the main role in scrutinizing government expenditures and monitoring unknown expenditures. This process matters for accountability in public finance management. Article 34 of the Law on SAO states that "The president of the SAO is elected or removed through the National Assembly Congress following a proposal by the President of the State." Furthermore, the President of the SAO monopolizes crucial responsibilities within the organization, such as supervising, monitoring, approving, and removing SAO officials, implementing the organizational policy, revising the Decree on the SAO, and approving and removing officials in the SAO (see more the Article 35 in Kod May Wa Douay Kan Kouad Sop Heng Lat, Sapha Heng Xat, 2016. p. 13–14). One of the former presidents of the SAO is Vienthong Siphandone, the daughter of the former Lao president Khamtay Siphandone. Her position reflects the political power of the Siphandone's clan, a fact that is, unfortunately, unlikely to be met with criticism in Laos.

The financial management capacity in Laos relates to financial decentralization at the local level. Even though the Lao government took an important step to decentralize its decision power over local authorities, it has not loosened control held by the central government. Article 39 of the Law on the State Budget (Sapha Heng Xat, 2015b) enacts the state's budget responsibilities, and details the central government's role in managing and approving government revenue and expenditure throughout the country, and in supporting the provinces, cities, districts, and municipalities that have encountered deficit problems to become more self-reliant. In terms of budget distribution, it is obvious to see that the central government has received a greater development budget than local organizations. In the fiscal year 2015/16, the total state budget expenditure implementation was 30,545,119 million Kip, 78 percent of which was spent by the central government and 28 percent of which was spent by local administrations. More importantly, the development budget allocation itself is also based on the development plan set by the central government via the Ministry of Planning and Investment.[69]

Despite the fact that local administrations spend the development budget to mitigate development issues and improve service delivery, the national development plan has limited their autonomy to do so. Central-planning in Laos has led to uneven development and a widening of the development gap in each province according to GRAPH 5.4, which reveals budget distribution in each province in the fiscal year 2015/16.

source: Ka Xouang Kan Ngeun, 2018

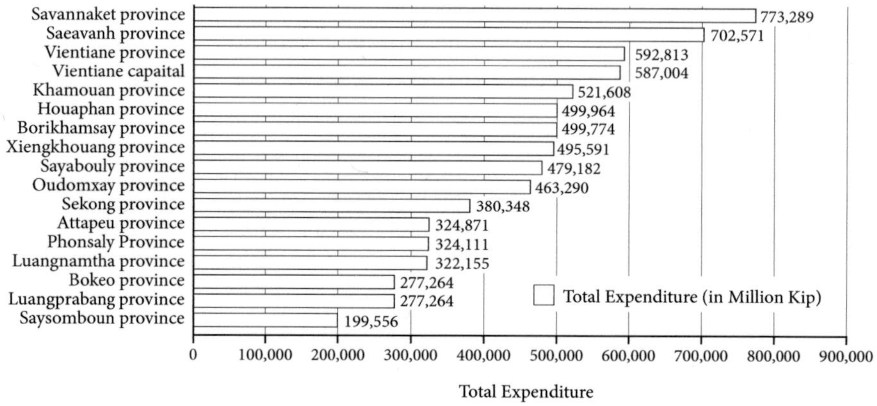

GRAPH 5.4 The government budget expenditure implementation of the local administration in the fiscal year 2015/16

Lastly, tax collection is another avenue for the government to generate more revenue in the development plan. Although, the statistics above show increasing tax revenue in Laos for 2011/12—2015/16 (see GRAPH 5.5), there is a problem unseen from this angle. According to a World Bank (2018b) report, income tax collection only contributes to 2.6% of Lao's GDP. This low figure reflects the ineffectiveness of the Lao government to tax small and informal businesses, and the consequences that have followed the increasingly loose tax exemption policy for certain sectors in the country. The composition of total revenue in Laos consists of tax revenue, non-tax revenue, and more importantly, grant funding. GRAPH 5.6 shows that the number of the grants

[69] Article 34 (1) of the Law on the State Budget stresses the scope of responsibility for the provinces and capital city that:
[In financial management and state budget, the provinces and capital city are responsible for] creating and implementing the development strategy, the development plan, and the fiscal plan every year and every five years in line with the national development plan, and the developmental and resource-related potentials, which reflect the state's actual capacity (Sapha Heng Xat, 2015b).

contributed and likely to be contributed by the development partners is on the increase, according to a prediction of the World Bank. This prediction illustrates the financial capacity of the Lao government in the next five years. The higher number of grants implies lower tax and non-tax revenue.

SOURCE: Fiscal Policy Department, Ministry of Finance, Lao PDR in KEOMIXAY, 2017, p. 10

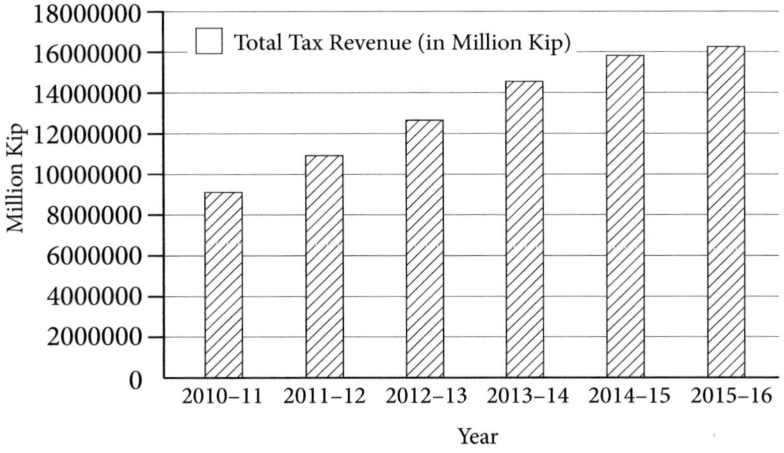

GRAPH 5.5 Total tax revenue from the fiscal year 2010/11–2015/16 (million Kip)

SOURCE: Lao Authorities, trading partners' data, staff calculations and projections, World Bank, 2018b, p. 38

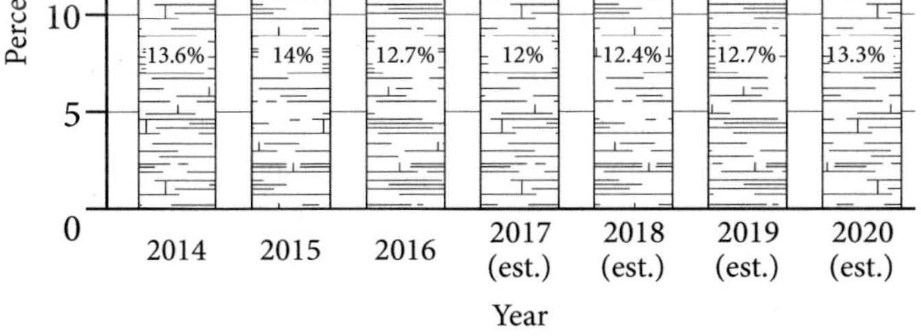

GRAPH 5.6 The government revenue indications and projections (Percent of GDP)

The indications and projections from the World Bank report clarify that the grants from development partners are needed as a source of government revenue. Keomixay (2017, pp. 22–26) analyzed the Value Added Tax (VAT) in Laos, noting that the registering system for small and medium-sized enterprises is inaccessible at local levels. Hence, tax collection in the country cannot reach small-scale enterprises, which lack the resources and accounting skills to keep formal business records. Moreover, IT systems are also important for checking and monitoring the business activities of small and medium enterprises. He proposes that local authorities should apply IT systems in tax collection. Two other constraints include: poor understanding of tax obligations by bureaucratic staff and the Lao people and considerable tax exemptions for the large agricultural and forest sectors.

For the problems above, the Lao government has sought to improve its capacity for tax extraction by applying IT systems via Smart Tax and Smart VAT (Laotian Times, 2017) and amending the Law on Tax in 2015. Harrison (2016) concluded that there have been few changes to profit taxes, income taxes, and excise taxes in the amended Law on Tax in 2015. The Lao government instead clarified more channels and lists of taxable products. In addition, tax collection by the local administrations is not autonomous enough to collect taxes and to spend the development budget without approval from the central government. In fact, the capacity to collect taxes is as important as the whole system of tax payment and auditing. An active system can enhance the ability of the government to collect taxes. In Laos, the foggy line between the Lao government and the Party blurs this system. The Ministry of Finance, especially the tax department is responsible for collecting direct and indirect taxes[70] from taxpayers, and the National Assembly, the State Audit Organization, the State Inspection Authority, and the Lao National Front Organization, which are subordinate to the Party, play a crucial role in auditing and inspecting tax payments. It thus remains an unanswered question how the government can possibly become autonomous in tax collection without the Party's sanction.

In conclusion, the financial capacity based on the international development standards to develop the country under the SDGs is currently inadequate since Laos is poor and its public debt remains high. Moreover, the socialist-style financial management in Laos is different from the develop-

[70] The Law on Tax amended in 2015 identifies direct taxes including the profit tax, the income tax, the lump-sum tax, the environment tax and fee and administrative charges, while indirect taxes consists of the value-added tax and the excise tax (see more Article 14–18 in Lao on Tax, Sapha Heng Xat, 2015).

ment partners' support. It can be seen that the main actor in public finance management in Laos is the Party. Even though the Lao government ostensibly amended the Law on the State Budget to bring transparency and accountability to public finance management, the Party's power on the inside has largely stifled the effort.

Human capital capacity: Degree of professionalization and the patronage system

Another aspect of state capacity to achieve the development goals includes, according to Fukuyama, the degree of professionalization of the bureaucratic staff that can deliver and implement the development policy and public services across the country. In this sense, human capital capacity through education is crucial to increase the competency of bureaucratic staff in the Lao government. Since development itself is progressive, it requires sophisticated knowledge and a robust skillset on the part of the bureaucratic staff to carry out the development plan effectively. This topic will focus on the human capital capacity of Lao officials.

Civil servants in Laos respond directly to commands from the top. The salary distribution system in Laos is based on proficiency grades and educational qualifications. Currently, there are five possible proficiency grades. The highest grade is grade 5 (Onxayvieng et al., 2015). With regard to holding the status of a least developed country, civil services struggle due to, as Onxayvieng et al. (2015, p. 19) address: the small number of key service delivery functions; low qualifications, competencies, and skills of officials; payment plans built on "qualification[s] and length of service rather than jobs and responsibilities"; ineffective systems and procedures of poor quality and slow speed; and a low level of transparency and accountability. Addressing the problems with civil servant management will require reforms of the Lao government with support from the development partners.

The Ministry of Home Affairs (MOHA) plays a crucial role in reforming civil services under the Civil Service Management Strategic Framework of 2011. This effort was intended to strengthen the civil servants in Laos through measures of accountability, responsibility, and transparency. Furthermore, the MOHA took an important step by implementing the Examination Recruitment System to enhance accountability and transparency in the recruitment process, as the result of the National GPAR Programme Secretary Support Project supported by the UNDP from 2012–2015.

Moreover, the Law on Civil Servants, revised in 2015, is one of the Lao government's great efforts to standardize the qualifications and work proficiency of Lao officials. This unprecedented decree creates an enforcement body that monitors officials at all levels.[71] Article 18 of the law in Laos requires each specific profession to be certified by the vocational and higher education systems (see Article 18 the Law on Civil Servants, Sapha Heng Xat, 2015). One could argue that the Lao government is demonstrating receptivity to the idea of improving its bureaucratic staff to become more specialized. As a result of this revision, in 2017, Laos had over 183, 000 civil servants, equal to 2.8% of the total population. Over 26,000 civil servants are employed in the central government, 36,000 at the provincial level, and 120,000 at the district level. Laos is ranked third highest for its total number of government officials among the ASEAN countries (Vientiane Times, 2018b).

Even with this effort placed on civil servant management, there is evidence that being an underdeveloped country has slowed its pace to improve public services due to a number of domestic constraints. First, the considerable rise in employment of civil servants has increased government expenses on wages and salary. However, the Lao government lacks the capacity to allocate salaries to officials regularly. This problem was highlighted by a scandal that leaked in 2017, in which a Lao news agency exposed late salary payments made to government officials. In an interview with a government official working in Attapeu's department of information, culture, and tourism it was stated that, "Late salary payments have become the norm in the province… This has been happening for the last 10 years" (Anonymous as cited in Radio Free Asia, 2017). As a consequence, public services in Laos have become degraded since many would rather spend their working time doing private work instead of public work (Radio Free Asia, 2017).

In order to mitigate this problem, the Lao government sought to regulate the number of bureaucratic staff in 2017, and to increase their salaries. However, another problem here is that the calculated number of civil servants is not accurate. Souvanny Lattanavong, the Director-General of the Civil Servant Management Department of the Ministry of Home Affairs, commented that "the number of civil servants is sometimes reported inaccurately… In an attempt to resolve this issue, officials plan to launch a first-hand inspection, issuing civil servant ID cards," according to a Lao news agency (Souvanny

[71] The Decree on Civil Service in 2003 did not apply to high-ranking officials (from ViceMinister level and above), members of the military and police forces, employees of State Owned Enterprises, or State employees working on a contractual basis (Ministry of Home Affairs [MoHA], 2018).

Lattnavong as cited in Laotian Times, 2017). This comment reveals one possible source of the issue. If the government does not even know how many employees they have, it may be difficult to issue accurate and timely pay checks.

The second domestic constraint to professionalization is that, although the Lao government has set qualifications for government officers, evidence shows that the higher education system in Laos cannot diversify its workforce or supply in-depth and technical knowledge. Currently, there are five universities and one college in Laos including the National University of Laos, Souphanouvong University, Champasak University, Savannakhet University, the University of Health Science, and Rattana Business Administration College (RBAC). The number of Lao students enrolled in these higher education institutions totals 708,514 students (UNESCO, 2018). In 2008, the Technical and Vocational Education and Training (TVET) was established, addressing 27 areas under four main fields of study, including: agriculture, business, industry, and handicraft. According to UNESCO, however, "Around 40% of all students enrolled in certificate programmes are in 'low skill programmes', such as business studies, while high skill labour is in greater demand and pays significantly more" (UNESCO cited in ICF Monitor, 2014). My interviews with the development partners also voiced the concern that many Lao officials do not have the experience and know-how to implement the development strategies effectively. They have to bring in technical experts from outside of the country to improve civil management in the government and arrange workshops and training for public servants (Informant No. 2, 4 and 10, 2017).

The third domestic constraint is widespread corruption and a lack of good governance practices. The Lao official interviewed commented "If you want to get a government job or go to a good university in Laos, you have to be willing to pay out bribes. Corruption is everywhere in Laos" (Informant No. 28, 2017). Another problem is, as already stated in chapter 3, the patronage system of the country. Most of the high-rank officials are those who have strong connections to Party members and nationalist leaders. This brings the question of how the Party recruits its members and proves their capability and professionalization to shape and implement the development plan. Lao political leaders may be able to justify their positions by their educational backgrounds and expertise at the central level, however, at the local level education appears to be lacking. Thus, even though the Lao government has attempted to improve its civil service sector, the lack of financial and institutional capacity remains an obstacle to its progress.

Institutional capacity and autonomy

Since the open economy in 1986, the domestic institutions of the country have been restructured to serve the economic purpose of guaranteeing political stability through trade and investment. In 1991, separation of powers was implemented to separate the government from the Party's structure and to institutionalize the state organizations, such as the National Assembly, the Lao government, and mass organizations from the Party. This political reform, in turn, has encapsulated the Party's power inside the government. In this section, institutional capacity with regard to Lao institutions and their ability to maintain autonomy while implementing the development goals and carrying out the government's wishes will be investigated. There are three main arguments of this section: 1) As a newly independent country, a massive amount of laws and regulations have to be modernized to meet developmental standards and to support new global trends; 2) the domestic institutions in Laos rather reflect the Party's power than genuinely contribute to good governance in the country; and 3) Lao domestic institutions are effective at sustaining political stability in the country as the Party organization is competent to control society.

The first argument requires consideration of laws and regulations approved by the National Assembly to pursue global, regional and sub-regional standards and to improve public services provided by the civil servants. Diversification of economic forces under regional and sub-regional economic integration can provide economic opportunities to utilize the development potential of the country. Currently, Lao institutions under the Lao government, from the development perspective of the development partners, are new and too young to implement sophisticated techniques. (Informant No. 15, 2017). There is no doubt that the Lao government is eager to improve the policy, law, and regulation to catch up with other countries, in particular its neighbor countries.

In terms of regional economic integration, Laos became a member of ASEAN in 1997. Its membership has connected trade and investment to the other ASEAN member countries. For example, the ASEAN Free Trade Area (AFTA) was initiated in 2007 to deregulate trade procedures among the ASEAN countries. Certain development partners that deal in technical support for economic integration sought to assist the government to be able to facilitate trade and investment and deregulate its complex procedures for the sake of regional economic integration, otherwise the whole system with the other countries in ASEAN could not work (Informant No. 10, 2017).

For the SDGs, implementing the goals at the local level is optimal for the development partners. One of their focal points is strengthening local institutional capacities to carry out their procedures with good governance. The Three Builds directive and the Provincial People's Assembly are currently the main institutions with this aim. As mentioned above, however, the challenges of implementing the SDGs through these actors are ongoing.

The second argument is derived from the fact that Lao domestic institutions rather reflect the Party's power than the principle of good governance. The Party has situated itself within state organizations, and plays a role in shaping the development plan and allocating resources under the Party-led development. Although the development partners have sought to diminish such power through the democratic process, the Party's power is embedded in the political structure beyond their estimation. Their support in developing procedures to support good governance and rule of law around these apparently democratic institutions cannot separate from the Party. As mentioned in chapters 3 and 4, Party members are pervasively embedded in all of the high-rank positions of the state and have controlled all areas of governance in the country. This sort of domestic institution is typical for the socialist regime which is incomparable with the democratic one.

The Party is thus the supreme organ determining national development. I argue that the Party-led development is both advantageous and disadvantageous with respect to institutional capacity and autonomy. On the positive side, policy implementation goes smoothly without political conflict. On the contrary, government authorities cannot decide by themselves and have to wait for the decision to be approved at higher levels. This process takes time and makes the development implementation run slower. It had led to a question of how to remove certain procedures to enhance autonomy in state organizations. The answers provided by the development partners are to support decentralization, especially with regard to the decision-making power of local authorities.

In spite of all this, domestic institutions are not totally dysfunctional. Indeed, I argue that the Lao state is efficient as a coercive apparatus maintained by the Party, which penetrates society in such a way as to flawlessly perpetuate political stability in the country. The Lao political structure has created favorable conditions for the Party to have to stabilize the country through mass organizations, the local administration, and the Party committees at both central and local levels. Most importantly, the Party has full control over the most significant sources of state power: the military and the police. Croissant and Lorenz (2018), points out that:

> [...] The Lao People's Armed Forces (LPAF)... are formally under the supremacy of the ruling party. The constitution charges the LPAF with defending the party's revolutionary accomplishments and contributing to national development... The president of the state—who is simultaneously general secretary of the Central Committee of the LPRP—is the commander-in-chief of the armed forces... Consequently, LPAF leaders are wellrepresented in the LPRP's top decision-making bodies (p. 132).

In conclusion, the adaptability of domestic institutions to new circumstances, such as implanting the SDGs, will require improvement. Overall, the Party and the Lao government are successful at maintaining social order and political stability. In the next section, I will specifically analyze how state capacity can contribute to the SDGs and to the country's overall development.

How can the state capacity support the SDGs in the country?

As mentioned in chapter 4, the Lao government has shaped the Lao domestic institutions and development policy based on the SDGs. Notably, the 8th Five Year National Development Plan is the concrete outcome of the Lao government's work toward attaining the requirements of the SDGs. The 18 goals contained in the SDGs in Laos, as previously mentioned, have been divided into the four pillars of economic development, environmental sustainability, social inclusion, and security. These pillars are the guidelines for the Lao government to take action to shape the national development plan, and are based on the assessed development potential of the country. State capacity, in this sense, matters in order to extract resources and to implement the SDGs through good governance. However, Lao's state capacity, as analyzed in this chapter, is insufficient to do so. This issue thus necessitates the continued assistance of the development partners to strengthen state capacity. Yet Laos's state capacity is only currently capable of successfully implementing the security pillar.

As already mentioned, domestic institutions are complex and serve both socio-economic and political purposes. It is no surprise that domestic institutions rather reflect the Party's power over given territories. More precisely, as noted in chapter 4, sustainability has been reinterpreted to mean political stability under the one-Party state. Viewed in this way, the Lao state's capacity to provide sustainability is thus achievable.

Looking at the numbers indicated by the World Bank,[72] political stability in Laos is solid, and Laos was ranked 3 out of 10 among ASEAN countries for political stability and lack of violence. GRAPH 5.7 illustrates overall political stability and lack of violence among the ASEAN countries in 2016.

source: The World Bank, 2016

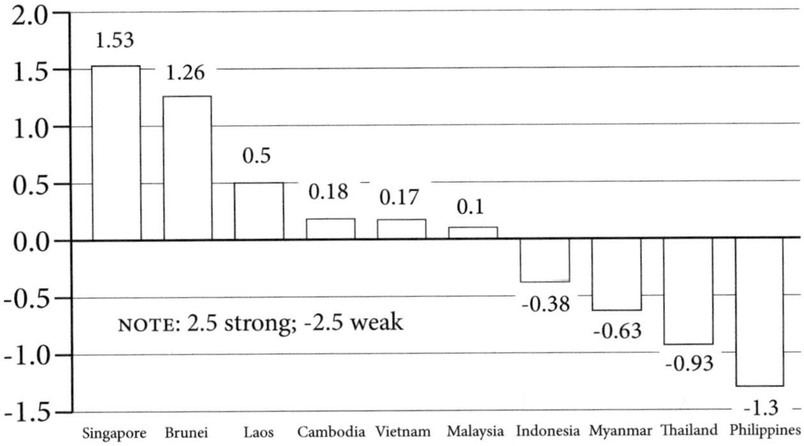

GRAPH 5.7 Political stability and lack of violence among the ASEAN countries in 2016

State capacity is thus highest with regard to the security pillar. The Lao government in fact emphasizes this capacity to the eyes of the public. For example, in 2016, Thongsing Thammavong, the former Prime Minister, told the National Assembly "Our country has actively participated in protecting peace and stability, and promoting friendship and cooperation towards development in the region and the world (Vientiane Times in Asian New, 2016b). Without a doubt, the Party has employed the coercive capacity to control the freedom of the Lao people and the press. Regarding freedom in Laos, the Freedom House, an independent watchdog organization, rated Laos at 12/100 on freedom out of 100 (Freedom House, 2018). The freedom rating of Laos signifies its general suppression of political and civil liberties. According to World Press Freedom,[73] Laos is ranked 170 out of 176 countries, pointing to its lack of free speech, press, and media.

72 The World Press Freedom ranking is arranged by the Reporters without Borders (RSF) as an independent non-governmental organization which is consultative with international organizations, such as the United Nations, UNESCO and the Council of Europe (see more Reporters without Borders, 2018).

73 The World Bank initiated the Worldwide Governance Indicators (WGI) project to assess governance in over 200 countries. Its indicators include: Voice and Accountability; Political Stability and Absence of Violence; Government Effectiveness; Regulatory Quality; Rule of Law and Control of Corruption (see World Bank, 2018c)

How does the Lao government strengthen its state capacity for the SDGs? The Lao policy-maker interviewed acknowledges that the consultation process between the Lao government and the development partners should be ongoing. As he said, "The indicators of the SDGs are vague. We are always engaged in discussions with the development partners to find common ground on what works with this country" (Informant No. 15, 2017). This led to the advisory process at the Round Table Meeting (RTM) to improve state capacity building in finance, human, and institutional development. Consequently, the Lao government and the development partners, in the national development plan, have promoted economic diversification, human development, and infrastructural accessibility. This sort of development has led to fruitful discussions on Lao development between the development partners, the Lao government, the INGOs and Lao scholars, who have all expressed their wish to see improved development in the country. In the following section, I will put a spotlight on the debate on Lao development and on contemporary developmental issues in Laos.

When expectations meet reality: Debates on Lao development

Lao development is controversial and ambiguous. According to interviews with the actors in Lao development, there are a variety of perspectives with regard to what should be expected of development. This leads us to the development debates in Laos, which can be categorized into two contemporary development issues including: 1) hydropower dam development and 2) the global pandemic and the graduation from the LDC status. The truth underlying these over-simplifications is reflected in the interplay between the expectations of the development partners, the reality of underdeveloped countries like Laos, and the specific political history of Laos. I will not suggest that the perspectives of those I interviewed amount to the final answer for each of these debates. Indeed, I will leave the discussion open for further study.

Hydropower dam development: Are things really flowing smoothly?

In 2017, the Lao economic monitor report launched by the World Bank displayed the headline "Lao PDR power sector: grow without sorrow." Its contents emphasized how the power sector, and hydropower dams in particular, rapidly contribute to economic growth, further reducing poverty in the country. As it points out, the expansion of the power sector "boosted growth and poverty reduction through investments, provision [sic] of reliable, clean, and affordable energy, higher exports, and government revenues" (The World Bank, 2017c, p. 37). The growth of the power sector contributes to exports to neighboring countries and allows for ample consumption within the country. Although investments and operations in the power sector are potentially risky, the Lao government and the development partners aim to strengthen the process to become more sustainable and environmentally friendly. According to the UNDP, the power sector in Lao contributed between 11,220 and 14,843 million Kips to the country's GDP in 2017. GRAPH 5.8 exhibits the rising growth of the power sector (represented in the chart as: "Mining, electricity, water and gas") and its contribution to Lao's GDP.

The growth of the power sector in Laos looks good for the Lao government. It is no surprise that the Lao government has been designated the Battery of Asia for its ability to utilize its potential by producing electricity through dams and alternative sources, like mines, thermal vents, and various renewable resources. Souphanh Keomixay, the Minister of Planning and Investment, told the National Assembly that, "The energy sector will be the major source that will push up economic growth to 7%" (The Nation, 2016a). Although Laos is low in its capacity to diversify economic activity due to its small population, it is on the fast track to accomplishing its economic development goals. As of 2016, 38 hydropower dam projects, including 13 dams owned by the Electricity du Laos (EDU) and 25 by independent power producers, are operating with a total installed capacity of 6,258.95 Megawatts (MW), and a production capacity of 33,324.6 million Kilowatt Hours (kWh) per annum. Moreover, the Lao government has signed off on 369 dam projects that are now undergoing construction (Ministry of Planning and Investment, 2016a, pp. 20–21). The increasing number of hydropower dams in Laos has roused debate, and a variety of pro and anti-dam views have been argued.

The pro-dam side includes some of the development partners, some Lao experts, and the Lao government. They support the building of hydropower dams mainly for the project's potential in bringing the Lao people out of poverty by increasing economic growth in the country. One of the interviewees representing the development partners stated that the Mekong River is the center of the Lao economic development strategy because Laos has a lot of hydropower potential to enhance its economy and reduce poverty, as well as to serve regional energy demands. For these reasons, the government dubbed the policy as the *battery of Asia*, despite the electrical capacity of the country being small—consisting less than 10 percent of the total output of the ASEAN region (Informant No. 7, 2017).

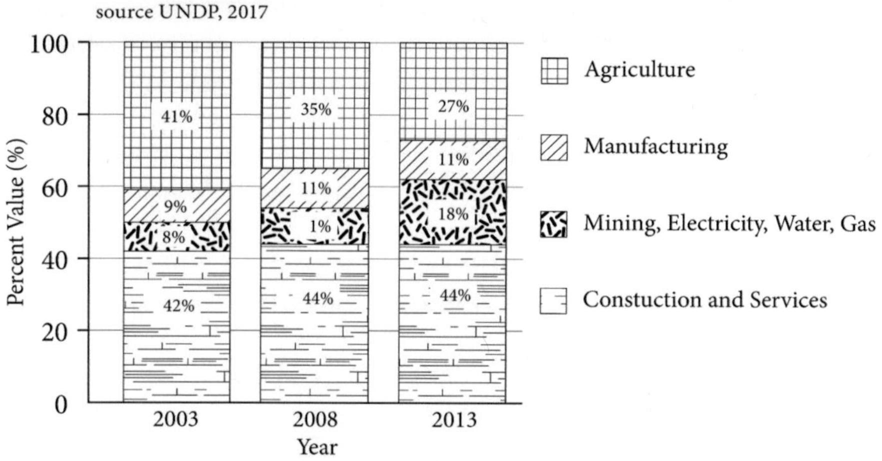

GRAPH 5.8 Sectorial composition of GDP by the amount of output produced (measured as value-added and expressed in percent of total value-added)

The economic growth that comes from building a dam is worth the risk, according to the Lao scholar I interviewed who studies hydropower dams in Laos. He believes that hydropower dams will contribute to long-term economic growth in the country. As that scholar strongly believed that the government will earn income from selling electricity once the hydropower dams operate. (Informant No. 22, 2017).

Dam supporters, moreover, do not overlook the fact that hydropower dams have caused unexpected harm to the physical environment, the ecological system, and the lives of local peoples. The development partners seek to help the Lao government to improve the quality of its hydropower dams to be more sustainable with regard to the assessment processes, operations, and compensation. The delegate I interviewed from the development partners pointed out his organization's role in hydropower dam development in Laos, which is called the "learning by doing" process. This process is that the development partners will work with the Lao government to design the environmental-friendly and sustainable hydropower dams at its best. Actually, the Lao government is more concerned with revising the legislation to assess the impacts of and protect the environment with regard to hydropower dams. The Lao government has played a role in negotiating between investors and local peoples, and providing useful insights on positive outcomes to building dams. There is an ad hoc committee appointed by the Lao government to deal with this matter, referring to the Lao scholar I interviewed (Informant No. 23, 2017).

The Lao government indeed took efforts to revise the Law on Electricity in 2017. Article 5 of the law emphasizes promoting environmentally friendly and clean processes that utilize modern technologies and work with natural resources in an economical, efficient and sustainable manner under green growth development (Sapha Heng Xat, 2017). In addition, Article 49 of the law sets up an initial assessment process and investment standard for approving dam developers. The Ministry of Energy and Mining takes responsibility for feasibility studies and financial analyses, which are part of the initial phase before auction (see more the Article 49, Sapha Heng Xat, 2017). The law justifies the positive direction of building dams in Laos in a more environment-aware manner. However, the questionable governance practices in Laos have left open the question regarding the effectiveness of law enforcement across the country. The dam collapse in 2018 provided damning evidence to the negative.

As mentioned earlier, concerning the dam's collapse in 2018, a technical error is believed to have caused the collapse, resulting in enormous damage to the Lao people. Countless international news reports have critically attacked the Battery of Asia policy. The backfire of the hydropower dam has dealt a blow to the legitimacy of the Lao government to facilitate sustainable development. For example, the Nation (2018) investigated hydropower development in Laos in order to examine how dams are beneficial to local communities. They concluded that, "revenues have yet to trickle down to village level… and farmers have complained that diverting river-water destroys farmland, while damming rivers interrupt fish flows." More harshly, Ives & Paddock (2018), a reporter from the New York Times, reveals the unspoken truth about the politics of dam building in Laos, stating that "companies get access to Laos' abundant natural resources; Laotian officials get some revenue; and no one will cast undue scrutiny on investment projects that exacerbate rural poverty—or, in this case, kill innocent villagers." The damage resulting from the failure of hydropower dams in Laos have earned the Battery of Asia policy some crucial criticisms, describing the policy as unfriendly to local communities and ecological systems. One of the Lao experts attempted to clarify the problem to local communities that even the Lao government and the investors compensated local people with the nice and modern houses in the resettlement areas, the problem is that they cannot catch fish due to changes to the ecological system. They will in the end feel insecure in their poverty, lack of sustainability. But they are not brave enough to tell the government this truth. (Informant No. 20, 2017).

The weakness of the civil society, analyzed in chapter 3, in Laos is another reason why the local people are mostly voiceless in Lao development, and why they always follow the orders of the Lao government. The interviewee quoted above points out that the local people believe that what the Lao government brings to their community is suitable for their livelihoods. Likewise, there are no real representatives for local people to voice concerns about development to the Lao government. Thus, INGOs who work in transborder development have become a delegate of people to advocate the unspoken truths of hydropower dams to the international community (see chapter 3). For instance, the interviewed representative of the INGO reflects another side of dam development in Laos that there are no participatory channels between local people, civil society, the government, and the monitoring systems from the development partners are not workable to assess the social and economic impacts to local people comprehensively (Informant No. 11, 2017).

As long as the Lao government places emphasis on hydropower development as a source of government income and the country's prosperity, the debate on hydropower dams will continue. As one INGO interviewee said,

> People are not like statues that you can place anywhere you want. They are alive and have their own lives. The government at the central level always thinks about their policy from an air-conditioned room and then pushes this policy on the lives of innocent people (Informant No. 12, 2017).

Laos under the global pandemic: Can Laos really graduate from its status as a Least Developed Country by 2026?

The year 2020 is a difficult year for many countries. The COVID-19 as the global pandemic has plunged the global economy into recession since many countries have announced the lockdown policy and introduced the "new normal" to control the number of virus infectious people. Many business sectors, particularly tourism, were severely affected and businesses have not yet returned to pre-pandemic conditions. Like other countries, Lao economy has suffered from the global economy as the country heavily relies on the tourism sector. The lockdown policy from the Lao government has restrained the numbers of tourists, workers and some business sectors. Without this income, the graduation from the LDC status by 2024 is out-of-reach for the Lao government. This goal, again, was postponed from 2024 to 2026.

Graduation from the Least Developed Country status by 2026 has been the ultimate long-term goal for the Party since the national development plan in 2001. With consideration for the three thresholds to graduate from the LDC status set by the United Nations Economic and Social Councils (ECOSOC), it seems like Laos may have already crossed two of these thresholds. According to the Committee for Development Policy, a subsidiary body of ECOSOC, Laos has crossed the threshold for obtaining $1,230 or on GNI per capita (Laos made it to $1,996) and scored at least 66 on the Human Assets Index (HAI; Laos made it to 72.8). Nevertheless, the Economic Vulnerability Index reached 33.7 and is yet to meet the threshold of 32 or below but it is close (UNDP, 2018a).

An analyst from the UNDP points out that natural disasters and inequality rates continue to pose major challenges for the Lao government, with regard to the Economic Vulnerability Index (UNDP, 2018b). Thongloun Sisoulith told the National Assembly,

> Lao has engaged [sic] on a path of development for 43 years. Since 2001, the Party and Government have tried their best to implement a national development plan with the goal of graduating from Least Developed Country status, an economic classification given to Laos by the United Nations based on three criteria. And for the first time since then, United Nations representatives have come to perform inspections and have concluded that Laos will not be able to free itself from this classification by 2020 for a number of reason" (Sisoulith as cited in Laotian Time, 2018).

To improve the EVI of the country and prepare to re-address the issue of graduating from LDC status, the Lao government decided to postpone the deadline from 2020 to 2024 and now appears to be working harder to accomplish this development goal.

However, my interview with the Lao government officials and the Lao scholar reveals graduation from LDC status carries a mythical quality for them for a few reasons. First, graduation from LDC status is a self-improvement process for the Lao government to reduce its dependency on development assistance from the international community. The National Assembly member I interviewed supports this argument. In his sense, development is progressive and motivates the Lao government to improve its capacity to pursue the development goals. Such self-improvement is a practical necessity to strengthen the capacity of the Lao government to be more effective and sustainable.

The second reason is that graduation from LDC status can prove the capability of the Party and the Lao government to fulfil the ultimate development goal. This achievement could serve as another source of regime legitimacy. The connection between the development goals and regime legitimacy is observable in the perspective of the Lao scholar I interviewed. He commented "If Laos is capable of achieving this, then I do not think international development assistance is necessarily important anymore for Laos at all" (Informant No. 22, 2017). Belief in developmental achievements, I argue, supports the Lao government, or the Party, to continually be the leading nucleus in Lao development.

The third reason is, the Lao government genuinely wants to change and do something new. The Lao government has recently become more receptive to restructuring domestic institutions and the development policy to bring about good governance in the country. The key informant of the Lao government I interviewed clarified the government's motivations by noting, "Graduation from the LDC status means a lot for the government… The government commits itself because the government wants to change and do something for its own sake." He further conceded that the development partners are still the critical agents for Lao development stating "the Lao government cannot get things done without support from the donors and the development partners. It takes time, patience and a lot of young blood… For very young institutions like those in Laos, it takes a lot of time" (Informant No. 15, 2017).

However, the consequences of the global pandemic from 2020 to 2021 have slowed down the pace to the graduation from the LDC status. It could be seen the economic disruption in Laos that could by no means reach the graduation thresholds. The report on the socio-economic impact assessment of COVID-19 in Lao PDR published by the UNDP shows the human development in Laos has been decelerated since the global pandemic. In 2020, for example, 23.4 percent of the Lao population lost their job and more than 300,000 people could be back into poverty. The poverty and unemployment of people could reduce the country's HAI and EVI scores to not meet the graduation thresholds since many people cannot afford the medical expenses and tuition fees for education (Lao PDR and UNDP, 2021).

Actually, many observers of Lao development are concerned about the Lao state's readiness to sustain the consequence of no longer being an LDC country and to avoid the middle-income trap.[74] One of the development

[74] The middle-income trap is the situation that a country encounters after reaching middle-income levels. It refers to the difficulties associated with slow growth, following the withdrawal of aid, as the country struggles to make it on its own (see Global, Economic Symposium, 2018).

partners stated, "the Lao government should not be in a rush to graduate from LDC status because there are many advantages to being a least developed country from the perspective of our organization" (Informant No. 4, 2017). Viewed in this light, the Lao government should not ignore the fact that the ODA is critical for enhancing Laos's state capacity (see GRAPH 5.9).

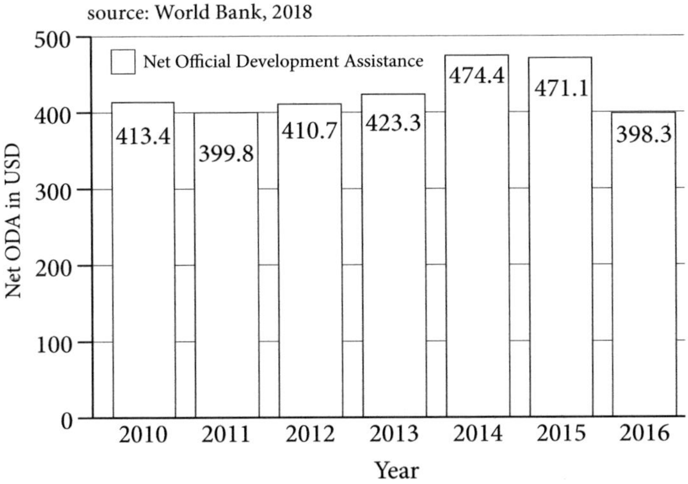

GRAPH 5.9 Net Official Development Assistance (ODA) (Currency in US$)

Therefore, graduation from LDC status amounts to a trade-off between more self-reliance and the ODA cut-off—it is difficult for the Lao government to balance these two-incompatible outcomes. In the following section, the readiness of the Lao government to sustain the consequences after graduation from LDC status will be explored.

After graduation from the Least Development Country status: What comes next?

I will begin this section by shedding light on the LDC identification status and what Laos gains and losses when it reaches its goal, thereby transitioning out of this status. The least developed country is a label that was coined in 1971 by the United Nations for nations suffering from the most "severe structural handicaps" (UNDP, 2012) who were to be given preferential trade-related financial assistance to better address their needs and to bring them up to speed with respect to the global economy. In Laos, being a landlocked country particularly has left the Lao government with few options for integrating with the global economy. Moreover, as a newly independent country, the Lao government needs international development assistance to enhance its state capacity to deal with new economic activities and meet the international development standards. As a result, the Lao government needs the ODA, but graduation from LDC status will inevitably reduce aid provided by the development partners.

However, every cloud has a silver lining. This development goal can bring an advantage to the country's development. Southichack (2017) points out that a tangible benefit is that if the Lao government achieves this development goal, it implies that the Lao government is economically stable and can cope with the market and shocks that follow natural disasters. On the one hand, Laos will have the intangible benefits of ensuring the place of direct foreign investors in human capacity and economic activity, strengthening the position of the Lao government in international negotiations, and motivating the Lao government and the Lao people to achieve more development goals.

On the other hand, the cost of graduating from LDC status is risky for the Lao government, particularly because Laos will lose aid that is a result of the "Generalised Scheme of Preferences" (GSPs).[75] In EU countries, for example, Laos is in the Everything but Arms (EBA) scheme, which allows free access to the EU Single Market for all products, except arms and armaments (European Commission, 2021). Therefore, Laos can export some products to EU countries to generate government revenue. Moreover, international development assistance, concession loans, and debt relief will be reduced, as in the case of special facilities of the WTO that allow flexibility in international trade rule enforcement, and which assist the Lao government in building up its capacity in trade negotiation and rule enforcement. The cost of graduating from LDC status will thus become a primary challenge for Lao state capacity to maintain independence and self-reliance so as to sustain development without international development assistance and low-interest loans.

With the Least Developed Country status, state capacity is still being enhanced. Both the Lao government and the development partners concede that avoiding the middle-income trap will be the next task for them. The informant I interviewed from the NA mentioned that the role of the Lao government in dealing with this task is to focus on human resource development. He believes that "Lao people should become ready to become more independent and to start thinking about the future" (Informant No. 16, 2017). Likewise,

---

75 The European Commission website points out the three main objectives of the Generalised Scheme of Preference, which include: 1) to contribute to poverty eradication by expanding exports from countries most in need; 2) to promote sustainable development and good governance; 3) to ensure that the EU's financial and economic interests are safeguarded (see more European Commission, 2021).

the policy-maker of the Lao government interviewed expressed his concern about the readiness of the Lao government to compensate the Lao people and manage the environment, as well as to protect the national culture due to the fact that the Lao government strives to achieve the development goals with a development plan that inevitably alters its natural resources and its people's ways of life. And yet he believes that investment in the next generation is also important. Another informant from the Lao government believes that young people will need to deal with the responsibility of making a healthier rural community by contributing well-educated and skilled labor (Informant No. 15, 2017).

Currently, the development partners have varied priorities in Lao development, as they work to help the Lao government improve its capacity and decrease social inequality. The prioritized domains primarily include human resource capacity, infrastructure development, good governance, and economic diversification. These issues have already been encapsulated in the Official Development Assistance mentioned in chapter 4. GRAPH 5.10 highlights its monetary disbursement by the Sector Working Group of the SDGs from 2015–2016.

source: Ministry of Planning and Investment, 2016c

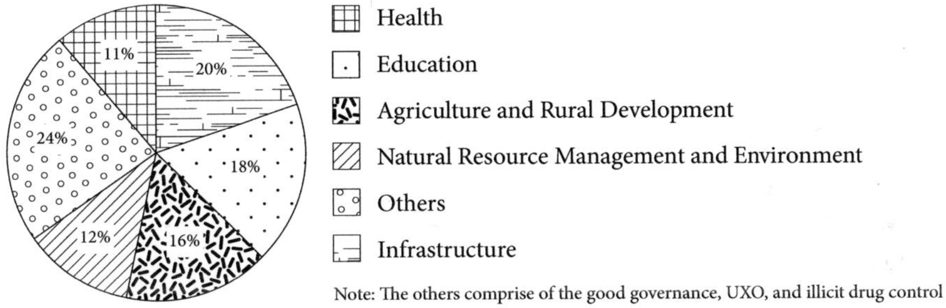

GRAPH 5.10 The ODA disbursement by Sector Working Group in the fiscal year 2015/16

Clearly the Lao government has to rely on development assistance in many sectors—both financial and technical. This leads to my last argument of the chapter: that the Lao government should not rush to push forward graduation from the LDC status unless its state capacity is ready to deal with the consequences. There are a few reasons for the argument that Laos is not ready.

First, it is obvious to see the inequality and the development gap between the rich and the poor in Laos, especially when comparing rural and urban areas. As shown in GRAPH 5.11, the Vientiane capital has the lowest poverty headcount at 8.5, whereas the highest poverty headcount is Saravan at 48.5. This gap is extremely wide.

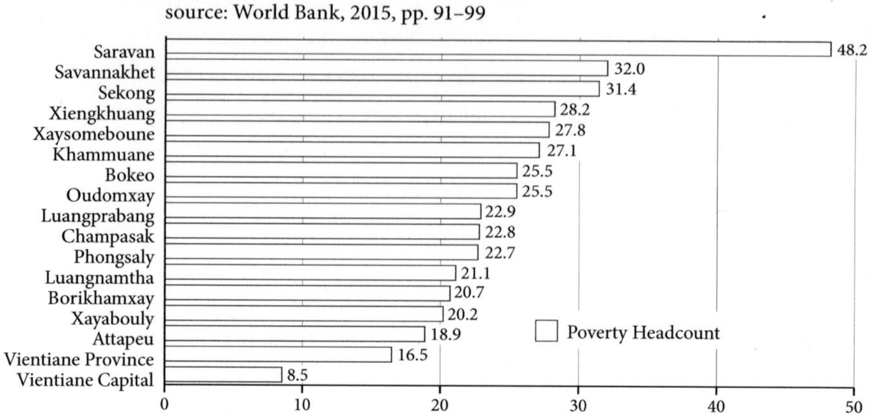

GRAPH 5.11 Poverty Headcount in 17 provinces and 1 capital city

With regard to the second argument, technical experts are essential to deal with new technologies and new circumstances that arise with global change. The education system should therefore be ready to provide the necessary support to increase the number of technical experts. On the other hand, based on UNESCO data there is a considerable number of out-of-school adolescents in 2017, shown in GRAPH 5.12.

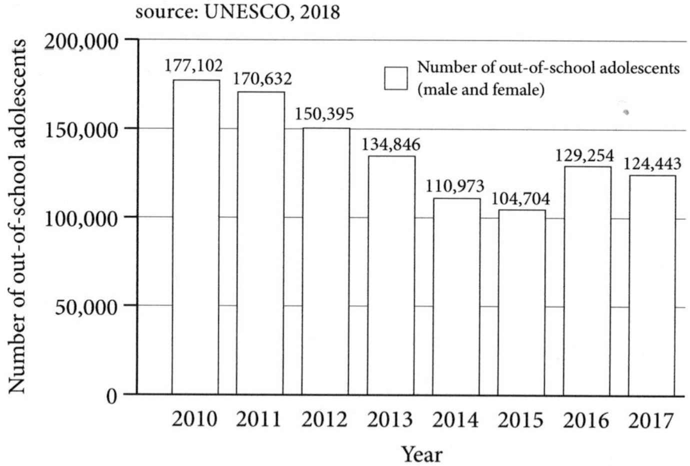

GRAPH 5.12 The number of out-of-school adolescents (male and female)

This total number of out-of-school adolescents affects the state's capacity for human development. The higher the number of student dropouts from schools and universities the lower the number of skilled-laborers[76] and general manpower that can be used to implement the development plan and sustainably utilize natural resources to generate income, mitigate environmental degradation and, most importantly, to bring sustainability into the next generation. This challenging issue in human development justifies the needed role of the development partners to continue to assist the Lao government.

The country is too young to deal with the complicated outcomes that will follow graduation. Therefore, the Lao government must strengthen its institutional capacity to deliver public services and implement the development plan effectively. In this light, good governance is an essential contribution to the country's accountability, transparency, and efficiency in dealing with new circumstances and the consequences that will follow graduation. If the Lao government cannot deal with them, development assistance that helps to improve the quality of governance in the country remains indispensable. The Lao government should thus consider that development assistance in good governance will be cut-off if Laos graduates from the LDC status.

Accordingly, the Lao government is capable of meeting the criteria to bring the country out of the LDC status in 2018. However, the global pandemic in 2020 decelerated the graduation path. Moreover, there is still a long way to go for the government to build up state capacity to deal with the consequences following graduation. The Lao government should focus more on issues related to inequality in the country to ensure that said consequences do not jeopardize the livelihood of its people or result in the exploitation of the natural resources that belong to the next generation.

Concluding remarks

The, graduation from the LDC status by 2020, and postponed to 2026 has been the ultimate goal for the Party since 2000. If the Party could achieve this goal, it could maintain the status quo of the leading nucleus in Lao development and stay in power in Lao politics. To achieve this goal, therefore,

76 The report from ADB reflects the number of high skilled workers in the labor force based on educational background, divided into three classifications. Its result shows that the percentage of high skilled workers in 2013 was 14.33% in the first classification (tertiary education and vocational education), 6.93% in the second classification (tertiary and vocational education and high-skilled occupation), and 3.30% in the third classification (tertiary education and high-skilled occupation) (see more Asian Development Bank, 2015, p. 92).

the Party has to be receptive to the criteria from the UNDP and improve the state capacity to meet the criteria. This state capacity investigated here is the financial, institutional and human capacities as these capacities are interconnected. As the least developed country, the development assistance from the development partners remains in need for the Lao government to improve its state capacity. This chapter does merely not investigate the assistance provided by the development partners in Lao state capacity but also analyze how the state capacity works in the socialist regime. For the financial capacity, the development partners support the public finance management to improve Lao financial capacity which has led to the debt trap in the country as the external debt of the country remains high. In reality, however, the public financial management in Laos is in the hands of the state organization dominated by the Party's members and the budget distribution in the country is centralized. For the institutional capacity, it could be seen that Laos needs to standardize the legal frameworks and domestic institutions to meet the global and regional cooperation. Regarding political stability, the Lao domestic institutions are capable of maintaining the political stability of the country. Last but not least, the human capacity is important to increase skilled laborers and experts in the country. The development partners thus support human development through education. The following investigation of the chapter is the development debate in Laos in two topics. First is the debate on the hydropower dam in Laos. The pro-dam side supports that the dams are able to generate income to the Lao government by selling the electricity to the neighboring countries. On the contrary, the anti-dam side contends that the dams have jeopardized the environment and ecological system in the river. This could have a negative impact on local people's.

The second debate is on the global pandemic in Laos and the graduation from the LDC status. The debate shows that the global pandemic has decelerated this goal of the Lao government and even if the country could graduate from LDC status, there are challenges that remain to be seen. The challenges further analyze in the last investigation of the chapter—the consequences after the graduation. The results show that if Laos graduates from the LDC status, the country will be more self-reliant. The development partners will decrease the development assistance to the Lao government. If the Lao state capacity is not sufficient to deal with the consequences after the graduation, the country could be in the middle-income trap.

6

CONCLUSION

The journey of the completion of the SDGs and graduating from the LDC status for Laos is far from over. It is rather infeasible to indicate, or even predict, the success or the failure of SDGs because 2030 is such a far-off mark. However, this chapter summarizes the "research" results analyzed in previous chapters. My main argument is that the development partners and the Lao government (or the Party) are struggling to implement their development goals in Laos. The development partners have implied the democratic process in the SDGs, which have shaped Lao domestic institutions and development policies to an extent, but cannot fully diminish the state power occupied by the Party. The Party, in turn, employs development as another source of political legitimacy to play a leading role in national development.

To understand why the SDGs, as a western development norm, is applicable in Lao development, this book traced back to the construction and reconstruction of Lao modernity from the colonial era. The French colony, at that time, attempted to modernize and civilize Laos based on the French model. Compared with the traditional culture in Laos, the French civilization seemed to be superior and more modern than the traditional one. Many Lao elite changed their way of life and dressing style and applied the French colonial architecture in their houses. Another wave of western modernity in Laos is from the influence of the USA during the cold war. This sort of modernity was widely accepted and localized by the Lao elite. Since then, western modernity has been influential in Lao people's mind-set which could not be backward to the pre-colonial era. Even the western modernity was replaced with the socialist one after the country's independence, this modernity reappeared after the open economy in 1986. The international development standards set by the international community reconstructed Lao modernity in which the

Party commits itself to willingly implement the standards in the national development. In conclusion, the Lao modernity is progressive and could be reconstructed based on the influence of external factors.

The first section represents the regime's legitimacy in post-socialist Laos. I contend that the Marxist-Leninist ideology alone is inadequate for providing an in-depth analysis of the regime's survival in Laos. Development legitimation should be taken into account as another source of the regime legitimacy for the Party, assisting them to stay in power. The second section of this chapter looks at how international development norms have shaped Lao domestic institutions and development policy. Prior to analyzing the domestic institutions and development policy, I begin with the role of the development partners in Lao development as a driver of decision-making inside the Party. After this, the Party is considered for its normative influence over domestic institutions and development policy. The last section of this chapter is to scrutinize the Lao state capacity since these matters for assessing the effectiveness of SDGs implementation and the likelihood of graduating from the LDC status. The three dimensions of Lao state capacity being explored in this chapter are the financial, human capital and institutional capacities.

Post-socialist Laos: development as another source of the regime legitimacy

This topic begins with the account for the Lao state power, which is how the Party obtains and maintains such power. The Lao government, or the Party, acts as the primary actor in Lao development in part by embedding itself in nominal democratic institutions and in order to deal with capitalism and legitimize its political power. Back in 1975, the victory of the Pathet Lao after the civil war in Laos legitimized the nationalist movement, allowing it to become the sole political institution, dubbed as the Lao People's Revolutionary Party (LPRP). The Party then introduced a blend of Marxist-Leninist and nationalist ideology as an underlying ideology in political socio-economic realms. In the beginning, the ideology was a political tool of the Party to control society, stabilize the new regime, and reconcile the conflicting political factions in the aftermath of the Lao civil war. However, the Party could not enjoy the fruit of the nationalist legacy for long since the failure of the centrally-planned economy left Laos with a massive downturn. As a result, Laos had opened its hermetic curtain in order to integrate itself with the global economy by unprecedentedly introducing capitalism to the country's economy under the New Economic Mechanism policy in 1986.

The consequence of this policy led to the socio-economic and political development of the country under the 1991 Constitution. The Party upheld its members to the Lao government while also introducing the separation of powers principle to guarantee political stability and the rule of laws for foreign investment. Moreover, the Party became receptive to the international community as the result of the failure of the Soviet Union, which was the major aid-donor before the open economy. Without a doubt, the condition attached in the ODA provided by the international community, or the development partner in Laos, always implies democratic principles that ultimately put the Party, as a socialist institution, into a dilemma.

The Party has encountered the dilemma of dealing with the contradiction between capitalism and socialism in the country. As capitalism on an international scale can deteriorate the Marxist-Leninist ideology, it becomes the burden of the Party to legitimize its existence in order to maintain the status quo of the one-Party state. The Party has thus initiated an optimal means to legitimize its power. I employ Saxonberg's framework to simplify regime legitimation. His framework requires analysis of ideological legitimacy, pragmatic acceptance of performance-based legitimation, and the revolutionary potential in the country to understand the regime's survival.

For ideological legitimacy, the Party remains positing the Marxist-Leninist ideology combined with the nationalist movement by emphasizing the contribution and the dedication of the nationalist leaders in the national liberation in the public sphere and the political rhetoric of the Party's member speech. Under the umbrella of capitalism and globalization, the Party plays the two main roles to protect the ideology: the supporter of the socialist ideology and the guardian of the national interest. Nevertheless, the ideological legitimacy alone is inadequate for the Party to maintain the status quo of the one-Party state.

Development achievements, according to my view, are used by the Party to serve the political purpose of pragmatic acceptance, to obtain more support from the Lao people and the development partners. Currently, graduating from the LDC and achieving the SDGs become the main tasks of the Party and the Lao government. The Party uses those development goals to tighten its control to Lao society by increasing the number of Party members at the local level and introducing the Three Build directive, which encloses the government officials at the central and local levels to justify the Party's action development.

Lastly, the framework contends the revolutionary potential from the proletariat, the intellectuals and the civil society could threaten the regime's survival if it lacks apparent legitimacy. In Laos, the control of these groups is absolute. They are mostly voiceless in Lao politics because the Law on Civil Society revised in 2017 tightens the Party's control over civil society, leaving little room for its participation in development issues. It can be concluded that the Party employs the Marxist-Leninist ideology to build trust among the Lao people with regard to the socialist utopia and to legitimize the role of the Party as the delegate of the Lao people in dealing with capitalism. As a consequence, the Party has a legitimate right to rule over the given territory and consolidates its power in the political structure.

The political structure reflects the consolidation of the Party's power embedded in the state organization. In this sense, the Party's power is autonomous and intact. Democratic institutions, such as the National Assembly, the Lao government and the People's Court, are just nominal due to the fact that the Party members occupy the high-rank position in these institutions. In terms of the intra-Party co-optation, a substantial amount of evidence reveals that the Party is the overarching medium for distributing economic and political goods to certain intra-Party-political factions based on their influence and charisma in Lao Lao politics.

Without a doubt, the Party is the leading actor to determine the country's developmental direction through its restructuring of the domestic institutions and development policy based on the development partners' recommendations and the Party's resolution. The Party Congress is a meeting that reveals the developmental achievements of the Party from the preceding four years, the future development direction, and changes in political leadership. The resolution of the Party Congress concretely transfers to the five-year National Development Plan. This plan covers development potential, natural resource distribution, and the local development project going on in the country. For example, the Tenth Party Congress focuses on the new global development agenda—the SDGs. Domestic institutions and development policies have been reshaped with help from the development partners in an attempt to meet them.

Sustainable Development Goals under the Party-led development in Laos

For the domestic institution and development policy under the SDGs, it is worth mentioning the development partners, their development agendas and how the Party interprets the SDGs in that end. As Laos relies on international development assistance over the last half-century, the development partners have played a supporting role by providing financial and technical assistance to the Lao government. As a result, Lao development is designated to adopt the international development standards attached in the ODA from the development partners.

The interplay between the development partners and the Party is observable through two big events. First, the Round Table Meeting (RTM), held every five years, is a consultative process intended to find a common ground between them, based on the current international development norms. The latest RTM in 2016 set the SDGs for Lao development to be attained by 2030. Both the development partners and the Lao government commit themselves to work together to implement the SDGs effectively. Besides the 17 goals of the SDGs identified, in Laos, there is one additional goal entitled "Lives Safe from UXO" to eradicate unexploded mines from the Lao civil war throughout the country. The development partners and the Lao government believe the unexploded mines are the main obstacle to natural resource utilization for economic development. With the 18 goals of the SDGs in Laos, the development partners assist the Lao government through the ODA in their partnership framework in order to make sure Laos meets the standards.

Since the trajectory of the SDGs began in 2016, there have been four main focal points of the development partners to standardize Lao development. These include: poverty reduction, capacity building, environmental protection, climate change resilience, and good governance to localize and implement the SDGs at every level. However, I argue that the development partners themselves have specific agendas for Lao development that are beneficial for their national and stakeholder interests. The development agendas I analyzed comprise: 1) the SDGs promotion, 2) the profit received from Lao natural resources, 3) the improvement of the connectivity between Laos and its neighbor countries to facilitate the economic integration, 4) the humanitarian reason, 5) advocating their national interests, and 6) democratizing in Laos. Indeed, ODA is like a double-edged sword. On the positive side, it can bring prosperity to the country and improve economic growth. On the contrary, it can also be a development trap for the Lao government to remain indebted and for Lao people to be more insecure and vulnerable.

The second event for Lao development is the Party Congress. This congress is a meeting between the Central Committee and the Party members from the local level to justify the contributions of the Party in national development and the development direction in the next five years. At the Tenth Party Congress in 2016, the Party interpreted the term sustainability to serve the political purpose for the political stability and social order under the one-Party state.

Consequently, the four pillars of the SDGs were set as the Lao-style development norm and issued in the 8th Five-Year National Development Plan (2016–2020) and the Lao domestic institution. These pillars consist of economic development, environmental sustainability, social inclusion, and security.

For restructuring domestic institutions and formulating the development policies, I employ Sach's framework (2012; 2015) that divides the SDGs into four scopes. The first is economic development. The Lao government currently promotes sustainable and inclusive growth in order to rise from the LDC status by the year 2026 and to reduce the poverty rate of the country. Second is social inclusion is to narrow the development and gender inequality gap, let alone the civil society empowerment. For instance, the Lao government supports the women employed in state and private organizations and encourages them to access education. Moreover, the Lao government revised and improved the law on women and development strategy supports the role of women in national and local development. The third scope is environmental sustainability. The Lao government advocates a green-growth agenda in governmental organizations. The Lao government references the Environmental Impact Assessment (EIA) before undertaking megaprojects like hydropower dams. Most importantly, the government issues the Law on Disaster Management which is expected to be enforced in 2017. The last scope is good governance. The Party and the Lao government play the main role to support good governance throughout the country with their political subsidiary body. The Lao government attempts to mitigate the worrying related to good governance by increasing more political participatory channels to Lao people, approving laws and regulations to guarantee the rule of law, tackling the corruption issues with the leadership, and decentralizing the political power to the Three Build directive.

However, the effort of the Party and the Lao government to implement the SDGs in national and local development has served both economic and political purposes. The Party has employed development achievements and challenges to legitimize its leading role. The Party claims itself as the delegate of Lao people to protect their national interest and contribute to political stability. This situation has broadened the debate from the observers upon the state capacity of the Lao government to cope with the new development goals, which I will shed additional light on in the following section.

Lao state capacity

I mainly employed Fukuyama's framework to investigate the state capacity of the Lao government to implement the identified SDGs. The state capacities investigated here are the financial management capacity, the human capital capacity, and the institutional capacity. This book particularly focuses on the capacity to graduate from the LDC status as this goal is ultimate for the Party and the Lao government. If the Party could achieve this goal, it could prove the Party's legitimacy as the leading nucleus in Lao development. In reality, being the least developed country, this book also helps to convey the fact that Lao state capacity is ineffective at bringing the country out of the LDC and that development assistance from the development partners remains indispensable.

According to the economic monitoring report, the Lao economy has become more vulnerable with the rise in public debt over the past five years. Almost 80 percent of the public debt is from external sources, such as the aid-donor countries and financial institutions. It implies that the Lao government lacks the ability to generate more government revenue and still relies on external sources for the country's development. The development partners thus support the public finance management as they believe that it could improve Lao economic performance and reduce the external debt. After that, the Lao government issued the vision 2030 to strengthen the public finance management to be transparent, modern, and fair. However, I argue that the institutional arrangement on the budget approval and auditing should be another main concern for the Lao government if the government genuinely intends to strengthen the public finance management.

This argument arises from the fact that the budget approving and auditing is currently in the hands of Party members in the NA and SAO and centralized by the MPI. This ministry is responsible for determining the development plan of each province. Budget distribution does not presently amount to be enough to meet the needs of the local development. Another financial capacity in Laos is tax collection to increase the government revenue. Acquired information on tax collection illustrates the Lao government has attempted to computerize the tax system via the so-called Smart Tax and VAT, and categorize the list of taxable products in the Law on Tax revised in 2015. Nevertheless, the ability of the tax collection is insufficient for the country's development, according to the statistical information, which has revealed the rising needs of the ODA from the development partners.

The second state capacity analyzed is the institutional capacity. There are three primary arguments that address institutional capacity in Laos. The first argument starts with the fact that Laos is a newly independent and least developed country; the massive number of laws and regulations should be modernized to meet the need for global and regional economies. Second, the domestic institutions of Laos are unique as it remains adhering to the democratic centralism principle. The Party-led development, and the top-down command line from central to local levels, have delayed the decision-making and implementation processes. Consequently, the Lao government should hasten these processes to adapt to the new circumstances. The institutional capacity, in turn, is effective to contribute political stability under the one-party system of the country. It could be concluded that Laos' state capacity is practical with regard to the security pillar of the SDGs, as the Party and its subordinates are competent to penetrate and control Lao society.

For the human capital capacity in Laos, evidence shows that the Ministry of Home Affairs took an important step to initiate the recruitment examination for the government officials and revise the Law on Civil Service in 2015. This law increases the degree of professionalization with respect to the educational qualifications of government officials. However, the reality is that Laos has slowed down its pace to improve civil service to deliver and localize the SDGs at every level. There are three constraints of human capacity building that come across in this book. The first constraint is the lack of financial capacity to pay the salaries of officials in time. The officials thus have little choice left but to do private work during their working time to earn more income. The educational system in Laos is the second constraint. This system cannot diversify the labor forces to deal with needed complex and in-depth technical knowledge. The last constraint is the patronage system and nepotism in the country. The interview information and Lao news implied that bribes are being paid in taking government positions. Ultimately, the Party's recruitment process cannot be viewed apart from the political clans inside the Party, which worsens the professionalization and the recruitment system in Laos.

To improve the state capacity to accomplish the development goals, moreover, the Lao government and the development partners formulated a development plan and strategies to diversify economic activities and labor forces, and to strengthen the good governance in the domestic institutions. The outcome of this development plan has led to development debates on two contemporary issues. These issues include the hydropower development in Laos, and Laos under the global pandemic and the graduation from the LDC status. I propose that these issues require the in-depth and comprehensive inclusion of diverse perspectives of Lao development stakeholders, at a certain time. However, I would not judge which development approach is right or wrong for Laos. Instead, this section will leave the question open for further study in Lao development.

Eventually, I address the question of the readiness of the Lao government to sustain the consequence of the graduation from the LDC status. The Lao government will both gain and lose some benefits after graduation. On the positive side, if the country is out of the LDC status, it implies the readiness of the country to become more self-reliant and independent from the development partners. On the other hand, Laos will lose the privilege of development assistance, the low-interest loan and exported product quota. Hence, I argue that the Party and the Lao government should not rush to push the country out of the LDC status unless the Lao state capacity to deal with its consequences is efficient enough. Even the efficiency in the state capacity takes time, I positively believe in what I often heard during the field trip in Laos that big changes can start with small steps.

BIBLIOGRAPHY

Asian Development Bank. (2006). *The Greater Mekong Subregion — Beyond Borders (2007–2009).* Retrieved September 15, 2018, from Asian Development Bank: https://www.adb.org/sites/default/files/institutional-document/32486/files/gms-rcspu-2006.pdf

Asian Development Bank. (2011). *Civil Society Briefs: Lao People's Democratic Republic.* Retrieved June 7, 2018, from https://www.adb.org/publications/civil-society-briefs-lao-peoples-democratic-republic

Asian Development Bank. (2015). *Lao People's Democratic Republic: Support for the Human Resource Development Strategy.* Retrieved November 23, 2018, from ADB: https://www.adb.org/sites/default/files/project-document/173734/46068–001-tacr.pdf

Asian Development Bank. (2016). *Governance and Capacity Development in Public Sector Management Program (RRP LAO 46059).* Retrieved October 14, 2018, from ADB: https://www.adb.org/sites/default/files/linked-documents/46059–001-lao-dc.pdf

Asian Development Bank. (2017). *Lao People's Democratic Republic, 2017–2020—More Inclusive and Sustainable Economic Growth.* Retrieved October 20, 2018, from ADB: https://www.adb.org/sites/default/files/institutional-document/360121/cps-lao-2017–2020.pdf

Almond, G., & Verba, S. (1963). *The Civic Culture: Political Attitudes and Democracy in Five Nations.* Newbury Park: Sage Publication.

ASEAN Today. (2018). *Thongloun Sisoulith's Losing Battle against Corruption.* Retrieved October 3, 2018, from ASEAN Today: https://www.aseantoday.com/2018/06/thongloun-sisouliths-losing-battle-against-corruption/

Asia Regional Integration Center. (1992). *Agreement on the Common Effective Preferential Tariff Scheme for the ASEAN Free Trade Area.* Retrieved August 28, 2018.

Baird, I., Shoemaker, B. P., & Manorom, K. (2015). The People and Their River, the World Bank and its Dam: Revisiting the Xe Bang Fai River in

Laos. *Development and Change, 46* (5), 1080–1105.

Bangkok Post. (2021). *Laos communist party holds leadership congress amid economic pain.* Retrieved January 14, 2022, from: https://www.bangkokpost.com/world/2050455/laos-communist-party-holds-leadership-congress-amid-economic-pain

Beach, D., & Peterson, R. B. (2013). *Process-Tracing Methods: Foundations and Guidelines.* Ann Arbor: University of Michigan Press.

Bennett, A., & Checkel, J. T. (2016). *Process Tracing: From Metaphor to Analytic Tool*. Cambridge: Cambridge University Press.

Blaikie, N. (2009). *Designing Social Research: The Logic of Anticipation* (2nd edition ed.) Cambridge, UK; Malden, MA: Polity Press

Bolesta, A. (2012). *China as a Post-Socialist Developmental State: Explaining Chinese Development Trajectory* . Retrieved March 9, 2018, from LSE Thesis Online: http://etheses.lse.ac.uk/536/

Bourdet, Y. (2002). Laos in 2001: Political introversion and economic respite. *Asian Survey*, vol. 42, no.1, 107–114.

Boute, V., & Pholsena, V. (2017). Introduction. In Boute, V. & Pholsena, V. (Eds.), *Changing Lives in Laos: Society, Politics, and Culture in a Post-Socialist State.* Singapore: NUS Press.

Brown, A. (2011). *The Rise and Fall of Communism.* New York: Ecco.

Brown, M. (1991). Communists in Coalition Government: Lessons from Laos. In Joseph J. Zasloff, & Leonard Unger (Eds.), *Laos: Beyond the Revolution* (pp. 41–66). New York: St. Martin Press.

Onxayvieng, C, et al., (2015). Public Service Improvement: A case study of One Door Service in Lao People Democratic Republic. *Journal of Public Administration and Governance*, 5 (1), 137–156.

Christie, C. (1982). Nationalism and the Pathet Lao. In M. Stuart-Fox (Ed.), *Contemporary Laos* (pp. 62–75). St.Lucia: University of Queenland Press.

Civil Society Consortium. (2015). *Civil Society Organizations (CSOs) in Laos.* Vientiane: Civil Society Consortium.

Committee for Economic Development. (2015). *Crony Capitalism.* Retrieved June 20, 2018, from Unhealthy Relations Between Business and Government: https://www.ced.org/pdf/Embargoed_Report_-_Crony_Capitalism.pdf

Creak, S. (2011). Laos: Celebrations and Development Debate. *Southeast Asian Affairs*, pp. 149–171.

Creak, S. (2014). Laos in 2013: International Controversies, Economic Concerns and the Post-Socialist Rhetoric of Rule . *Southeast Asian Affairs, 2014*, 149–171.

Croissant, A., & Lorenz, P. (2018). *Comparative Politics of Southeast Asia: An Introduction to Governments and Political Regimes.* Cham: Springer International Publishing.

CVCE. (2015, July 3). *Agreement on Ending the War and Restoring Peace in Vietnam (Paris, 27 January 1973).* Retrieved August 12, 2018, from CVCE: https://www.cvce.eu/content/publication/2001/10/12/656ccc0d-31ef-42a6-a3e9-ce5ee7d4fc80/publishable_en.pdf

Department of International Cooperation, Ministy of Planning and Investment, Lao PDR. (2016). *Background Document.* Vientiane: Ministry of Planning and Investment.

Dore, A. (1982). The Three Revolutions in Laos. In M. Stuart-Fox (Ed.), *Contemporary Laos* (pp. 101–115). St. Lucia: University of Queenland Press.

Easterly, W. (2006). *The White Man's Burden: Why the West's Efforts to Aid the Rest Have Done So Much Ill and So Little Good.* New York: Penguin Press.

Easterly, W. (2013). *The Tyranny of Experts: Economists, Dictators, and the Forgotten Rights of the Poor.* New York: Basic Books.

Edwars, R., & Holland, J. (2013). *What is qualitative interviewing?* London: Bloomsbury Academic. Retrieved from National Centre for Research Methods: http://eprints.ncrm.ac.uk/3276/1/complete_proofs.pdf

European Union. (2017). *Environmental Impact Assessment of Projects: Guidance on the preparation of the Environmental Impact.* Retrieved 10 15, 2018, from European Commisson: http://ec.europa.eu/environment/eia/pdf/EIA_guidance_EIA_report_final.pdf

European Commission. (2019). Everything but Arms (EBA). Retrieved June 4, 2021, from: https://trade.ec.europa.eu/access-to-markets/en/content/everything-arms-eba

Evans, G. (1995). *Lao: Peasants under Socialism & Post-Socialism.* Chiang Mai: Silkworm Books.

Evans, G. (1998). *Politics of Ritual and Remembrance Laos since 1975.* Hawai'i: University of Hawai'i Press.

Faure, G. (2010). The Asian Development Bank and Chinese and Japanese

Power Plays. In G. Faure (Ed.), *New Dynamics between China and Japan in Asia: How to Build the Future from the Past?* (pp. 173–185). Singapore: World Scientific Publishing.

Fukuyama, F. (2013). What is Governance? *Governance: An International Journal of Policy, Administration, and Institutions,* 3, pp. 347–368.

FIDH and LMHR. (2016). *Laos: Sham election cements one-party rule.* Retrieved June 30, 2018, from International Federation for Human Rights: https://www.fidh.org/IMG/pdf/20160317_laos_briefer_en.pdf

FAO. (2016). *Government aims to restore forest cover to 70 percent by 2020.* Retrieved October 20, 2018, from Food and Agriculture Organization of the United Nations: http://www.fao.org/laos/news/detail-events/en/c/454719/

Freedom House. (2018). *Laos Profile.* Retrieved November 1, 2018, from Freedom House: https://freedomhouse.org/report/freedom-world/2018/laos

Gans-Morse, J. (2004). Searching for Transitologists: Contemporary Theories of Post-Communist Transitions and the Myth of a Dominant Paradigm. *Post-Soviet Affairs, 20* (4), 320–349.

George, A. L., & Bennett, A. (2005). *Case Studies and Theory Development in the Social Sciences.* London: MIT Press.

Ghosh, N. (2016). *Chemicals are killing Laos' farmlands.* Retrieved October 7, 2018, from The Strait Times: https://www.straitstimes.com/asia/se-asia/chemicals-are-killing-laos-farmlands

Glassman, M, R,. *The new middle class and democracy in global perspective.* New York: St. Martin's; London: Macmillan, 1997.

Global Economic Symposium. (2014). *Escaping the Middle Income Trap.* Retrieved November 3, 2018, from Global Economic Symposium: https://www.global-economic-symposium.org/knowledgebase/escaping-the-middle-income-trap

Government of Lao PDR. (2015, December). *National Nutrition Strategy to 2025 and Plan of Action 2016–2020.* Retrieved September 25, 2018, from Country Planning Cycle Database: A World Health Organization Resource: http://www.nationalplanningcycles.org/sites/default/files/planning_cycle_repository/lao_peoples_democratic_republic/final_lao_version_nnspa_2016_matrix_updated_21_dec_2015_-_part_1_rta_-.pdf

Gunn, G. C. (2008). Laos in 2007: Regional Integration and International Fallout. *Asian Survey*, 48 (1), 62–68.

Haber, S. (2002). *Crony Capitalism and Economic Growth in Latin America: Theory and Evidence*. Washington, DC: Hoover Institution Press.

Harrison, D. (2016). *Tax Alert: Revised Tax Law Pending*. Retrieved November 28, 2018, from Arion Legal: http://arionlegal.la/revised-tax-law-pending/

Hartley, R. (2015). *Japan and the Greater Mekong Sub-region: Hegemony in the Making or Hegemony Already Established?* Retrieved September 29, 2018, from Tohoku University Repository: https://tohoku.repo.nii.ac.jp/index.php?action=pages_view_main&active_ action=repository_action_common_download&item_id=68855&item_no=1&attribute_id=18&file_no=1&page_id=33&block_id=38

High, H., & Petit, P. (2013). Introduction: The Study of the State in Laos. *Asian Studies Review*, 37 (4), 417–432.

Hlaing, K. T. (2006). Laos: The State of the State. *Southeast Asian Affairs*, pp. 127–147.

Holt, J., & Manning, N. (2014). Fukuyama Is Right about Measuring State Quality: Now What? *An International Journal of Policy, Administration, and Institutions,*, 27 (4), 717–728.

Howe, B. (2018). *National Security, Statecentricity, and Governance in East Asia*. New York: Palgrave Macmillan.

Howe, B. M., & Park, S. (2015). Laos: The Danger of Developmentalism. *Southeast Asian Affairs, 2015*, 165–185.

Hulme, D. (2015). *Global Poverty: How Global Governance is Failing the Poor People in the Post-2015 Era* (2nd Edition ed.). New York: Routledge.

Human Right Watch. (2017). *Laos: No Progress on Rights*. Retrieved October 3, 2018, from Human Right Watch: https://www.hrw.org/news/2017/07/17/laos-no-progress-rights

Hunt, J. (2012). Aid and Development. In D. Kingsbury, J. McKay, J. Hunt, M. McGillivray, & M. Clarke (Eds.), *International Development: Issues and Challenges* (2nd Edition ed., pp. 79–111). Hampshire: Palgrave Macmillan.

Hunt, L. (2017). *New Guard, Old Problems: What Sombath Somphone's Continued Disappearance Says About Rights in Lao*. Retrieved June 20, 2018, from The Diplomat: https://thediplomat.com/2017/12/new-guard-old-problems-what-sombath-somphones-continued-disappearance-says-about-rights-in-laos/

Huntington, S. P. (1991). *The Third Wave: Democratization in the Late Twentieth Century.* University of Oklahoma Press.

Hutt, D. (2017a). *Little Laos Tackles Big Corruption.* Retrieved October 4, 2018, from Asian Times: http://www.atimes.com/article/little-laos-tackles-big-corruption/

Hutt, D. (2017b). *Is Laos' New Leader Really a Reformer?* Retrieved November 21, 2018, from The Diplomat: https://thediplomat.com/2017/04/is-laos-new-leader-really-a-reformer/

Hutt, D. (2018a). *Beware the Destruction of Civil Society in Laos.* Retrieved June 1, 2018, from The Diplomat: https://thediplomat.com/2018/01/beware-the-destruction-of-civil-society-in-laos/

Hutt, D. (2018b). *How Worried Should Laos Be About Its Debt Problems?: The issues poses significant challenges for the Southeast Asian state's future trajectory.* Retrieved November 6, 2018, from The Diplomat: https://thediplomat.com/2018/07/how-worried-should-laos-be-about-its-debt-problems/

ICF Monitor. (2014). *Market Snapshot: Laos.* Retrieved October 20, 2018, from ICF Monitor: http://monitor.icef.com/2014/09/market-snapshot-laos/

Inglehart, R., & Welzel, C. (2009). *How Development Leads to Democracy.* Retrieved September 20, 2018, from Foreign Affairs: https://www.foreignaffairs.com/articles/2009–03–01/how-development-leads-democracy

International Rivers. (2018, July 30). *Save the Mekong Statement on the Collapse of the Xe Pian—Xe Nam Noy Hydropower Project.* Retrieved September 10, 2018, from International Rivers: https://www.internationalrivers.org/resources/save-the-mekong-statement-on-the-collapse-of-the-xe-pian-xe-nam-noy-hydropower-project

Ivarsson, S. (2008). Creating Laos: The Making of a Lao Space between Indochina and Siam, 1860–1945. Copenhagen: NIAS Press.

Ivarsson, S. & Gosha, C. (2007). Prince Phetsarath (1890–1959): Nationalism and Royality in the Making of Modern Lao. *Journal of Southeast Asian Studies* 38(01), 55–81.

Ives, M., & Paddock, R. C. (2018). *In Laos, a Boom, and Then, 'The Water Is Coming!'.* Retrieved November 21, 2018, from The New York Times: https://www.nytimes.com/2018/07/25/world/asia/laos-dam-collapse-rescue.html

J&C Laos. (2017). *Government To Limit Number Of Civil Servants.* Retrieved October 15, 2018, from J&C Laos: http://jclao.com/government-to-limit-number-of-civil-servants/

Ka Xouang Kan Ngeun. (2018). *Chod May Het: Sa Rup Kan Chod Tang Patibat Lai Hap Lai Chay Ngop Paman Heng Lat Sok Pee 2015–2016* . Retrieved August 10, 2018, from Ministry of Finance: https://www.mof.gov.la/

Kana Kosana Aob Hom Soun Kang Pak. (2015). *Hoksip Pee Pak Paxaxon Pativad Lao.* Vien Chan: Kana Kosana Aob Hom Soun Kang Pak.

Keomixay, D. (2017). *Value Added Tax in Lao PDR: Agenda for the Future.* Retrieved October 16, 2018, from Ministry of Finance, Japan: https://www.mof.go.jp/pri/international_exchange/visiting_scholar_program/Keomixay2.pdf

Khennavong, P. (2014). *Aid to Laos in the Twenty-First Century: Engagement and Change.* Crawford School of Public Policy Australian National University .

Kikuchi, Y. (2017). *Japanese Involvement in Laos: From the Invasion of the Japanese Army in Northern French Indochina in 1940 to the End of World War Two.* Retrieved August 14, 2018, from Waseda University Repository: https://waseda.repo.nii.ac.jp/?action=pages_view_main&active_action=repository_view_main_item_detail&item_id=39274&item_no=1&page_id=13&block_id=21

Kollmorgen, R. (2013). Theories of Postcommunist Transformation. Approaches, Debates, and Problems of Theory Building in the Second Decade of Research . *Studies of Transition States and Societies,* 5 (2), 88–105.

Kuo, L., & Kommenda, N. (2018). *What is China's Belt and Road Initiative?* Retrieved October 2, 2018, from The Guardian: https://www.theguardian.com/cities/ng-interactive/2018/jul/30/what-china-belt-road-initiative-silk-road-explainer

Langer, P. F., & Zarloff, J. J. (1970). *North Vietnam And The Pathet Lao: Partners in the Struggle for Laos.* Cambridge: Harvard University Press.

Civil Society Woring Group. (2017). Decree on Association 2017 (Unofficial English translation), Retrieved October 6, 2019, from the laocs-kis.org: https://laocs-kis.org/resources/decree-association-2017-unofficial-english-translation/?fbclid=IwAR1B4zPxXOUSz5NlVQqQQ8shJhWNkQAFIeDsfu716_i0OekkbkHwfLxx_WM

Lao PDR. (2004). *National Growth and Poverty Eradication Strategy* . Retrieved November 25, 2018, from IMF: https://www.imf.org/external/pubs/ft/scr/2004/cr04393.pdf

Lao PDR. (2015). *Vientiane Declaration on Partnership for Effective Development Cooperation (2016–2025).* Retrieved August 1, 2016, from Lao People's Democratic Republic National Round Table Process: https://rtm.org.la/wp-content/uploads/formidable/Vientiane-Partnership-Declaration.pdf

Lao PDR and UNDP (2021). *Socio-economic Impact Assessment of Covid-19 on Lao PDR.* Retrived December 10, 2021, from https://laopdr.un.org/sites/default/files/2021–04/UN%20Lao%20PDR%20SEIA%20COVID-19_EnglishFA2web.pdf

Laotian Times. (2017). *Cash Will No Longer Be Accepted for Tax Payments in Laos.* Retrieved November 28, 2018, from Laotian Times: https://laotiantimes.com/2017/04/29/cash-no-longer-accepted-tax-payments/

Laotian Times. (2018). *PM: Laos Won't Graduate From Least Developed Country Status by 2020.* Retrieved November 20, 2018, from Laotian Times: https://laotiantimes.com/2018/06/11/laos-not-graduate-least-developed-country/

Larrabure, et al. (2014). *GPAR Assessment and Concept Development, Lao PDR.* Retrieved October 2, 2018, from Multi-Partner Trust Fund Office, UNDP: http://mptf.undp.org/document/download/18028

Le Hong Hiep. (2012). Performance-based Legitimacy: The Case of the Communist Party of Vietnam and "Doi Moi". *Contemporary Southeast Asia*, 34(2), 145–172. Retrieved from http://www.jstor.org/stable/41756339.

Lintner, B. (2008). Laos: At the Crossroads. *Southeast Asian Affairs,* pp. 171–183 .

Linz, J. J., & Stephan, A. (1996). *Problems of Democratic Transition and Consolidation: Southern Europe, South America, and Post-Communist Europe.* London: The John Hopkins University Press.

Mann, M. (1984). The Autonomous Power of the State: Its Origins, Mechanism and Result. *European Journal of Sociology, 25* (2), 185–213.

Maierbrugger, A. (2012). *Laos To Set Up 41 Special Economic Zones.* Retrieved August 10, 2018, from Investvine: Southeast Asia's Business News Site: http://investvine.com/laos-to-set-up-41-special-economic-zones/

Mike Ives. (2018). *Laos Dam Failure Exposes Cracks in a Secretive Government's*

Agenda. Retrieved November 1, 2018, from The New York Times: https://www.nytimes.com/2018/07/29/world/asia/laos-dam-response-government.html

Minh, H. C. (1968). *On revolution: selected writings, 1920 - 66*. (H. C. Minh, Ed., & B. B. Fall, Trans.) New York: New American Library.

Ministry of Agriculture and Forestry. (2015). *Agriculture Development Strategy to 2025 and Vision to the Year 2030*. Retrieved September 25, 2018, from Ministry of Agriculture and Forestry: http://www.maf.gov.la/wp-content/uploads/2016/01/MDS-2025-and-Vision-to-2030-Eng.pdf

Ministry of Finance. (2018). *State Budget Implementation Fiscal Year 2015–2016*. Retrieved October 15, 2018, from Ministry of Finance: http://www.mof.gov.la/sites/default/files/docs/budget/2015–2016(English).pdf

Ministry of Finance. (n.d.). *Vision to 2030 and Public Finance Development Strategy to 2025*. Retrieved from Ministry of Finance, Lao PDR: https://www.mof.gov.la/wp-content/uploads/2018/11/6

Ministry of Foreign Affairs of Japan. (2016). *The Japan-Lao PDR Joint DevelopmentCooperationPlanfortheSustainableDevelopmentofLaoPDR*. Retrieved October 6, 2019, from the mofa.go.jp: https://www.mofa.go.jp/ic/cap1/page22e_000791.html?fbclid=IwAR1pi7sXqEWd4eH2HbZdIZoZkYxGdpfBxQXJ1WQaIbDFqWqfZXm0ZtrGMis

Ministry of Home Affairs. (2017). *Decree on Association 2017 (Unofficial English translation)*. Retrieved August 12, 2018, from Lao Civil Society Knowledge and Information System: https://laocs-kis.org/wp-content/uploads/2017/11/English-translation-of-Decree-238-on-Association-002.docx

Ministry of Home Affairs. (2018). Law on Civil Servant 2003. Retrieved November 20, 2018, from Ministry of Home Affairs: www.moha.gov.la

Ministry of Planning and Investment. (2016a). *8th Five-Year National Socio-Economic Development Plan (2016–2020)*. Retrieved September 17, 2018, from UNDP: http://www.la.one.un.org/images/publications/8th_NSEDP_2016–2020.pdf

Ministry of Planning and Investment. (2016b). *Progree Report of Sector Working Group*. Vientiane: Departmet of International Cooperation, Ministry of Planning and Investment.

Ministry of Planning and Investment. (2016c). *Foreign Aid Implementation*

Report (FAIR) Fiscal Year 2015/16. Retrieved November 2, 2018, from Lao People's Democratic Republic National Round Table Process: https://rtm.org.la/wp-content/uploads/2017/01/8-FAIR-2016.pdf

Ministry of Planning and Investment & UNDP. (2017). Graduation From Least Developed Country Status Lao PDR, 2017. Vientiane, Lao PDR: Ministry of Planning and Investment, and United Nations Development Programme in Lao PDR.

Mocci, N. (2016). Laos 2016: The 10th congress of the Lao People's Revolutionary Party (LPRP) and its domestic and international aftermath. *Asia Maior*, 221–224

National Assembly. (2013). *Law on Local Administration of the Lao People's Democratic Republic*. Retrieved June 19, 2018, from Vientiane Times: http://www.vientianetimes.org.la/Laws%20in%20English/49.%20Law%20on%20Local%20Administration%20(2003)%20Eng.pdf

National Assembly. (2004). *Law on Development and Protect Women*. Retrieved September 30, 2018, from International Labour Organization: http://www.ilo.org/dyn/travail/docs/1425/Law%20on%20the%20Development%20and%20Protection%20of%20Women%202004.pdf

National Assembly. (2015). *Constitution of Lao People's Democratic Republic (Revised 2015)*. Retrieved June 19, 2018, from National Reform Steering Assembly of Thailand: https://www.parliament.go.th/ewtadmin/ewt/ac/ewt_dl_link.php?nid= 119&filename=parsystem2

National Commission for Advancement Women. (2015). *Summary Report: A Study on Violence against Women in Lao PDR*. Retrieved October 20, 2018, from UNDP: http://www.la.one.un.org/images/publications/Lao_PDR_Violence_Against_Women_Summary_Report.pdf

O'Donnell, G., & Schmitter, P. C. (1986). *Transition from Authoritarian Rule: Tentative Conclusions about Uncertain Democracies*. Baltimore: The John Hopkins University Press.

Onphanhdala, P., & Suraga, T. (2013). *Chinese Outward FDI in Agriculture and Rural Development: Evidence from Northern Laos*. Retrieved October 9, 2018, from Graduate School of International Cooperation Studies, Kobe University: http://www.research.kobe-u.ac.jp/gsics-publication/gwps/2013–25.pdf

Organisation for Economic Co-operation and Development. (2011). Busan Partnership for Effective Development Co-operation. Retrieved October

6, 2019, from the oecd.org: https://www.oecd.org/dac/effectiveness/49650173.pdf?fbclid=IwAR0eJAXL46rPVlb9EGsfrra2yfxFUHbCpBV1siB3nLKXH-g0R42hFojTwT4

Pak Pasason Pativad Lao. (2016). *Kong Praxum Yai Khang Thee X Khong Pak Pasaxon Pativad Lao* . Vieng Chan: Xam Nak Pim Le Cham Nai Pum Heng Lat.

Palma, G. D. (1991). Legitimation from the Top to Civil Society: Politico-Cultural Change in Eastern Europe . *World Politics,* 44 (01), 49–80.

Parson, T. (1951). *The Social System.* London: Free Press of Glencoe.

PEFA. (2016). *History.* Retrieved October 29, 2018, from PEFA: https://pefa.org/content/history

Paik, C., & Vechabanyongratana, J. (2018). Mandala matters: Former tributary states and modern civil society conflict in Thailand. Retrived July 16, 2021, from: https://www.eh.net/eha/wp-content/uploads/2018/06/Vechbanyongratana.pdf

Penumetcha, S. (2016). *Democratic Governance: Unlocking the Keys to the SDG Agenda.* Retrieved August 30, 2018, from Centre for Internationa Private Enterprise: https://www.cipe.org/blog/2016/09/21/democratic-governance-unlocking-the-keys-to-the-sdg-agenda/

Phimphanthavong, H. (2012). Economic Reform and Regional Development of Laos. *Modern Economy* (3), 179–186.

Pholsena, V. & Banomyong R. (2005). LAOS IN 2004: Towards Subregional Integration: 10 Years on. *Southeast Asian Affairs,* 173–188.

Pholsena, V. (2006). *Post-War Laos: The Political of Culture, History and Identity.* Chiang Mai: Silkworm Books.

Phomvihane, K. (1985). Sip Pee Heng Kan Kosang Pak Lae Xao Pee Heng Kan To Sou Pativad. In K. K. Pak, *Ni Phon Luak Fen 1.* Vieng Chan.

Phraxayavong, V. (2009). *History of Aid to Laos: Motivations and Impacts.* Chiang Mai: Mekong Press.

Porter, I. C., & Shivakumar, J. (2010). *Doing a Dam Better: The Lao People's Democratic Republic and the Story of Nam Theun 2.* Retrieved October 10, 2018, from The World Bank: http://documents.worldbank.org/curated/en/200041468044952974/pdf/584400PUB0ID161Better09780821369852.pdf

Prime Minister's Office. (2010). *Decree on Special Economic Zone and Specific Economic Zone in the Lao PDR* . Retrieved June 14, 2018, from World

Trade Organization: https://www.wto.org/english/thewto_e/acc_e/lao_e/WTACCLAO20A1_LEG_3.pdf

Radio Free Asia. (2016). *Obama to Make, and Face, History in Laos*. Retrieved 10 15, 2018, from Radio Free Asia: https://www.rfa.org/english/news/laos/obama-to-make-and-face-history-in-laos-09022016152317.html

Radio Free Asia. (2017). *Salary Delays Slow Government Work in Laos*. Retrieved October 16, 2018, from Radio Free Asia: https://www.rfa.org/english/news/laos/delays-01062017142322.html

Radio Free Asia. (2018). *Civil Society Groups in Laos Delayed Funding, Forced to Disband Under New Law*. Retrieved June 19, 2018, from Radio Free Asia: https://www.rfa.org/english/news/laos/csos-01242018122715.html

Rathie, M. (2017). The History and Evoluion of the Lao People's Revolutionary Party. In V. Pholsena, & V. Boute (Eds.), *Changing Lives in Laos: Society, Politics, and Culture in a Post-Socialist State* (pp. 19–55). Singapore: NUS Press.

Rehbein, B. (2007). *Globalization, Culture and Society in Laos*. London: Routledge.

Rehbein, B. (2016). Democracy and Middle Class in Laos. In C. B. Wangaeo, B. Rehbein, & S.

Rehbein, B. (2017). *Society in Contemporary Laos: Capitalism, Habitus and Belief*. New York: Routledge.

Reporters without Borders. (2016). *Our Value*. Retrieved November 1, 2018, from Reporters without Borders: https://rsf.org/en/our-values

Rigby, H. T. (1982). Introduction: Political Legitimacy, Weber and Communist Mono-organisational Systems. In Rigby, H. T and Feher, F. (Eds), Political Legitimation in Communist States. London: The Macmillan Press.

Richards, D. (1996). Elite Interviewing: Approaches and Pitfalls. *Politics*, 16(3), 199–204.

Ruane, K. (1995). *War and Revolution in Vietnam, 1930–1975*. London: Routhledge.

Sachs, J. (2012). From Millennium Development Goals to Sustainable Development Goals. *The Lancet*, *379*, 2206–2211.

Sachs, J. (2015). *The Age of Sustainable Development*. New York: Columbia University Press.

Sachs, J. D. (2005). *The End of Poverty: How We Can Make It Happen in Our Lifetime*. London: Penguin Books.

Santi. (2018). *Nayok Nen Tong Han Pien Kan Dam Hong Se Vit Bab Kin Ngay You Ngay Kay Pen Kheng Khan Lae Pattana*. Retrieved October 7, 2018, from Lao Edaily: https://laoedaily.com.la/30918/

Sapha Heng Xat. (2015a). *Kod May Wa Douay Souay Akon*. Retrieved October 15, 2018, from National Assembly: http://www.na.gov.la/files/laws

Sapha Heng Xat. (2015b). *Kod May Va Douay Ngop Paman Heng Lat*. Retrieved October 14, 2018, from The National Assembly: http://www.na.gov.la/files/laws/

Sapha Heng Xat. (2015c). *Kod May Wa Douay Pha Nak Ngan - Lat Ta Kon*. Retrieved October 18, 2018, from National Assembly: http://www.na.gov.la/files/laws/

Sapha Heng Xat. (2016). *Kod May Wa Douay Kan Kouad Sop Heng Lat*. Retrieved October 15, 2018, from State Audit Organization: http://sao.gov.la/law

Sapha Heng Xat. (2017). *Kod May Wa Douay Fay Fa*. Retrieved November 1, 2018, from National Assembly: http://www.na.gov.la/files/laws/elec tric_law.pdf

Saxonberg, S. (2013). *Transitions and Non-transitions from Communism: Regime Survival in China, Cuba, North Korea and Vietnam* . Cambridge: Cambridge University Press.

Sayalath, S., & Creak, S. (2017). Regime Renewal in Laos: The Tenth Congress of the Lao People's Revolutionary Party. *Southeast Asian Affairs 2017*, 179–196.

Scott, J. C. (1972). Patron-Client Politics and Political Change in Southeast Asia. *The American Political Science Review*, 66 (1), 91–113.

Sengdara, S. (2015). *Party meetings hightlight authority, sector achievement* . Retrieved September 17, 2016, from Vientiane Times: www.vientiane times. org.la/Freecon tent / FreeConten_party.htm

Shleifer, A. (1997). Government in Transition. *European Economic Review*, 41, pp. 385–410.

SIDA. (2003). *Governance and Participation in Laos*. Retrieved October 2, 2018, from Sida: https://www.sida.se/contentassets/136b3ec257224f139 b85f926bccd4e48/governance-and-participation-in-laos_577.pdf

Skocpol, T. (1985). Bringing the State Back In: Strategies of Analysis in Current Research. In P. B. Evans, D. Rueschemeyer, & T. Skocpol (Eds.),

Bringing the State Back in (pp. 3–37). Cambridge: Cambridge University Press.

Smith, J. & Gladstein, A. (2018). *How the UN's Sustainable Development Goals undermine democracy.* Retrieved August 30, 2018, from Qaurtz Africa: https://qz.com/africa/1299149/how-the-uns-sustainable-development-goals-undermine-democracy/

Sotheary, P. (2018). *Activists push for Pak Lay Dam studies.* Retrieved November 21, 2018, from The Khmer Times: https://www.khmertimeskh.com/50535755/activists-push-for-pak-lay-dam-studies/

Soukamneuth, B. (2006). *The Political Economy of Transition in Laos: From Peripheral Socialism to the Margins of Global Capital.* Retrieved August 8, 2015, from Cornell University: https://ecommons.cornell.edu/bitstream/handle/1813/3430/The %20Political%20Economy%20of%20Transition%20in%20Laos.pdf?sequence=1&isAllowed=y

Souksavanh, O. (2016). *Lao Politburo Forces Officials to Give Up Their Luxury Cars.* Retrieved 11 20, 2018, from Radio Free Asia: https://www.rfa.org/english/news/laos/lao-politburo-forces-12302016143614.html

Southichack, M. (2017). *LDC Status Graduation, the Ways Forward for Lao PDR.* Retrieved November 24, 2018, from The UNESCAP: https://www.unescap.org/sites/default/files/Lao%20PDR%20LDC%20Graduation%20PPT-revised-MSouthichack.pdf

Stuart-Fox, M. (1986). Laos in 1985: Time to take stock. *Southeast Asian Affairs,* 1986, 165–181.

Stuart-Fox, M. (1995). Laos: Towards Subregional Integration. *Southeast Asian Affairs*, pp. 177–195.

Stuart-Fox, M. (1996). *Buddhist Kingdom Marxist State: The Making of Modern Laos.* Bangkok: White Lotus.

Stuart-Fox, M. (1997a). *A History of Laos.* Cambridge: Cambridge University Press.

Stuart-Fox, M. (1997b). Laos in 1997: Into ASEAN. *Asian Survey,* 38 (1), pp. 75–79.

Stuart-Fox, M. (2005). *Politics and Reform in the Lao People's Democratic Republic.* Retrieved September 30, 2016, from Murdoch University: https://www.murdoch.edu.au/Research-capabilities/Asia-Research-Centre/_document/working-papers/wp126.pdf

Stuart-Fox, M. (2009). Laos: The Chinese Connection. *Southeast Asian Affairs*, pp. 141–169.

Szelenyi, I. (2016). Weber's Theory of Domination and Post-communist Capitalisms. *Theory and Society*, 45, 1–24.

Tan, D. (2014). *China in Laos: Is There Cause For Worry?* Retrieved September 13, 2018, from The Institute of Southeast Asian Studies: https://www.iseas.edu.sg/images/pdf/ISEAS_Perspective_2014_31.pdf

Tani, S. (2018). *Laos 'not concerned' about debt from China's Belt and Road: Prime Minister downplays fiscal risk from $5.8bn high-speed rail project.* Retrieved November 6, 2018, from Nikkei Asian Review: https://asia.nikkei.com/Spotlight/The-Future-of-Asia-2018/Laos-not-concerned-about-debt-from-China-s-Belt-and-Road

Tappe, O. (2017). Shaping the National Topography: The Party-State, National Imageries, and Question of Political Authority in Lao PDR. In V. Boute, & V. Pholsena (Eds.), *Changing Lives in Laos: Society, Politics, and Culture in a Post-Socialist State* (pp. 56–80). Singapore: NUS Press.

Thang, N. X. (2018). *Ho Chi Minh's thought on the Vietnamese revolution, and Kaysone Phomvihane's thought on the Lao revolution.* Retrieved September 4, 2018 from Political Theory: *Research Joutnal and Scien tific Voice of Ho Chi Minh National Academy of Politcs*: http://lyluanchinhtri.vn/home/en/index.php/theory-research/item/529-ho-chi-minh%E2%80%99s-thought-on-the-vietnamese-revolutionand-kaysone-phomvihane%E2%80%99s-thought-on-the-lao-revolution.html

Thayer, C. A. (1983). Laos in 1982: The Third Congress on the Lao People's Revolutionary Party. *Asian Survey, 23* (1), 84–93.

The ASEAN Post Team. (2018). *Lao PDR's Battle Against Corruption.* Retrieved 11 20, 2018, from The ASEAN Post: https://theaseanpost.com/article/lao-pdrs-battle-against-corruption

The ASEAN Post. (2018). *Lao's Controversial Hydro Ambitions.* Retrieved November 2, 2018, from The ASEAN Post: https://theaseanpost.com/article/laos-controversial-hydro-ambitions

The Japan Times. (2000). *Aid-funded Laos Bridge Open.* Retrieved September 29, 2018, from The Japan Times: https://www.japantimes.co.jp/news/2000/08/03/national/aid-funded-laos-bridge-open/#.W4aqHZP7SgQ

The Lao National Institute of Social Science and Humanities. (2011). *Sa Roup*

25 Pee Kan Pien Paeng Mai Yoo Sor Por Por Lao (1986–2010). N.P.

The Laotian Times. (2017). *Audit Uncovers Over One Trillion kip of Unauthorized Spending.* Retrieved October 4, 2018, from The Laotian Times: https://laotiantimes.com/2017/10/19/audit-uncovers-one-trillion-kip-unauthorized-spending/

The Nation. (2016a). *Energy Sector to be 'Big Contributor to Laos' GDP'.* Retrieved November 1, 2018, from The Nation: http://www.nationmultimedia.com/detail/asean-plus/30298657

The Nation. (2016b). *Laos Prohibits New Banana Plantations.* Retrieved September 5, 2018, from The Nation: http://www.nationmultimedia.com/detail/aec/30299906

The Nation. (2018). *Power Failure in the 'Battery of Asia'.* Retrieved November 21, 2018, from: http://www.nationmultimedia.com/detail/opinion/30350924

The New York Times. (2016). *Obama Acknowledges Scars of America's Shadow War in Laos.* Retrieved August 28, 2018, from The New York Times: https://www.nytimes.com/2016/09/07/world/asia/obama-laos-bombs-war.html

The Redd Desk. (2010). *Strategy on Climate Change of the Lao PDR.* Retrieved October 1, 2018, from The Redd Desk: https://theredddesk.org/countries/policies/strategy-climate-change-lao-pdr

The Strait Times. (2019). Victims of Xe Pian-Xe Namnoy dam Collapse in Laos Languish in Shelters as Aid, Supplies Dry Up. Retrieved January 29, 2019, from The Strait Times: https://www.straitstimes.com/asia/se-asia/victims-of-xe-pian-xe-namnoy-dam-collapse-in-laos-languish-in-shelters-as-aid-supplies

The Strait Times. (2018). *Lao PM's Call for 'Open Doors, Minds and Barriers' is Opportunity for Change.* Retrieved October 5, 2019, from the straits times: https://www.straitstimes.com/asia/se-asia/lao-pms-call-for-open-doors-minds-and-barriers-is-opportunity-for-change-vientiane?fbclid=IwAR24p7iy69HeD68idqn4QsjcndJ8dMICPrfnw OaAiJ9iyoV Tf9XkjjaJvfs

The White House President Barack Obama. (2016). *Joint Declaration between the United States of America and the Lao People's Democratic Republic.* Retrieved September 12, 2018, from The White House President Barack Obama: https://obamawhitehouse.archives.gov/the-press-office/2016/09/06/joint-declaration-between-united-states-america-and-lao-peoples

Transparency International. (2018). *Laos*. Retrived October 20, 2018 from: https://www.transparency.org/en/cpi/2021/index/lao

Time Reporter. (2015). *President's speech on the 40th anniversary of Lao National Day*. Retrieved June 20, 2018, from Vientiane Times: www.vientianetimes.org.la

Tommasoli, M. (2012). Rule of Law and Democracy: Addressing the Gap Between Policies and Practices. *UN Chronicle*, *XLIX* (4).

Trading Economy. (2019). *Lao Government Budget*. Retrieved October 15, 2018, from Trading Economy: https://tradingeconomics.com/laos/government-budget

U.S. Department of State. (2018). *Lower Mekong Initiative*. Retrieved August 28, 2018, from U.S. Department of State: https://www.state.gov/p/eap/mekong/

UNDP. (2006). *Vientiane Declaration on Aid Effectiveness*. Retrieved September 4, 2018, from UNDP Lao PDR: http://www.la.undp.org/content/dam/lao pdr/docs/Reports%20and%20publications/UNDP_LA_Vientiane%20 Declaration_finalJune07.pdf

UNDP. (2012). *The Lao Development Journey toward Graduation from LDC Status*. Retrieved November 2, 2018, from UNDP: http://www.la.one.un.org/images/publications/UNDP_LA_LDC_Pamphlet_2012_EN.pdf

UNDP. (2016). *Lao PDR - United Nations Partnership Framework 2017–2021: A Partnership for Sustainable Development*. Retrieved October 2, 2018, from UNDP: http://www.la.one.un.org/images/publications/LaoPDR_UNPF-FINAL-22082016_web.pdf

UNDP. (2017a). *Human Development Report 2016: Human Development for Everyone*. Retrieved April 3, 2018, from UNDP: http://www.la.undp.org/content/dam/laopdr/docs/Reports%20and%20publications/2017/HDR16%20Report.pdf

UNDP. (2017b). *Lao PDR—United Nations Partnership Framework 2017–2021 Progress Report 2017*. Retrieved October 15, 2018, from UNDP: http://www.la.one.un.org/images/publications/UNPF-ProgReport-2017_web.pdf

UNDP. (2018a). *Lao PDR's eligibility for graduation from LDC status confirmed*. Retrieved November 2, 2018, from UNDP: http://www.la.undp.org/content/lao_pdr/en/home/presscenter/pressreleases/2018/3/19/lao-pdr_s-eligibility-for-graduation-from-least-developed-countr.html

UNDP. (2018b). *As Lao PDR prepares for LDC Graduation, inequality has to be overcome*. Retrieved November 3, 2018, from UNDP: http://www.la.undp.org/content/lao_pdr/en/home/presscenter/pressreleases/2018/10/as-lao-pdr-prepares-for-ldc-graduation--inequality-has-to-be-ove.html

UNDP. (2018c). *Human Development Reports*. Retrieved December 20, 2018, from UNDP: http://hdr.undp.org/en/composite/HDI

UNDP. (2018d). *Goal 5: Gender Equality*. Retrieved September 30, 2018, from UNDP: http://www.la.undp.org/content/lao_pdr/en/home/sustainable-development-goals/goal-5-gender-equality.html

UNDP. (2018e). *Goal 2: Zero Hunger*. Retrieved September 20, 2018, from UNDP: http://www.la.undp.org/content/lao_pdr/en/home/sustainable-development-goals/goal-2-zero-hunger.html

UNDP. (2018f). *Goal 15: Life on Land*. Retrieved September 30, 2018, from UNDP: http://www.la.one.un.org/sdgs/sdg-15-life-on-land

UNDP. (2018g). *Goal 13: Climate Action*. Retrieved September 30, 2018, from UNDP: http://www.la.one.un.org/sdgs/sdg-13-climate-action

UNDP. (2018h). *Goal 1: No Poverty*. Retrieved September 30, 2018, from UNDP: http://www.la.undp.org/content/lao_pdr/en/home/sustainable-development-goals/goal-1-no-poverty.html

UNDP. (2020). *Lao People's Democratic Republic*. Retrieved June 12, 2021, from UNDP: http://hdr.undp.org/sites/default/files/Country-Profiles/LAO .pdf

UNESCO. (2018). *Lao People's Democratic Republic*. Retrieved October 20, 2018, from UNESCO: http://uis.unesco.org/country/LA

United Nations. (2015a). *The Millennium Development Goals Report*. Retrieved September 22, 2016, from The United Nations: http://www.un.org/millenniumgoals/2015_MDG_Report/pdf/MDG%202015%20rev%20(July %201).pdf

United Nations. (2015b). *Discussion Paper: The Sustainable Development Goals in the context of the Lao People's Democratic Republic*. Retrieved October 3, 2018, from United Nations in Lao PDR: http://www.la.one.un.org/images/publications/SDG_adaptation_to_Lao_PDR.pdf

United Nations. (2015c). *Handbook on the Least Developed Country Category: Inclusion, Graduation and Special Support Measures*. Retrieved February 19, 2018, from The United Nations: http://www.un.org/en/development/desa/policy/cdp/cdp_publications/ 2015cdphandbook.pdf

United Nations. (2015d). *Sustainable Development Goals.* Retrieved August 20, 2016, from The United Nations: http://www.un.org/sustainabledevel opmentp/sustainable-development-goals/

United Nations. (2015e). *Paris Agreement.* Retrieved October 2, 2018, from UN Climate Change: https://unfccc.int/sites/default/files/english_paris_ agreement.pdf

UN-OHRLLS. (2006). *Brussels Programme of Action: Addressing the needs of Least Developed Countries.* Retrieved October 10, 2018, from UN-OHRLLS: http://unohrlls.org/UserFiles/File/Publications/bpoa.pdf

UN-OHRLLS. (2018). *Criteria for Identification and Graduation of LDCs.* Retrieved November 26, 2018, from UN-OHRLLS: http://unohrlls.org/ about-ldcs/criteria-for-ldcs/

US Embassy in Laos. (2016). *Laos signs the Paris Agreement on Climate Change in New York.* Retrieved October 1, 2018, from US Embassy in Laos: https://la.usembassy.gov/laos-signs-paris-agreement-climate-change-n ew-york/

Vaenkeo, S. (2015). *Economic growth tops NA development debate.* Retrieved June 20, 2018, from Vientiane Times: www.vientianetimes.org.la

Vientiane Times. (2015). *Laos Marks 40 Years of National Pride.* Retrieved November 9, 2016, from Embassy of Lao People's Democratic Republic in United States of America: http://laoembassy.com/Lao%20PDR%20 Marks%20the%2040%20Founding%20Anniversary%20of%20its%20 Founding.pdf

Vientiane Times. (2016a). *Violence against Women a 'Hidden Scourge' in Laos.* Retrieved 09 29, 2018, from Asia News Network: http://www.asianews. eu/content/violence-against-women-%E2%80%98hidden-scour ge%E2%80%99-laos-11289

Vientiane Time. (2016b). *Laos enjoys political stability, strong economic growth, parliament told.* Retrieved 11 15, 2018, from Asia News Network: http://www.asianews.eu/content/laos-enjoys-political-stability-strong-economic-growth-parliament-told-14919

Vientiane Times. (2016c). *Sustainable Development Goals Spur Progress in Laos* . Retrieved September 26, 2016, from Vientiane Times: http://www. vientianetimes.org.la /FreeContent/FreeConten_Sustainable224.htm

Vientiane Times. (2018a). *Quality Infrastrucutre Proving Useful, Effective,*

PM says in Japan. Retrieved October 10, 2018, from The Vientiane Times: http://www.vientianetimes.org.la/freeContent/FreeConten_Quality237.php

Vientiane Times. (2018b). *Govt slashes 2019 civil servant intake by half*. Retrieved November 30, 2018, from Vientiane Times: http://vientianetimes.org.la/freeContent/FreeConten_Govt278.php

Vilaysack, S. (2018). *Humanitarian assistance vital to sustain flood victims*. Retrieved 8 29, 2018, from Vientiane Times: http://www.vientianetimes.org.la/sub-new/Opinion/Opinion_Humanitarian180.php

Vu, T. (2010). *Paths to development in Asia: South Korea, Vietnam, China, and Indonesia*. Cambridge: Cambridge University Press.

Walder, A. (1995). China's Transitional Economy: Interpreting Its Significance. *The China Quarterly*, 144 (Special Issue: China Transitional Economy), 963–969.

Wan, M. (1995). Japan and the Asian Development Bank. Pacific Affairs, University of British Columbia, Vol. 68, No. 4 (Winter, 1995–1996), pp. 509–528.

Warr, P., Menon, J., & Rasphone, S. (2015). Public Services and the Poor in Laos. *World Development*, *66* (C), 371–382.

Weber, M., Roth, G., and Wittich, C. (1978). Economy and society: An outline of interpretive sociology. Berkeley: University of California Press.

Winichakul, T. (1994). *Siam Mapped: A History of Geo-body of a Nation*. Honolulu: University of Hawaii Press.

World Bank Policy Research Reports. (1993). *The East Asian Miracle: Economic Growth and Public Policy*. New York: Oxford University Press.

World Bank. (2010). *The Lao People's Democratic Republic Public Expenditure and Financial Accountability (PEFA): Public Financial Management Assessment*. Retrieved October 13, 2018, from PEFA: https://pefa.org/sites/default/files/assements/comments/LA-Jun10-PFMPR-Public_0.pdf

World Bank. (2015). *Driver of Poverty Reduction in Lao PDR*. Retrieved September 20, 2018, from World Bank: http://documents.worldbank.org/curated/en/590861467722637341/pdf/101567-REPLACENENT-PUBLIC-Lao-PDR-Poverty-Policy-Notes-Drivers-of-Poverty-Reduction-in-Lao-PDR.pdf

World Bank. (2016). *Political Stability, No Violence*. Retrieved November 15, 2018, from TCdata 360: https://tcdata360.worldbank.org/

World Bank. (2017a). *Country Gender Action Plan FY2017–2021 for Lao People's Democratic Republic.* Retrieved September 30, 2018, from World Bank: http://documents.worldbank.org/curated/en/824181495177203647/pdf/115142-WP-LaoPDRCGAPFINAL-PUBLIC.pdf

World Bank. (2017b). *Country Partnership Framework for Lao People's Democratic Republic for the Period FY2017–FY2021.* Retrieved October 10, 2018, from World Bank: http://documents.worldbank.org/curated/en/617471493517642342/pdf/Lao-Country-Partnership-Framework-2-March-2017-clean-03152017.pdf

World Bank. (2017c). *Lao PDR Economic Monitor: Lowering Risks and Reviving Growth.* Retrieved October 12, 2018, from World Bank: http://documents.worldbank.org/curated/en/677161512735183133/Lao-PDR-economic-monitor-lowering-risks-and-reviving-growth

World Bank. (2017d). *Lao PDR to Adopt Green Growth, with World Bank Support.* Retrieved October 1, 2018, from World Bank: http://www.worldbank.org/en/news/press-release/2017/05/31/lao-pdr-to-adopt-green-growth-with-world-bank-support

World Bank. (2017e). *Lao PDR to Adopt Green Growth, with World Bank Support.* Retrieved 10 2, 2018, from The World Bank: http://www.worldbank.org/en/news/press-release/2017/05/31/lao-pdr-to-adopt-green-growth-with-world-bank-support

World Bank. (2018). *Worldwide Governance Indicators.* Retrieved 11 15, 2018, from The World Bank: http://info.worldbank.org/governance/wgi/index.aspx#doc

World Bank. (2018a). *Belt and Road Initiative.* Retrieved October 2, 2018, from World Bank: https://www.worldbank.org/en/topic/regional-integration/brief/belt-and-road-initiative

World Bank. (2018b). *Lao PDR Economic Monitor, June 2018: Safeguarding Stability—An Ongoing Agenda.* Retrieved October 17, 2018, from World Bank: https://openknowledge.worldbank.org/bitstream/handle/10986/29920/127222-WP-P164978-PUBLIC-LEMJuneFinalforweb.pdf?sequence=1&isAllowed=y

World Bank. (2018c). *The Worldwide Governance Indicators (WGI) project.* Retrieved October 20, 2018, from World Bank: http://info.worldbank.org/governance/wgi/#home

World Bank. (2018d). *Net official development assistance received (current*

US$). Retrieved November 2, 2018, from World Bank: https://data.worldbank.org/indicator/DT.ODA.ODAT.CD

Southivongnorath, S. (2015). *Speech by Comrade Choummaly Sayasone, Party Secretary General and President of the Lao PDR delivered at the Grand Meeting to mark the 60th Anniversary of the Founding of the Lao People's Revolutionary Party*. Retrieved October 6, 2019, from Vientiane times: http://www.vientianetimes.org.la/FreeContent/FreeConten_Special%20Report_Speech1.htm

Southivongnorath, S. (2015). *Speech by Comrade Choummaly Sayasone, Party Secretary General and President of the Lao PDR delivered at the Grand Meeting to mark the 60th Anniversary of the Founding of the Lao People's Revolutionary Party Part 2*. Retrieved October 6, 2019, from Vientiane times: http://www.vientianetimes.org.la/FreeContent/FreeConten_Special%20Report_Speech2.htm

Southivongnorath, S. (2015). *Speech by Comrade Choummaly Sayasone, Party Secretary General and President of the Lao PDR delivered at the Grand Meeting to mark the 60th Anniversary of the Founding of the Lao People's Revolutionary Party Part 3*. Retrieved October 6, 2019, from Vientiane times: http://www.vientianetimes.org.la/FreeContent/FreeConten_Special%20Report_Speech3.htm

Southivongnorath, S. (2015). *Speech by Comrade Choummaly Sayasone, Party Secretary General and President of the Lao PDR delivered at the Grand Meeting to mark the 60th Anniversary of the Founding of the Lao People's Revolutionary Party Part 4*. Retrieved October 6, 2019, from Vientiane times: http://www.vientianetimes.org.la/FreeContent/FreeConten_Special%20Report_Speech4.ht

Xinhua. (2017). *Full text of Chinese Presiden Xi's signed article on Lao media*. Retrieved 8 29, 2018, from Xinhuanet: http://www.xinhuanet.com/english/2017-11/13/c_136749157.htm

Xinhua. (2018). *Mining Sector to Contribute Less to Lao Economy: Report*. Retrieved November 20, 2018, from Xinghua: http://www.xinhuanet.com/english/2018-05/03/c_137153271.htm

Yamada, N. (2018). Legitimation of the Lao People's Revolutionary Party: Socialism, Chintanakan Mai (New Thinking) and Reform. *Journal of Contemporary Asia*, 1–22.

Yap, J. (2017). *The Paris Climate Agreement and How it Affects Laos*. Retrieved

October 6, 2019, from Laotian times: https://laotiantimes.com/2017/06/06/paris-climate-agreement-affects-laos/?fbclid=IwAR1E_0hKeDGC5rFHdZZioYwiWE0Yy-Mxla5cNpvMk8I27QYU2UuOiY5fWYg

Zasloff, J. J. (1991). Political Constraints on Development in Laos. In Joselp J. Zasloff, & Leonard Unger (Eds.), *Laos: Beyond the Revolution* (pp. 3–40). New York: St. Martin Press.

Ziai, A. (2015). *Development Discourse and Global History: From Colonialism to the Sustainable Development Goals.* New York: Routledge.

Interviews cited in the text

Informant No. 1. (2017, January 18). Personal interview.

Informant No. 2. (2017, January 19). Personal interview.

Informant No. 3. (2017, January 27). Personal interview.

Informant No. 4. (2017, March 16). Personal interview.

Informant No. 5. (2017, January 25). Personal interview.

Informant No. 6. (2017, January 30). Personal interview.

Informant No. 7. (2017, December 7). Personal interview.

Informant No. 8. (2017, December 8). Personal interview.

Informant No. 9. (2017, December 6). Personal interview.

Informant No. 10. (2017, March 9). Personal interview.

Informant No. 11. (2017, February 10). Personal interview.

Informant No. 12. (2017, February 6). Personal interview.

Informant No. 13. (2017, December 5). Personal interview.

Informant No. 14. (2017, December 6). Personal interview.

Informant No. 15. (2017, December 5). Personal interview.

Informant No. 16. (2017, December 6). Personal interview.

Informant No. 17. (2017, December 1). Personal interview.

Informant No. 18. (2017, December 1). Personal interview.

Informant No. 19. (2017, March 6). Personal interview.

Informant No. 20. (2017, February 6). Personal interview.

Informant No. 21. (2017, February 12). Personal interview.

Informant No. 22. (2017, December 1). Personal interview.

Informant No. 23. (2017, December 7). Personal interview.

Informant No. 24. (2017, December 7). Personal interview.

Informant No. 25. (2017, November 20). Personal interview.

Informant No. 26. (2017, November 20). Personal interview.

Informant No. 27. (2017, November 18). Personal interview.

Informant No. 28. (2017, December 8). Personal interview.